THE UNITED STATES OF THE UNITED RACES

The United States of the United Races

A Utopian History of Racial Mixing

Greg Carter

NEW YORK UNIVERSITY PRESS
New York and London

819717789

NEW YORK UNIVERSITY PRESS
New York and London
www.nyupress.org

© 2013 by New York University

LIBRARY OF CONGRESS CATALOGING-IN-PUBLICATION DATA
Carter, Greg, 1970–
The United States of the united races : a utopian history of racial mixing / Greg Carter.
pages cm   Includes bibliographical references and index.
ISBN 978-0-8147-7249-2 (cl : alk. paper) — ISBN 978-0-8147-7250-8 (pb : alk. paper) —
ISBN 978-0-8147-9048-9 (ebook) — ISBN 978-0-8147-7251-5 (ebook)
1. Racially mixed people—United States—History. 2. Miscegenation—United States—
History. 3. United States—Race relations—History. 4. Post-racialism—United States. I.
Title.
E184.A1C337   2013
305.800973—dc23   2012045598

References to Internet Websites (URLs) were accurate at the time of writing.
Neither the author nor New York University Press is responsible for URLs that
may have expired or changed since the manuscript was prepared.

New York University Press books are printed on acid-free paper,
and their binding materials are chosen for strength and durability.
We strive to use environmentally responsible suppliers and materials
to the greatest extent possible in publishing our books.

Manufactured in the United States of America

c 10 9 8 7 6 5 4 3 2 1
p 10 9 8 7 6 5 4 3 2 1

Contents

Acknowledgments

I would like to thank everyone everywhere who ever helped me with anything ever, but that would be an infeasible task. Instead, I will acknowledge sets of people, institutions, and associations who have aided me since this project's beginning.

As an adviser, Neil Foley urged me to ask the truly important questions during the early stages. I thank him for treating my work with the same seriousness that he treats his own. Janet Davis, John Hartigan Janet Staiger, and Shirley Thompson also offered necessary guidance during the formative stages.

The faculty and staff of the Department of American Studies at the University of Texas at Austin provided the training that I draw from daily. Fellow graduate students, whether senior, peers, or junior added the necessary camaraderie. They continue to this day, even though we have gone to different locales.

As a graduate student at the University of Texas, I also received support from departments beyond my own, including the Center for African and African American Studies, the Center for Asian American Studies, and the Louann Atkins Temple Endowed Presidential Fellowship.

At the University of Wisconsin–Milwaukee, I have the honor of working with an exceptional set of colleagues, mentors, and activists in the Department of History. I have also received support from Comparative Ethnic Studies, Cultures and Communities, the Graduate School Research Committee, the Institute on Race and Ethnicity, and the Office of Undergraduate Research. Founding the Mixed Race Studies Group brought me in contact with others in the U.W.M. community interested in mixed race. I thank Lee Abbott, Shelleen Greene, Nikki Wallschlaeger, Kathleen Farrell Whitworth, and Yanmei Jiang for their cross-disciplinary perspectives on racial mixing globally.

Conversations with students, both undergraduate and graduate, helped me articulate many of the concepts I employ throughout this book. It has been my pleasure to counsel, to develop friendships, and to follow their successes. Kudos to the founding officers of U.T's Mixed Student Union—Desire

Taylor, Kevin Jackson, Alexandria Bills, and Susannah Osegi—whom I advised during their inception! (I have named only a few students, but I have many more in mind.)

Beyond these two universities, I want to name some of the individuals who have helped move this project into book form with substantive feedback, professional advice, or insights into academic publishing: Heidi Ardizzone, Amy Bass, Philip Deloria, Julie Dowling, Shelley Fisher Fishkin, Benita Heiskanen, Mark Anthony Neal, Justin Ponder, Peter Rachleff, David Roediger, Carole Stabile, Paul Spickard, James Brewer Stewart, and Siva Vaidhyanathan.

Editors of journals and edited collections I have contributed to guided me in refining my writing, and in turn the effectiveness of my ideas. These include Ron Bayor, Mary Beltrán, John Bukowczyk, G. Reginald Daniel, Camilla Fojas, Heather Kaufman, Jack McKivigan, Anju Reejhsinghani, Madeline Shu, and Hettie V. Williams.

Panelmates and audiences at conferences hosted by the University of Southern California's Annenberg School of Communications, Harvard University's W. E. B. Du Bois Society, the National Association for Ethnic Studies, the American Studies Association, and the American Educational Research Association have contributed to the development of the ideas within.

Membership in the American Studies Association, the Organization of American Historians, and the National Association for Ethnic Studies has brought me to wider communities of scholarly work. Within the A.S.A., the Students Committee, the Committee on Ethnic Studies, and the Minority Scholars Committee have contributed to my sense of belonging within the field since I first started as a master's student. It is a pleasure to serve on the third with Ernesto Chavez, Denise Cruz, Sandra Gunning, Christina Hanhardt, Adriane Lentz-Smith, Gabriela Nunez, and Lisa Thompson. During the writing of this book, WeiMing Dariotis, Camilla Fojas, and Laura Kina organized the inaugural Critical Mixed Race Studies conference, which took place at DePaul University in 2010. (It was a phenomenal success!) I thank them for this forum and the opportunity to contribute to the program committee, History Caucus, and Black and Asian Caucus.

In addition to U.T. and U.W.M., archivists at the University of Virginia, Harvard University's Houghton Library, the Boston Public Library, the Massachusetts Historical Society, the Library of Congress, and the New York Public Library were great aids with primary documents research. Similarly, the following offered assistance with illustrations: the Muscarelle Museum at the College of William and Mary, the American Antiquarian Society, the McClurg Museum of the Chautauqua County Historical Society, the

Frederick Douglass National Historic Site, Yale University's Beinecke Library, the Michigan State University Museum, Seaweed Productions, the Japanese American National Museum, the University of Southern Mississippi, and Mexico's National Museum of Viceroyalty.

At New York University Press, I thank Eric Zinner, Ciara McLaughlin, and other staff members for making this book a reality.

To my three hundred best friends on Facebook, thank you for your good humor, good news, and good connections to the world beyond this project.

I cannot name each relative one by one, but I thank them all—near, far, and departed—for their love and support.

Clarice Carter, my mother, has been my longest ally, supporter, and role model. All good work here traces back to her excellent job as a parent.

Natasha Borges Sugiyama, my wife, is my partner in all things. I cannot imagine having completed this without her.

Lastly, to our daughter, Nina Sugiyama Carter: you are special, beautiful, and full of potential for reasons beyond your racial makeup.

Introduction

In April 2010, the White House publicized Barack Obama's self-identification on his U.S. census form. He marked one box "Black, African Am., or Negro," settling one of the most prevalent issues during his 2008 presidential campaign: his racial identity. This choice resounded with the monoracial ways of thinking so prevalent throughout U.S. history. People who believed he was only black because he looked like a black person or because many others (society) believed so or because of the historical prevalence of the one-drop rule received confirmation of that belief. The mainstream media had been calling him the black president for over a year, so they received confirmation of this moniker.

Many people who had followed the adoption of multiple checking on the census found his choice surprising. Surely, as president, he would be aware of the ability to choose more than one race. To pick one alone went against everything activists wanting to reform the government's system of racial categorization had worked for in the 1990s. Many found it surprising that the man who had called himself "the son of a black man from Kenya and a white woman from Kansas" would choose one race. After all, he had used this construction far more times than he had called himself black, giving the impression that he embraced his mixture along with identifying as black. That snippet, along with images of his diverse family, had been part of what endeared him to mixed-race supporters. Similarly, his campaign's deployment of his white relatives built sympathy with white voters. Some people argued that he had failed to indicate what he "was" by choosing one race. He made the diverse backgrounds in his immediate family a footnote. But, recalling Maria P. P. Root's "A Bill of Rights for Racially Mixed People," a pillar of contemporary thought on mixed race, they had to respect his prerogative. He had the right to identify himself differently than the way strangers expected him to identify.[1]

Three lessons emerged from this episode: How one talks about oneself can be different from how one identifies from day to day. How one identifies from day to day can be different from how one fills out forms. And on a form with political repercussions, such as the census, one may choose a political statement different from both how one talks and how one identifies. Obama had always been a political creature; he never did anything for simple reasons. By the regulations, the administration could have withheld the information for seventy-two years. Instead, it became a small yet notable news piece in real time. Publicizing his participation in the census could motivate other minorities (beyond those who knew the history of multiple checking) to do so as well. More likely, he was thinking about the 2012 election. His response to the 2010 census could influence voters later on. If the number of those who would have hurt feelings over a singular answer was less than those who would find offense in a multiple answer, then a singular answer was the best to give. Even though mixed-race Americans took great pride in Obama's ascendance, they were a small faction to satisfy.

Then why did Obama take so much care to cast himself as a young, mixed-race hope for the future? Because even though the number of people who identify as mixed race is small, they hold immense figural power for the nation as symbols of progress, equality, and utopia, themes he wanted to associate with his campaign. In other words, he piggybacked onto positive notions about racially mixed people to improve his symbolic power. At the same time, he nurtured the stable, concrete, and accessible identity that people so used to monoracial thought could embrace, not the ambiguous one that challenged everyone.

Interpretation of current events such as this can disentangle the complexities we encounter here and now. However, while historical analysis always enriches the understanding of current events, writing history about current events presents a pitfall: they are moving targets resisting our attempts to focus on them. Similarly, following figures such as Obama lures us into announcing sea changes in racial conditions. Americans of all walks like indicators of progress. But addressing racial inequality calls for more than well-wishing. As a guiding principle, we should remember to appreciate that these are stories that have no resolution, much like the story of racialization in general. The meanings of mixture, the language we use to describe it, and its cast of characters have always been in flux.

Even before colonial Virginia established the first anti-intermarriage laws in 1691, efforts to stabilize racial identity had been instrumental in securing property, defending slavery, and maintaining segregation. The study of interracial intimacy has labeled racially mixed people either pollutants to society or the last hope for their inferior parent groups. To this day, many Americans label each other monoracially, interracial marriage remains a rarity, and group identities work best when easy to comprehend. However, at the same time that many worked to make racial categorization rigid, a few have defended racial mixing as a boon for the nation. Ever since English explorer John Smith told the story of the Indian princess Pocahontas saving his life in 1608 (a founding myth of the United States), some have considered racial mixing a positive. These voices were often privileged with access to outlets. Many were men, and many were white. This study reconsiders the understudied optimist tradition that has disavowed mixing as a means to uplift a particular racial group or a means to do away with race altogether. Instead, this group of vanguards has praised mixture as a means to create a new people, to bring equality to all, and to fulfill an American destiny. Historians of race have passed over this position, but my narrative shows that contemporary fascination with racially mixed figures has historical roots in how past Americans have imagined what radical abolitionist Wendell Phillips first called "The United States of the United Races."

Each of this book's seven chapters explores how tensions in our intellectual history have revised themselves in every period since the early republic. In the 1780s, Hector St. John de Crèvecoeur, author of *Letters from an American Farmer*, defined America as new and composite, while Thomas Jefferson warned against whites mixing with blacks. The future president's secretary, William Short, proposed recognizing mixed offspring, transitioning slaves toward tenant farming, and offering universal citizenship. During the Civil War era, Wendell Phillips deemed interracial marriage inevitable for a multicultural democracy, while most others shied away from the controversial topic. Not only did the defense for the 1896 *Plessy v. Ferguson* case use a racially mixed defendant to challenge categorization, but its lead attorney, Albion Tourgée, imagined an interracial future for the United States. Unfortunately, the Supreme Court rejected this position, sanctioning segregation. Dramatist Israel Zangwill first considered blacks and Asians participants in his famous engine of intermarriage, the melting pot, in his 1908 play of the same name, but he then acquiesced to pressure and removed them. It would take Jean Toomer and José Vasconcelos, two writers more sensitive to racial difference, to address the vagaries of this American symbol. The middle decades of the twentieth century featured a hush around mixed race, but a closer look reveals that foreign wars, changes in immigration, and progressive mass media maintained the relevance of this topic at a different frequency. In the fall of 1993, racial mixing became fodder for the front pages of *Time* magazine via its computer-generated New Face of America and for newspapers such as the *New York Times* that covered the social movement aiming to include a multiracial identifier on the U.S. census. Intellectuals within and outside the Multiracial Movement looked to racially mixed people to bring about the end of all labels. Since 2000, the tension between racial ambiguity and certainty has played out in the popularity of consumer genomics tests, the allure of racially mixed fashion models, and the symbolic value of a variety of mixed-race figures.

Using analytic tools from the fields of U.S. history, ethnic studies, American studies, and media studies, I challenge the centuries-long conversation about the morphology, capacity, and status of racially mixed people. Through this work's deeper historical perspective, it diverges from what some scholars call "mixed-race studies," a set of titles from the past two decades that work against past, negative conceptions. This field began with three edited collections from the early 1990s: Maria Root's *Racially Mixed People in America* (1992); her follow-up, *The Multiracial Experience* (1995); and Naomi Zack's *Race and Mixed Race* (1993). As groundbreaking texts, they employed many disciplines but explored few of them in depth. Among more recent collections, Jayne Ifekwunigwe's *Mixed Race Studies* (2004) spanned 150 years, but its reliance on excerpts diluted the context of any of the selections. Others go into greater depth concerning one type of mixture, including Kerry Ann Rockquemore's *Beyond Black* (2002), Kip Fulbeck's *Part Asian, 100% Hapa* (2006), and Teresa Williams-León and Cynthia Nakashima's *The Sum of Our Parts* (2001). Many single-author titles from the past dozen years have focused on the negative associations around the topic. Leading this approach are Werner Sollors's *Neither Black nor White yet Both* (1997), which covers the tragic mulatto trope; Gerald Horne's *The Color of Fascism* (2006), a biography of racial passing through the life of white supremacist Lawrence Dennis; and Peggy Pascoe's *What Comes Naturally* (2009), which surveys prohibitions to interracial marriage in U.S. law. Last among mixed-race studies titles are those of the congratulatory model, focusing on the transformative potentiality of a "new multiracial consciousness," for example, Reginald Daniel's *More than Black?* (2002) and Maria Root's *Love's Revolution* (2001). Justifying the attention their work received, their writing negotiated a line between drawing the potential of mixed race and promising its cures, often favoring the latter.

Instead, I avoid arguing for progress, especially since one of this book's main goals is to interrogate the notion that racial mixing indicates progress. Following the liberal arts conventions, I have attempted to trace change as a means to avoid the same pitfalls I critique. However, progress does happen. Over time, through activism, legislation, and other social forces, conditions can improve, not just change. (I am thinking of the span between 1896 and now, not 1967 and now.) Merely recording the mutations of racism is a safe way to practice evenhanded analysis, but it is shortsighted—and masochistic.

I eschew equating progress with mixture, but I also want to convey that optimism is reasonable.

This study is unique for three reasons: First, it uncovers a narrative of positive notions just as important as the negative. Second, it puts both the positive and the negative in historical context, recovering past advocates for or against racial mixture and amplifying the resonances across time. Third, instead of privileging one kind of racial mixing (for example, black and white), it interrogates mixture in any configuration as an engine for positive change. This is crucial to understanding the themes of progress, utopia, and inclusion that underlie positions on racial mixing more broadly. This book presents the career of an idea more so than the biographies of particular writers, orators, or activists. My unified approach shows that in every period, an optimistic stance has been as central to the American conversation on race as the pessimist. Because antipathy toward mixture is so established, and because critics of the dominant position have no formal connection to predecessors, each must re-create the position in new ways.

Defenders of racial mixing have been highly visible commentators on the making of Americans, or ethnogenesis. Werner Sollors put this process in context of typology, or "a form of prophecy which sets two successive events into a reciprocal relation of anticipation and fulfillment."[2] This involves repetition of a prophecy to the point of overshadowing the promise. But it also means that the anticipation increases with repetition, making signs of fulfillment, such as increasing intermarriage or mixed-race birthrates, more prophetic. Those who rely on a linear, upward path toward racial equality repeat their optimistic prophecy to the point of overshadowing any original promise, making the anticipation of racial equality more important than achieving it. Even an everyday statement such as "In the future, everyone will be mixed" expresses positive ideas about racial mixing, place, and time by predicting an ideal America full of improved, mixed citizens. But predictions alone are not enough for achieving racial equality.

In contrast to such narratives, I illustrate the interplay between dominant and alternative discourses over the span of U.S. history. By presenting a chronological narrative around race mixing, my approach offers a way to appreciate temporal as well as spatial discontinuity in discourse around mixture, progress, and utopia. Rather than islands one can only connect by sailing between them, I maintain that expressions in favor for racial mixing constitute a coral reef that pokes through the surface at various points. A change in perspective reveals that these expressions connect beneath the expansive ocean. With that in mind, a new organizing principle emerges in this book, one with radical implications in the historiography of race in the United States.

Because of the potential of mixed race to disrupt racial categorization, it is one analytical tool for understanding how reconfigurations of race go hand in hand with the creation and dissolution of racial terms. But a historical work of this breadth requires some attention to terms such as *race* and *mixed race*, especially since they are constantly in flux. I follow Michael Omi and Howard Winant in defining *race* as "a concept which signifies and symbolizes social conflicts and interests by referring to different types of human bodies."[3] This definition resists pinpointing what those signifiers and symbols are, but its attention to bodies does acknowledge that persons and physical appearances are the objects of signification. Omi and Winant's assertion that race is "a social construction which alters over the course of time due to historical and social pressures" is especially useful.[4] The meanings of race change, depending on the social organization of the time and place, and these endless possibilities result in vagary about exactly what race is. However, certain concepts have prevailed through U.S. history, from Blumenbach's hierarchy by continental origin to Morton's hierarchy by physical features to the Chesapeake colonies' hierarchy by labor status. In each of these, it is hard to pinpoint which came first, racial categories or the processes of racialization. With the approach of the twentieth century, main currents in racial thinking shifted toward cultural positivism, social Darwinism, and eugenics. Even with the shame that the Nazi regime brought to racial science, many of its ideas have become common sense to Americans.

The arc of these paradigms tends to obscure particular meanings of race that individuals cobble together. At any moment, popular understandings reinterpret, contradict, and undermine accepted racial logics. They are socially constructed, much like Stuart Hall's expansion on the processes of encoding and decoding, which highlights the importance of active interpretation within relevant semiotic codes. Rather than mere absorption of discourse on a topic, Hall categorizes readings as dominant, negotiated, or oppositional. The moment of encoding describes when producers inscribe meanings into texts. The moment of decoding describes when audiences make their own meanings from the texts, perhaps very different from the originals. This theory applies to the meanings of race just as it applies to meanings of texts. However, race is one ideology out of many useful for analyzing the world; we also rely on gender, class, religion, and other lenses to make sense of society. This individualism further disrupts the linear narrative that insists on societal progress through time.

Some people take this subjectivity to an extreme, saying that race does not exist. They argue that the language around race is faulty, so we ought to jettison the whole way of thinking. But racism, the practice of determining outcomes by racial heritage, is relevant to this day. This is true even though legislation has removed racial barriers to education, employment, voting, and immigration. Even though the public outcry against derogatory statements indicates a high level of racial etiquette, reticence, paranoia, and resentment prevail. Though there is more visibility for interracial intimacy, intermarriage, and racial mixing, great inequalities remain. The vast majority of relationships and families in the United States today are monoracial. We cannot compel interracial intimacy to all, nor can we celebrate the integration of a few without making equality the charge for us all.

Omi and Winant explain the practice of racism through their theory of racial formation, "the process by which these socio-historical designations of race are created and manipulated," organizing racial projects into the micro- and macro-level.[5] This approach can lead to two dangerous conclusions: that race is trivial or that it is institutional. One can interpret micro-level racial projects as individual prejudice or ignorance. For example, a bus driver made Rosa Parks give up her seat; Ebens and Nitz beat Vincent Chin; my new neighbors thought I was the gardener. Or one can interpret macro-level racial projects as the product of forces beyond our reach. For example, blackface minstrelsy grafted the mockery of blacks into American popular culture; Congress passed the Chinese Exclusion Act; neighborhood associations plan private Halloweens rather than participate in the citywide event. Both of these poles hinder our ability to pinpoint that racism is a system and discourage us from doing anything about it.

For historical analysis of post-civil-rights white supremacy, Eduardo Bonilla-Silva's guidelines are especially useful. He discerned, "In contrast to race relations in the Jim Crow period, however, racial practices that reproduce racial inequality in contemporary America are (1) increasingly covert, (2) embedded in normal operations of institutions, (3) void of direct racial terminology, and (4) invisible to most whites."[6] The racialized social system that oppressed minorities for much of U.S. history has persisted, in different forms, despite the social movements of the mid-twentieth century. Because Bonilla-Silva's totalized racial system appreciates racism as "society-wide, organized, and institutional," rather than the work of a powerful few, I believe it augments Omi and Winant's racial formation theory. Together, they help make racism tangible, a set of practices we can address. This understanding of racism as changing values, practices, and beliefs is especially useful in discussing notions around racial mixing.

Surely, the protection of racial purity has been central in U.S. history; for many racial projects around property, labor, and access, "white racial purity as thus defined" was the objective.[7] However, the definitions of whiteness have changed, bestowing privilege to members of previously undesirable groups, such as Irish, Italians, Jews, fair Latinos, and mixed grandchildren of Asians in America, and showing that purity is unnecessary for membership. Even as a tool for civil rights enforcement, the census concerns itself with racial stabilization. It works best when we answer the questions in ways that fit Census Bureau models, and the work the agency does between decennials is in hope that fewer people choose nonconforming answers such as "Other." Many minorities strive for stabilization or consolidation under a monoracial label, rather than negotiating a mixed-race experience, calling for a distinction between racially mixed people and people with racial mixing in their backgrounds. The former refers to those with parents from different racial groups, with an appreciation for how "racial" varies. The latter refers to groups that acknowledge a high degree of mixture in their past, that do not label themselves mixed but, rather, prefer some other label, such as black.

The minority adoption of consolidation emphasizes unity over variable heritages. Following the lead of African Americans, other minority groups have discouraged mixing to promote unity, cultural pride, and mass action toward civil rights. Brown, Red, and Yellow Power movements emulated Black Power, but just as Black Nationalism of the 1960s built on previous consolidation efforts, the other minority youth rearticulated cultural nationalism for their situations. In the 1970s, the umbrella ethnicities of Asian American and Latino/Hispanic arose, exercises of strategic essentialism that collected groups with some similar experiences but many disparate ones. Past animosities are energized when national origins outweigh the collective label, and new divisions are fortified when those within umbrella ethnicities who achieve material success consider themselves higher than others who have not.

Considering how the stabilization of racial identity has affected all racial groups, I address many configurations of racial mixture, so that the impact of race as an organizing principle, the ways many people have worked to stabilize it, and the potential that mixed race has to disorganize it will be more apparent. While the drama around slavery, emancipation, and civil rights figures centrally in U.S. history, by no means do I wish to suggest that racism against blacks has been exclusive. Likewise, while some people have elevated their status by denigrating blacks, other minority groups have received similar treatment. Asians have experienced exclusion from citizenship, internment, and the backhanded platitude of the model minority. Hispanics and Latinos have experienced an array of discrimination in education, employment, and social services that aligns with physical appearances and degrees of acculturation. Native Americans have faced removal and marginalization since first contact and now operate under a system of blood quantum that requires minimum fractions of Indian parentage to claim membership and resources. These dynamics become more apparent when we loosen the American story from the conventional, east-to-west narrative, uncovering the racial situations of other regions. In regard to mixture, this project is relevant to all racial minorities, as the protection of racial stability has plied laws of purity on all of them.

Continuing this discussion of terminology, I prefer *mixed race* over *multiracial*, to distance myself from those who wanted to create a new category for racially mixed people. Coverage of the 2000 census gave the impression that all within the Multiracial Movement wanted this. In reality, most wanted some useful identifier of mixed heritage, and the decision to implement multiple checking was satisfactory to them. The faction that did want a new category tended to believe that there was a true, singular, multiracial consciousness that united racially mixed people across race, class, gender, and geography. Because mixed-race experiences are so varied, I reject this notion. Similarly, I avoid labels that connote specific configurations of mixing, for example, *hapa* or *biracial*. The former hails from the native Hawaiian term *hapa haole* and often refers to mixed Asian and white individuals. It is a term popular with racially mixed Asian Americans to express pride in their mixture. At the hands of scholars of mixed race, Multiracial Movement activists, and journalists, the latter term often refers to mixed black and white individuals. Although the word is indeterminate, its use reinforces the notion that race in the United States is only about blacks and whites.

Because nicknames for mixture veer too close to epithet, I also dislike terms such as *blasian*. Similarly, I follow the lead of Maria Root, Rebecca Walker, and Katya Gibel Azoulay in rejecting the language of fractions—for example, *half Indian*. Lastly, unless employing the vocabulary of a historical period, I avoid antiquated terms such as *mulatto*, *quadroon*, *mongrel*, or *half-breed*. We have seen provocative redeployment of offensive terms, but we have also seen episodes involving *Seinfeld* actor Michael Richards, radio personality Don Imus, and the rapper Nas showing we are far from demobilizing racial slurs. In the end, I use an additive language that is both appropriate for current mores and encompassing of the complexity of mixed-race identity.

Chapter 1 begins in the year 1782, when Thomas Jefferson updated *Notes on the State of Virginia* and Hector St. John de Crèvecoeur published *Letters of an American Farmer*. The former set forth a defense of racial purity that was becoming the standard in the republic. Slavery vexed Jefferson and other founding fathers, but *Notes* used both science and law to defend the slave system. While Jefferson wrote that "all men are created equal" in the Declaration of Independence, he was also a son of prominent planter families. Like them, he was deeply invested in Virginia's systems of privilege, land, and labor. He is famous for his relationship with Sally Hemings, but his public legacy is one that argued that free blacks "be removed beyond the reach of mixture."[8] The *Letters*, written by a French immigrant who adopted the new nation, bound together mixture and newness as centrally American traits. Speaking from Orange County, New York, which had a slave population of 5.2% in 1790 (compared to Virginia's 35.1%), Crèvecoeur's narrator marveled at a family "whose grandfather was an Englishman, whose wife was Dutch, whose son married a French woman, and whose present four sons have now four wives of different nations," calling them quintessentially American.[9]

Later conceptions of race coalesced around pseudoscientific differences, but at this time, the mixing of European nationalities was remarkable. Mixing between indigenous people, colonists, and Africans from different nations had been part and parcel of American life since the 1600s, so Crèvecoeur was describing a way of life in practice for over 150 years. Crèvecoeur's experience in New France introduced him to paradigms that relied more on trade and intimacy with Indians than Virginia's racial dynamics did. While he denounced slavery in Charlestown, South Carolina, he also spoke of blacks and Indians in terms we would now find condescending. However, not once did he exclude these groups from participating in the secular life of the United States, and this is the main difference between these two authors. Jefferson's *Notes* and Crèvecoeur's *Letters* have both a descriptive mission and a prescriptive one; they shed light on the early republic and offer paths toward the ideal America of the future. Even though ideas about race and mixture have changed since then, their legacies persist, with one defending racial purity and the other celebrating mixture. Starting at this historical moment, I show how the relationship between the dominant and alternative positions began over two hundred years ago.

Over the next fifty years, the American racial order solidified, with white supremacy the norm, blacks as servile, and mixture an unwelcome saboteur. At the same time that territorial expansion incorporated more land and more types of people, lines of inclusion remained tenuous. Most relevant during this interim is the array of reform movements that arose, including abolitionism. Wendell Phillips, among others, combined a belief in making God's kingdom on earth with a sense of individual responsibility. Born into Boston's upper class in 1811, he became active in the abolitionist movement in 1836, becoming a sort of Aaron to William Lloyd Garrison's Moses, tempering prophetic fervor with a lawyer's clarity.

Phillips's willing defense of amalgamation set him apart from his more cautious fellow radicals. In 1838, he became legal counsel for an Antislavery Society campaign to eliminate Massachusetts's anti-intermarriage laws. Unlike others, he continued to defend "honorable marriage" between racial groups through the following decades, his response to our founding documents, the sin of slavery, and antiabolitionist violence. In fact, his statements became the model for the *Miscegenation* pamphlet of 1864, a hoax that suggested amalgamation was a platform of the Republican Party. This product of Democratic journalists in New York attacked Abraham Lincoln's Emancipation Proclamation by lampooning Phillips's rhetoric, just as blackface minstrelsy attacked fair labor by satirizing black cultural forms.

The Civil War years provide a tumultuous intersection between slavery, politics, and popular culture, but I use Wendell Phillips's statements to show that the defense of racial mixing existed well before and after the war. In my reading in chapter 2, Phillips did more than target the conflict at hand; he also addressed racial inequality of the decades since Jefferson and Crèvecoeur, amending their statements with the knowledge that fighting for equal rights meant including all in the intimate making of future Americans. His 1853 editorial in the *National Era* (the inspiration for this book's title) named Chinese and East Indians as worthy of citizenship, a statement prescient of the Supreme Court's expansive decision in *United States v. Wong Kim Ark* (1898). Phillips's assertions resound in almost every defense of racial mixing that I present in this book. While some historians mention these optimistic statements about racial mixing in passing, I show that they are crucial to debates around equality, politics, and constructing a post–Civil War America.

Chapter 3 opens in the late nineteenth century, when Chinese laborers settled in more areas of the South and West but also received the label "aliens ineligible for citizenship." Battles throughout the plains subdued the Native American population to a point where many thought they would vanish. The residents of the former Mexican territory found they were the wards of colonization, rather than the beneficiaries of the supposedly inclusive Treaty of Guadalupe Hidalgo. After Radical Reconstruction ended, southern whites developed a retrograde system of segregation that disciplined blacks for exercising political agency or interracial intimacy. In fact, the conflation of these two threats was essential to arguments against social equality and remained so through the modern civil rights movement. In 1892, the Comité de Citoyens, a Louisiana social justice organization, and former Republican Superior Court judge Albion Tourgée deployed Homer Plessy, a racially mixed person, to challenge uses of racial categorization. They levied his white parentage against his black parentage, hoping the white seven-eighths would outweigh racial conclusions based on the black one-eighth. Plessy identified himself as a colored person sitting in the white section of a train, and his arrest led to a Louisiana Supreme Court case and then an appeal.

Tourgée's brief to the U.S. Supreme Court described the Fourteenth Amendment as the source of "new rights, privileges and immunities, derivable in a new manner" that would result in interracial families of various combinations and a wholesale disruption of racial categories.[10] He spelled out what the Reconstruction Amendments attempted to do: expand the Declaration of Independence to include all. However, nearly twenty years into Jim Crow, the defense wielded an underdog's position. The Court delivered a decision devastating to Tourgée, the Comité, and activists of the period, sanctifying racial segregation. But it also made degrees of mixture irrelevant, leading to the institution of hypodescent for all racial minorities.

The *Plessy* defense stands as an example of progressive thinkers on race (both mixed and unmixed) using mixture to disrupt racial order. The coalition employed positive ideas about racially mixed people that later became central to twentieth-century assimilation theory, the later foundations of the Multiracial Movement, and Barack Obama's victory in 2008. In placing racial mixture at the center of the long struggle for civil rights in the United States, chapter 3 provides a case of mixed-race activism that appreciated civil rights more broadly rather than espousing one variety of identity politics.

Chapter 4 picks up in the early twentieth century, when African American leaders articulated a meaning of race that brought together everyone of African descent, transforming the one-drop rule into a unifying tool for a diverse set of people. In particular, W. E. B. Du Bois established a definition of race that emphasized shared experience and group progress more than biology. However, descent remained central to this concept, ultimately influencing other minorities in their efforts for progress. At the recommendation of Du Bois and other scholars, the "Mulatto" category disappeared from the census, and hypodescent became the standard for all minorities. Rather than intermarriage, the collective focus for traditional racial groups was in mass action, litigation, and executive intervention. Likewise, racial pride, unity, and strategic essentialism became priorities for groups seeking progress. The umbrella ethnicities of "Latino" and "Asian American" solidified in the 1970s, reflecting the government's acknowledgment of the disadvantages these groups faced. The use of these terms attempted to smooth out matters of identity, making diverse collections of people monoracial. During the 1980s and 1990s, multiculturalism elevated minority experiences but also led to a pigeonholing of race, ethnicity, and culture.

President Theodore Roosevelt, a believer in imperialist expansion, racial hierarchy, and robust patriarchy, promoted the United States as a liberal democracy that could bestow equality on people of all nations. His counterpart in the arts was Israel Zangwill, the Jewish-British author of *The Melting-Pot*. Since the 1908 debut of Zangwill's play, "the melting pot" has become the most popular, positive description of American diversity of the twentieth century. In his 1914 revision of *The Melting-Pot*, Zangwill plucked out blacks and Asians, and the symbol has remained utterly vague regarding racial minorities ever since. Rather than intolerance, both of these men expressed the best of qualified liberalism. Their contradictions show that this period, like others, hosted an array of ideologies, not just a battle between inclusion and xenophobia.

Two contemporaries of Zangwill, José Vasconcelos and Jean Toomer, offered statements regarding mixing that continued where he stopped. Both had heard of the melting pot but chose their own tropes to describe a future mixed race that would actively participate in an egalitarian society, possess a higher consciousness, and advance society by creating art. They provided positive metaphors that differed from both the Americanization programs and the cultural pluralists of the time. In 1925, Vasconcelos, a Mexican educator and politician schooled in the United States, wrote "La Raza Cósmica," a manifesto praising the mixed Latin American race. His essay influenced several generations of thought on *mestizaje*, including the founders of the League of United Latin American Citizens (LULAC), the La Raza movement of the late 1960s, Gloria Anzaldúa's *Borderlands/La Frontera* (1987), and Richard Rodriguez's catch phrase "the browning of America." Toomer, author of *Cane* (1923) and descendant of Washington, D.C.'s mulatto elite, repeatedly described the United States as a "great stomach into which are thrown the elements which make up the life blood."[11] This organ was already in the process of producing a new, mixed, American race neither white, black, nor yellow. Vasconcelos and Toomer answered questions Zangwill and Roosevelt evaded: What will the Americans look like? What do they do? Do they participate in creating the Americans of the future? While Zangwill's symbol has been in the limelight for the past century (even inspiring a *School House Rock* segment), Vasconcelos's and Toomer's writings have remained obscure. I offer them here to demonstrate how intellectuals addressed issues of mixed race even if few noticed at the time.

Chapter 5 covers the greater part of the twentieth century, which included the rise of a new mixed race in the United States: the white race, fulfilling a narrow conception of Zangwill's vision. From 1914, when Robert Park and Ernest Burgess first described assimilation as "interpenetration and fusion,"[12] up to Mary Waters's *Ethnic Options* (1990), which finally drew the connection between white privilege and flexibility in identification, assimilation literature elevated interethnic marriage rates as the prime measure of incorporation into the mainstream. Edward Reuter's *The Mulatto in the United States* (1918), Everett Stonequist's "The Problem of the Marginal Man" (1935), and Joel Williamson's *New People* (1980) echoed Josiah Nott and George Gliddon's infamous antebellum proslavery text *Types of Mankind* (1854) in describing racially mixed people as superior to their minority racial group yet intermediary in social status and prone to confusion. However, these twentieth-century scholars hoped to address racial inequality, so they promoted the idea that mixed people were inseparable from their minority parent groups.

Along with suggesting that interracial intimacy and racially mixed people are new phenomena, scholars and students of civil rights cast them as tangential to the social movements of the twentieth century. However, these were the decades when American soldiers married women in Asia and petitioned to bring them to the States. Mass media broadened American influence, exporting our rhetoric of inclusion but also opening us to scrutiny. Transracial and international adoption aimed to reform the nation by bringing diverse members into families. By removing racial barriers, the Immigration Act of 1965 initiated a change in the way we define assimilation today. Lastly, in a struggle many authors omit from the traditional civil rights movement, the Supreme Court deemed seventeen states' remaining anti-intermarriage laws unconstitutional with its 1967 *Loving v. Virginia* decision. Chapter 5 recovers the centrality of racial mixture during these middle decades by integrating these currents into the master narrative of civil rights.

Chapter 6 picks up in the early 1990s, a period that featured a major shift in the visibility of racially mixed people in the United States, thanks to various media, scholars, and activists who charged racially mixed Americans with precipitating the end of race. While small support organizations for interracial families had existed since the 1890s, these grew after the 1988 and 1991 founding of Association of MultiEthnic Americans and Project R.A.C.E. (Reclassify All Children Equally). In July 1993, the presidents of these two national organizations testified before Congress, advocating the implementation of a Multiracial identifier on the U.S. census.

At the same time, a body of academic writing challenged racial categorization as oppressive, if not obsolete. While these titles provided an intellectual basis for the Multiracial Movement, both the praise and the demonization of racial mixing gained greater visibility in 1993, when *Time* put a mixed-race star on the cover of its fall special issue. The magazine's staff used Morph 2.0 software to combine features of seven ethnic types to symbolize the effects of immigration and intermarriage on American diversity. The New Face was young, comely, and hygienic, revealing the designers' aesthetic choices. Her creation, her physical appearance, and her lack of history supported the impression that racial mixing was a new phenomenon, one that in a matter of generations would produce a nation of people who appeared 15% Anglo-Saxon, 17.5% Middle Eastern, 17.5% African, 7.5% Asian, 35% southern European, and 7.5% Hispanic. Besides this visual tour de force, the magazine's articles echo earlier hopes in racial mixing as a means to overcome divisions in America. Scholars such as David Roediger, Donna Haraway, and Mike Hill have articulated many of the New Face's possible meanings, often arguing that she expresses a wish for racelessness—that is, the obsolescence of race through its blurring. However, I emphasize how the cover star supposes that it is through mixing race, not obliterating it, that Americans can shape "the world's first multicultural society," as the issue's cover promised. In other words, the country's diversity will produce a mixed future that will celebrate its constituent parts. Just as racially mixed people have an abundance of race, so does the New Face, and that quality is at the core of her potency.[13]

Concurrently, as chapter 6 shows, the Multiracial Movement created a sense of community, employed the nascent uses of the Internet, and appeared in major media outlets. However, it also created opposition, mostly from traditional civil rights organizations that perceived the addition of a new category as a threat to their representation. Such opposition came from the National Urban League, the National Council of La Raza, and the Asian American Legal Defense and Education Fund. The Census Bureau tested proposed changes, desiring to make the data collection most useful for equal employment, civil rights, and fair housing. Then in 1996, racially mixed golf pro Tiger Woods rose in the limelight, disavowing any monoracial label. More Americans outside the movement acknowledged the relevance of changing racial categories, and some made Woods a poster boy for color-blind meritocracy. In October 1998, the federal Office of Management and Budget settled on a system of multiple checking rather than an umbrella category, disappointing some activists. As many demographers anticipated, this decision complicated enumeration, but "mark all that apply" has popularized an idea Crèvecoeur articulated in 1783: that Americans can be many things at the same time. Looking back on the 1990s, it is easy to compartmentalize Census 2000, the rise of academic writing on mixed race, and the New Face as separate events. I bring them together to show how this moment fits with previous and following hopes for racial mixing in the United States. Altogether, this chapter reveals the multiple voices that were influential during the 1990s.

Census 2000 provided a detailed description of the nation's racial makeup, indicating that 97.6% of Americans identified with one race, with 75.1% white, 12.3% black, 3.6% Asian, 0.9% American Indian, 0.1% Native Hawaiian, and 5.5% some other race. Hispanic or Latino, an ethnic designation, made up 12.5% of the population, with members across many of the traditional racial groups. Those who checked two or more races made up 2.4%, or 6.8 million, of the population. Along with those who checked "Other," 7.9% of the population (or one out of every thirteen) chose to identify in ways divergent from monoracial categorization. After spring 2001, the topic of multiple checking went dormant, indicating that Census 2000 was a gratifying exploration. While the public has bestowed popularity on celebrities who refuse to reveal their racial makeup (e.g., Vin Diesel, star of *Pitch Black*, *The Fast and the Furious*, and *XXX*), it is more accurate to say that Americans praise racial ambiguity, but in reality they prefer certainty. Colonial Virginia's rules to categorize mixed offspring, terms such as *mulatto*, *quadroon*, and *octoroon*, eugenicists wishing to discourage mixing, and the mathematics of the New Face show that this has been true throughout U.S. history.

In chapter 7, I bring together three phenomena that show how the use of mixed-race people as signs of racial progress, harmony, and the future of America has always worked best when satisfying the need for quantifiable racial makeup. The increase in mixed faces and bodies in advertising and marketing reversed the decades-long patterns of white standards of beauty. These prejudiced norms displayed themselves in plain sight, and minority supermodels did not appear until the 1970s and later. Consideration of racial minorities in marketing strategies rose with the appreciation of them as consumers, and now there are many products and many kinds of people to sell them to. By 2001, advertisers, marketers, and casting directors praised a "multiracial look," often in the same breath as reflections on the latest decennial census data. In emphasizing mixed Americans under eighteen years old, these movie makers, advertisers, and casting directors would have us believe that less than 1% (or three million) youth embodied the future. In addition to this rationalization, the increased visibility came with the tendency to reveal subjects' backgrounds. Whether magazine covers, art photography, or cognitive psychology experiments, areas of contemporary discourse persist in quantifying racial makeup in order to make racial ambiguity more manageable.

Consumer D.N.A. tests have recast the tension between purity and mixture in a new way. Even though genomics can recover family histories and broaden minds concerning race, the percentages they provide do far more to naturalize eighteenth- and nineteenth-century notions of hybridity. They simplify mixed race via the figurative power of D.N.A., just as Census 2000 simplified mixed race via the figurative power of checking boxes. While the Multiracial category was a concern of Americans who knew they were racially mixed, these tests appealed mostly to those who did not. I suggest that many people desired to learn they were mixed so they could claim the positive qualities they associate with mixture, such as exoticism, ambiguity, and cultural richness. These tests have grown in popularity because they suggest that everyone is mixed to a certain percentage.

A decade after Tiger Woods appeared, another racially mixed figure, Barack Obama, reached or surpassed his fame, speaking at the Democratic National Convention in 2004, winning a seat in the U.S. Senate, and then leading a monumental presidential campaign. Like the golf protégé, Obama disclosed his racial makeup upon entering the national spotlight, satisfying the need for certainty. Unlike minority politicians of the previous decades, he concentrated on being accessible to all, rather than foregrounding the concerns of one group. Commenting on race only when necessary, Obama practiced a sort of symbolic ethnicity that one usually associates with ethnic whites. Most important, the candidate exercised a multiple-checking way of describing his background: "I am the son of a black man from Kenya and a white woman from Kansas," leaving the enumeration of his identity to his audiences. If the president is supposed to be heroic, forward thinking, and inclusive, then Obama's black and white and mixed-race image befits the position he sought. Throughout his campaign, questions of mixed-race character challenged the public just as they have since the early republic. Some people simplified his identity to simply black—or not black enough. Others attributed his leadership style to his racial makeup, suggesting he was able to see two sides of issues because of it. These tendencies show how the conflict between demonizing and heroizing racial mixture persists. Putting these cases in conversation produces a warning against taking twenty-first-century praise of racial mixing at face value. Considering Barack Obama, the terms regarding race shifted, but the tensions between racial stabilization and the praise of mixing have remained. Along with the changing vocabularies, the contexts are always in motion, making efforts around either pole constantly difficult. One way Americans have come to terms with this flux is to imagine some kind of utopia or dystopia. Each chapter of this book features versions of these, with racial mixing playing a central role.

While it is premature to propose a resolution to the narrative I present in *The United States of the United Races*, I do point to the optimism that my cases employ. Each requires critical analysis, but they also dare to propose a nation correcting its racial past. Although they have been the underdogs for much of U.S. history, their expansive optimism has opened up far more inclusive possibilities than their opposition could.

1

Thomas Jefferson's Challengers

In the late eighteenth century, *race* possessed a much different meaning than it does now, denoting what we call *variety*. *Ethnic* was a term that stood for foreigners, with connotations similar to *gentile* in the Old Testament, and its usage remained rare until the nineteenth century. The French natural scientist George Louis Leclerc, Count de Buffon, suggested six races with differences between them "arbitrary operations of our own fancy."[1] The German Enlightenment scholar Johann Von Herder also believed in one human race, holding differences as superficial matters of lifestyle and physical appearance. Carolus Linneaus, who gave us scientific nomenclature, suggested four varieties of mankind within a hierarchy that placed Europeans at the top. His pupil Friedrich Blumenbach argued for five races, all equal in intellect. However, he placed Caucasians (his coinage) at top because he believed the region by Mount Caucasus produced "the most beautiful race of men."[2]

However, along with the growth of the British colonies in the New World, racial categorization developed contours recognizable in the United States to this day. Social positions, including white supremacy, hinged on classification. Racial mixture complicated the fixity of these classifications, especially when determining who was a slave and who was free. Positions on racial mixture reflected attitudes toward other racial topics. For example, antipathy toward mixture meant antipathy toward freedom for the racially mixed. Defense of slavery meant conscribing mixed offspring to the station of their nonwhite parents. Because of the constant increase of racially mixed bodies, a short distance separated recognition of their rights and the recognition of the rights of unmixed slaves. In the United States, legitimizing racially mixed offspring meant dismantling slavery. In the new nation full of revolutionary fervor, states such as Massachusetts and New Hampshire abolished slavery completely, and delegates to the Constitutional Convention worked to include a condemnation of the international slave trade in 1787. Mostly northerners, they knew that the choices they made would shape American life for posterity. At the same time, they desired to halt the political and economic power of the southern states. Still, prominent Virginians resolved to remove slavery from their own estates. George Washington stipulated the release of his slaves once his wife's passing made their bondage irrelevant. George Wythe, mentor to Thomas Jefferson, signer of the Declaration of Independence, and America's first legal scholar, recognized his mixed off-spring in his original will, giving an example of personal conscience, abolitionism, and equality. Robert Carter III, one of the most prosperous landowners in Virginia, began the process of manumitting his slaves during his lifetime, leading to over 450 of them going free. His gradual plan also made steps to transition the recently freed slaves into independence, sometimes renting parts of his land to them. However, most of his peers were silent on the matter of interracial intimacy, providing a quiet denial of its persistence.[3]

French Enlightenment thinkers, including especially Guillaume Thomas François Raynal, Jean-Jacques Rousseau, and Montesquieu, influenced the revolutionary generation with a belief in natural rights, which were universal and permanent. Following these *philosophes*, Thomas Jefferson maintained that natural rights superseded social rights, which governments bestowed. They gave equality to all humankind, licensing people to separate from or rise against their socially appointed leaders. He had these natural rights in mind while writing "A Summary View of the Rights of British America" in 1774 and the Declaration of Independence in 1776. The second quality all humans possessed was moral sense, or the potential to be virtuous. Leading people away from this moral sense was a crime; in Jefferson's original draft of the Declaration of Independence, he indicted King George III for this act of war on human nature. The Declaration also followed Rousseau, instead of John Locke, naming happiness more important than property. This alteration reflected how Jefferson wrote the document as an appeal to natural feelings rather than to quantifiable logic.[4]

However, a second meaning of nature, as in the environment, led to differences between groups of people and, in turn, to different stations in society. Environmentalism, a popular notion among Jefferson and his peers, said that people were mutable to their surroundings. On a physical level, darker peoples would become lighter from exposure to northern climes. Likewise, Europeans would become darker from exposure to southern climes. People in less fortunate stations in society could improve themselves over time, but this would fail if the more fortunate neglected their side of the bargain. In other words, with natural rights and moral sense, blacks could act morally and virtuously. But slavery barred them from that and blocked whites from behaving at the best of their potential. As more time passed, blacks would become more resentful of their station. At various moments in Jefferson's life, he devised plans for emancipation, but he believed that blacks were likely to turn against those who had oppressed them.[5]

The production of a class of semifree people jeopardizing peaceful, gradual emancipation was the basis of Jefferson's public opposition to racial mixing. With both white, free parents and black, enslaved parents, they would complicate the process. So Jefferson censured mixing, relying on the distinctiveness of blacks from whites. But considering his intimacy with Sally Hemings, the favor he showed to their children, and his acquaintance with successful blacks, his subscription to the one-drop rule was as inconsistent as the concept itself. But it answered the questions of who was a legitimate mate (not Sally), who had a claim to his estate (none of Sally's children: Harriet, Beverly, Thenia, Madison, or Eston), and who possessed true genius (not Phillis Wheatley).

Thomas Jefferson's paradoxes revolve around three questions: If he believed all men were created equal, why did he license slavery? If he licensed slavery, why did he produce offspring who challenged the idea of black inferiority? When he encountered exceptions, why did he not revise his position? Addressing these questions reveals a career of contradictions, missed opportunities, and compromises that are discomfiting to engage.

Some close associates of Jefferson considered mixture as a positive. The French expatriate Hector St. John de Crèvecoeur equated America with newness, progress, and mixture. The narrator of his novel *Letters from an American Farmer* announces, "From this promiscuous breed, that race now called Americans have arisen."[6] Of course, combinations that qualified as mixture then would barely raise an eyebrow now. But for him, a family with French, Dutch, and English backgrounds was notable. While Crèvecoeur and his protagonist often spoke in Eurocentric terms, he never excluded racial minorities from civic participation. Just as Jefferson's prohibitions influenced generations of Americans abhorring mixture, Crèvecoeur's praise echoes in discussions of mixture in American identity, assimilation, and American ethnogenesis. *Notes* and *Letters* presented early forms of the two most prevalent attitudes toward mixture in the United States from that period onward. This is why Jefferson is worth treading over again and why Crèvecoeur is worth recovering. By repositioning them in the big picture, the former becomes more than the lothario of Monticello, and the latter, no less than the founder of assimilation theory in the United States.[7]

Even more notably, Jefferson's "adoptive son," the diplomat William Short, suggested the acceptance of racially mixed people as part of a plan to replace slavery with land leasing. In comparison to the crime against humanity that slavery presented, mixture was insignificant. Like Crèvecoeur, Short joined the French abolitionist organization La Société des Amis des Noirs (Society of the Friends of the Blacks). When he challenged Jefferson in 1798, his proposal also allowed for blacks and mixed-race people to stay in the United States as citizens.[8]

At the same time that Jefferson warned against mixing, doubted the fitness for citizenship of black (and mixed-race) people, and ceased making steps toward abolition, some of his associates saw no harm in mixture, acknowledged the possibility of black citizenship, and developed an active abhorrence of slavery. I incorporate Crèvecoeur, Jefferson, and Short into a snapshot of the early republic, along with the locales they inhabited and the events they witnessed. Virginia, home to Jefferson and Short, was the first colony to enact laws against interracial intimacy. Mixture persisted even though the state's genteel planter class denied it. France followed the United States with its own revolution striving to bring equality to all. At the same time, turmoil in its most profitable colony increased, with the status of its mixed inhabitants as a central concern. Saint-Domingue's free people of color joined abolitionists in the French legislature in expanding citizenship. These events concerned Jefferson in his highest posts, but they also concerned Short, who remained in Europe, and Crèvecoeur, who was never able to return to his adoptive nation. All three were associates, and all three owned slaves at some point. However, their experiences led them to different conclusions about interracial intimacy.

From the 1780s to the 1820s, all three friends' perspectives developed in stutters, halts, and bounds. I survey these to resist the notion that white supremacy was always fully formed, to demonstrate that perspectives on racial mixture were more complex than for-or-against, to show that roles were more complex than master-or-slave, and to give examples of relationships more complex than superior and inferior. These all changed over time, especially in such a transformative period. Most of all, I show that racial mixing was at the center of discussions of citizenship, freedom, and independence.

Who was the man who wrote, "What then is the American, this new man?" His biography differed from that of James the Farmer, rough-hewn, practical, and semieducated protagonist of *Letters*. Born on January 31, 1735, in Caen, Normandy, Michel Guillaume Jean de Crèvecoeur was a member of French nobility. After completing a Jesuit education, he lived with relatives in England, where he learned English and fell in love with a merchant's daughter. She died before their marriage, and Crèvecoeur sailed to Canada, joining the French militia as the French and Indian War was beginning. An officer, surveyor, and cartographer, he had some successes. However, after recovering from wounds in the defense of Quebec, he sold his commission in October 1759. The details are lost, but it is likely that some intrigue led to his resignation. Either shame or restlessness led him to assume a new identity, James Hector St. John de Crèvecoeur, the name he assumed when he arrived in New York City, December 1759.

For the next six years, Crèvecoeur explored the colonies as a trader and surveyor, possibly going as far north as the Great Lakes, as far south as Virginia, and as far west as the Ohio Valley. For him, this was a period of deep immersion into American life, in both urban and rural areas. In 1765, he met Mehitable Tippet, the daughter of a Westchester County landowner, and he became a naturalized citizen of New York. They married four years later, and soon after, he bought 120 acres of land in Orange County, the site of his farm, Pine Hill. While rural, this area was an active community. The road to New Jersey ran through his property, and he associated with nearby intellectuals. Reflecting his adoption of his new homeland, the couple named their first daughter America-Frances.

While slavery in New York City and the surrounding counties differed from that on Virginia's plantations, the region had nearly as high a rate of slave ownership as its southern counterpart. Many New Yorkers, whether merchants, craftsmen, or farmers, possessed slaves. Reflecting these vocations, duties varied from domestic work to helping in shops to loading vessels. Direct supervision and close living quarters influenced the relations between masters and slaves. Some apparent differences led witnesses to attest that slavery was gentler in New York. Notable visitors wrote that slaves were content and well fed, that owners spared the lash. This produced a sort of plantation myth of the North that Crèvecoeur purveyed in his writings.[9]

Yet it is a mistake to label the master-slave relationship in New York as kinder than the southern plantation system, in which overseers were the ones with direct contact, while masters managed from a distance. Servitude in New York was different but not necessarily gentler than in the South. With fewer numbers, it was harder for slaves to create social connections with other blacks. Families were far more vulnerable because of the low population, the uneven sex ratios, and the whims of slave owners. This was especially true in the more sparse counties surrounding the city. The labor was no easier. Slaves were an integral part of agricultural life in New York, and they surely did the work Crèvecoeur wrote of—clearing the land, tending to livestock, plowing, and sowing.

After settling at Pine Hill, Crèvecoeur began work on what became *Letters from an American Farmer*. By 1774, he had completed sketches based on his travels across different colonies. He augmented these with more about customs, manners, and experiences. With America's separation from Britain, he wrote more about the devastation of the war. Similarly, James the Farmer praises America as a colony but despises the brutality the war has brought. Crèvecoeur's in-laws were Loyalists, and it remains ambiguous where his allegiances lay. He took an oath of loyalty to the revolutionary government, but this may have been to avoid the confiscation of his land. Similarly, he convinced a friend to take the same oath, but the motivations may have been the same. On the other hand, it is possible that the former surveyor's descriptions of landscapes, resources, and customs were in service of the British army.[10]

In 1779, Crèvecoeur's father's failing health compelled him to travel to Europe. Securing his family inheritance required presenting his oldest son in France. Embarking from New York City meant crossing both sides' military lines with the six-year-old boy, surely involving tactics he developed as a soldier. The British knew about the revolutionary oath, so they arrested him as a spy. After three months in captivity with precarious health and separated from his son, he received permission to sail for Dublin and then London, where he arranged for the publication of *Letters from an American Farmer* with Davies and Davis.

Through his father, he met Madame d'Houdeton, the noblewoman hosting one of the most prominent intellectual salons of the time. She introduced the author to Benjamin Franklin, who was securing funds and supplies for the revolution. The elder used simple clothes, simple speech, and great wit to create an attractive personification of America. This self-fashioning made him a likely mentor for the literary newcomer. Just as Crèvecoeur had transformed from a French officer into an Orange County Loyalist, he fashioned himself into a Patriot to promote his book. So, even though he was a Frenchman by birth, he made his reputation as a frontiersman when he visited France.

Since then, his glowing reputation came from three legacies, beginning with his invention of the American character as resourceful, hardworking, and egalitarian. Writing about the New World had been popular in Europe since Christopher Columbus, but *Letters* describes the colony from the perspective of a native. Spanning various regions and covering many ways of life, it provides readers a guide to a large part of the American experience. The narrator speaks of America as his home, rather than as a place he is visiting, giving the book an air of authenticity. Published in 1782, near the end of the Revolutionary War, it provides a description of the underdog victor. Contemporary readers relied on it to learn more about this upstart, which had no unifying language, religion, or ruling family. Instead of those traditions, Crèvecoeur offers civic practices as central to how a modern, new, diverse nation succeeds.

Crèvecoeur's disapproval of slavery further ensured his reputation. Letter IX, in which James visits Charlestown, South Carolina, rivals Letter III in its number of citations. He encounters materialism unlike that of the northern colonies. Here, within "liberal constitutionalism and the form of subjectivity it engenders," lawyers thrive as administrators of this excess.[11] They protect personal property and the freedom to accrue more, wielding a tangle of law, nature, and liberty to rationalize their way of life, including large-scale chattel slavery. The narrator delays coming to terms with it or condemning it and continues his visit. The chapter's portrait of slavery added to Crèvecoeur's favorable reputation. In reality, Crèvecoeur probably had never been to South Carolina. He assembled the passage from other sources. For decades, analysis of this chapter has made the same mistakes as that of the other: assuming the Farmer and Crèvecoeur were the same person, reading that chapter as straight reportage, and treating each letter as a distinct unit. Examining the narrative without considering the context removes each chapter from the literary norms of the time, when creative writing guided the moral sense of readers and commented on timely issues. As Doreen Alvarez Saar suggests, Letter IX uses slavery in South Carolina to comment on the relationship between the colonies and Britain, as well as the cruel treatment of chattel in the southern colony. This analogy resonated with contemporary readers, who saw slavery as "the loss of power by an independent people, usually the result of a corruption in the body politic."[12] This complication makes it harder to label Crèvecoeur in 1782 as an antislavery author, but it does make his writing more relevant to its time.

The best way to appreciate the author's and the narrator's contradictions is to remember that *Letters* is a novel, not just a collection of essays. The plot, characters, and locales serve a broader cosmology, rather than a simple nom de plume framing Crèvecoeur's persona. The Farmer has his own story, even if its elements resemble the author's life. The chapters beyond the third and the ninth complete this story, going from the idyllic opening to the portrayal of Nantucket as a functioning society and on to southern decadence, dehumanization, and disregard for republican values. This narrative parallels a version of the nation's development, from simple agriculture to harmonious society to a cruel system with characteristics like those of the wilderness. In this, the Charles-Town episode is a turning point for the Farmer. On his way to dine with a local plantation owner, he encounters a slave by the side of the road. As a punishment for killing an overseer, the captive is held in a cage above ground.

For two days, he has suffered birds plucking his eyes, blood dripping from his wounds, and industrious yet vicious bees stinging his skin. Emotionally overwhelmed, the traveler is unable to do more than offer him water before gathering his composure and continuing toward his dinner date with the slave's master. When his host explains that "the laws of self-preservation rendered such executions necessary," James does not engage with the rationalizations for slavery, dealing only with the sentiments that the "melancholy scene" has produced.[13] The author possibly built into this episode a critique of James's superficial response to oppression, plus a reminder that slavery of fellow humans was real, not just a metaphor for British rule over the colonies.

However, considering the varieties of cruelty and greed across regions throughout the novel, Crèvecoeur may have had a more comprehensive indictment of slavery in mind, both northern and southern. As Jeff Osborne has written in *Early American Literature*, "James's language of affect and sympathy actually perpetuates the subjugation of blacks, reinforces racial, regional, and class hierarchies, and, most importantly, assuages the liberal conscience of Americans. Crèvecoeur reveals just how much liberalism's radical redefinitions of the family and social relations conceal what once was explicit, namely, how citizenship requires the domination of multiple social segments."[14] Very subtly, the author may have been reflecting on his own experience as a slaveholder, as well as the rationalizations of his associates, including Thomas Jefferson.[15]

Crèvecoeur's most important legacy for this study, though, was his articulation of the making of the Americans, which suggested that true Americans cast off the old ways of their ancestors and consented to a new way of life based on equality. In this, mixture was a positive. The American was intrinsically new and mixed, just as the society was new and mixed and the way of life was new and mixed. The new and mixed nation was the way of the future, a utopia. The people in that utopia would be new and mixed. However, besides a practice of equality more inclusive than the present, the particular features of this utopia were unknown. Neither Crèvecoeur nor many who echoed his positive regard for mixture could say exactly what the future utopia would consist of. Crèvecoeur presented a way of speaking positively about the war, the demise of old regimes, and mixture. In turn, he influenced nearly all who addressed these themes in the future. Mixture was acceptable as long as it happened in certain combinations, and mixed offspring were viable as long as they subscribed to normative values. This set the model for qualified acceptance of mixture and qualified grants of inclusion.[16]

Given these contributions, it is easy to gloss over the complexities of Crèvecoeur and the Farmer, conflating both. But Crèvecoeur was probably a Loyalist. Mehitable's family was, and the *Letters'* descriptions of the land were possibly surveying reports for British generals. Within the book, the Farmer denounces the colonists and constantly expresses an anglophilic tendency. He is unabashedly Eurocentric. Crèvecoeur focused on European descendants, even if he never cursed blacks and Indians. Likewise, the Farmer describes the American as white: "He is either an European, or the descendant of an European, hence that strange mixture of blood, which you will find in no other country."[17] Lastly, both Crèvecoeur and his protagonist owned slaves. Even when gradual emancipation began to take shape after the war, residents of Orange County were some of the most adamant against the change.

After the Treaty of Paris negotiated the peace between the United States and Britain, Crèvecoeur accepted the position of consul from France to the United States. When he returned to New York City, where he was to promote trade between the two nations, he learned that Indians had attacked Pine Hill, killing Mehitable. The two children still at home had taken refuge with a neighbor and then moved to Boston to live with a new, adoptive family. Most likely, he lost his slaves too. If he had antislavery tendencies before this point, then this misfortune may have eased his conscience in the matter, emboldening him to accept the loss. In addition to his post, his book brought him fortune. Working in New York City, he established a packet boat that moved goods, people, and documents across the Atlantic. He became a member of the American Philosophical Society. He published a two-volume edition of *Letters* in 1784 and a three-volume edition in 1787.

Born eight years after Crèvecoeur in Virginia, a colony with an established plantation system, Thomas Jefferson embodied just as many contradictions about mixture and slavery, but in different ways. His mother was from the prominent Randolph family, and his father was a successful planter and surveyor in Albemarle County with business connections to the Randolph family. Peter Jefferson died when Thomas was age fourteen; at age twenty-one, he inherited five thousand acres of land, fifty-two slaves, and livestock, among other possessions. He graduated from William and Mary College in 1762. He continued his classical education, reading law with George Wythe.

In 1772, Jefferson married Martha Wayles Skelton, daughter of John Wayles and Martha Eppes. When the elder Martha married, she brought two slaves with her as part of her dowry: Susanna Hemings and her eleven-year-old daughter, Elizabeth Hemings, who was racially mixed. As part of that marriage agreement, they were to be property of the elder Martha and her heirs forever. After she died, John Wayles initiated an intimate relationship with Elizabeth, producing six racially mixed offspring, including Sally Hemings. As Isaac Jefferson, a former Monticello slave, described them, "Sally Hemings' mother Betty was a bright mulatto woman, and Sally mighty near white. . . . Sally was very handsome, long straight hair down her back."[18] When Wayles died in 1773, the younger Martha inherited the Hemings family and brought them to the early site of Monticello, the home plantation Jefferson was building in Charlottesville.

Regarding slavery, Jefferson's dilemma in this period was between appeasing personal gain and personal convictions. On one hand, he gained from the slave system, and it marked his membership in a network of families of the same class. On the other hand, he found slavery distasteful and contradictory to the Enlightenment values he had adopted. In 1769, he attempted to legislate for emancipation in Virginia, an effort the colonial governor rejected. Jefferson's original draft of the Declaration of Independence included an indictment against King George III for involving the colonies in the slave trade, another matter meeting with royal indifference.

In 1776, reflecting the revolutionary sentiment for freedom, the Virginia General Assembly commissioned Jefferson, Wythe, and Edmund Pendleton to propose a plan for emancipation in the state. In 1778, Jefferson proposed ending the importation of slaves, and the next year, the three published their plan, which involved separating new black offspring from their parents, training the youth in republican values, and then deporting them. This would contribute to an all-white nation rather than promoting racial equality, but it was radical for its time. During this period, Jefferson was better able to stand by his personal convictions, even working against the spread of slavery.

As governor of Virginia from 1779 to 1781, Jefferson witnessed the British invade the state twice, barely escaping a cavalry column the second time. Disapproval of his performance led to a hiatus in his public service, and he never held office there again. Soon afterward, he began work on *Notes on the State of Virginia*, which began as a series of responses to queries from François Barbé-Marbois, secretary of the French legation in Philadelphia. The book was as much a natural history as it was a work of boosterism. Much of the writing, especially the sections that address blacks and Indians, adopted the tropes of eighteenth-century anthropology. The result was a series of hierarchies of intellect, comeliness, and even body odor.

Martha Jefferson died in 1782, devastating Thomas. He expanded *Notes* and published a limited edition in French, in 1784. Its first public English edition appeared in 1787. *Notes* expressed the same paradox present through much of Jefferson's life. On one hand, in Query 14, he argued blacks' lower capacities: "I advance it therefore as a suspicion only, that the blacks, whether originally a distinct race, or made distinct by time and circumstances, are inferior to the whites in the endowments both of body and mind."[19] Likewise, even with a proposal for gradual emancipation, he warned of the black slave, "When freed, he is to be removed beyond the reach of mixture."[20] Beyond that warning, Jefferson never addressed mixture at all.

On the other hand, Jefferson portrayed the United States as a beacon of freedom. To patch this incongruity, he had to rationalize the exclusion of blacks. Since his usual favor for natural feelings would amplify his hypocrisy, he abandoned his core beliefs about equality. So natural science became the foundation for his social prescriptions, and his conclusions about race were firm before his explication began. American racial science of the coming decades was to do the same. Jefferson practiced this same rationalization in two cases where he encountered black genius: In *Notes*, he dismissed the black poet Phillis Wheatley as a mere imitator. Later, in 1791, he praised the author, scientist, and mathematician Benjamin Banneker, whom George Washington had appointed to the team to design Washington, D.C. Yet he insinuated that Banneker owed his successes to his supervisor on that project, Andrew Ellicott.[21]

However, in Query 18 (Manners) of *Notes*, Jefferson returned to the belief that all humans have a moral sense that makes them equal. This chapter contains one of his most prominent condemnations of slavery:

It is more difficult for a native to bring to that standard the manners of his own nation, familiarized to him by habit. There must doubtless be an unhappy influence on the manners of our people produced by the existence of slavery among us. The whole commerce between master and slave is a perpetual exercise of the most boisterous passions, the most unremitting despotism on the one part, and degrading submissions on the other.[22]

As in "A Summary View of the Rights of British America" and the draft of the Declaration of Independence, slavery was not a natural state but rather an institution that man had imposed, degrading both master and slave. As "imitative animals," future generations would perpetuate slavery, regardless of how immoral it was. Still fond of revolutionary reversals, Jefferson imagined that emancipation would come one way or another: by the consent of the masters or by the uprising of the slaves. Query 18 appealed to the reader's senses, rather than Query 14's appeal to anthropology. Jefferson was proficient at either argument, and he was sincere in both. *Notes*, like the whole archive of Jefferson's statements on race, gives two contradictory messages that force us to confront our "ambiguous and ambivalent values" to this day.[23]

In August 1784, Jefferson sailed the Atlantic, joining Benjamin Franklin and John Adams as a minister to France, taking over Franklin's duties in 1785. There, he delighted in the arts, philosophy, and architecture that he had only read about in books. He resolved to bring European elements back to Monticello, including French cuisine by enrolling James Hemings in culinary classes. Jefferson had come from the upper class in Virginia, but he was a country farmer compared to the circles he orbited in Paris. The change in social norms and the distance from observation by his kin allowed him liberties that his home lacked. When he learned of his daughter Lucy's death in 1785, he sent for his elder daughter, Mary, to join him in France. She made the journey in 1787, accompanied by Sally Hemings, who was fourteen at the time, a young girl with no notable skills. Abigail Adams wrote Jefferson, describing the girl as needing more attention than his daughter did, "wholy incapable of looking properly after her, without some superiour to direct her"[24] As a widower, he lived a sort of bachelor's life at the Hôtels de Landron and Langeac. Now with two girls in close proximity, he was the man of the house with no lady to tend to the feminine realms of the household. The intimate relationship between Thomas Jefferson and Sally Hemings initiated within this context.

Jefferson sailed back to the States in 1789 and soon stepped into the post of secretary of state under George Washington. According to an 1873 memoir by Madison Hemings, Sally Hemings's son born in 1805, she became pregnant by Thomas Jefferson while in France. She was conversant in French, and she had interacted with free blacks in Paris. Some of these were the offspring of *pla-çage*, the extralegal system of concubinage in the French and Spanish colonies, which exchanged a committed sexual relationship for the white man and support for the black woman and their offspring. Sally and her brother James could have petitioned the French for their freedom, but they returned to family and home in Virginia. In the same recollection, Madison asserted that Sally ensured privileges for herself and her offspring in exchange for her return to Virginia as Jefferson's concubine. This first child was born in 1790, but it died in infancy.

After that point, Sally had six surviving children, ostensibly with Thomas Jefferson as their father. Madison's interview indicated his belief in the man's paternity, and documentary sources indicate that Jefferson was at Monticello for each of the children's conceptions. However, it would take DNA testing showing that he likely was the father for many historians to accept the notion. In part, because of changing mores regarding interracial intimacy in the past two hundred years, it is easier now to accept that Jefferson was the father. More importantly, though, scholarship has dared us to reconsider the relationships between the Jeffersons and the Hemingses. Annette Gordon-Reed's work accepts Jefferson's paternity and grounds it in the social mores of Virginia's planter class. The relationship may not have been romantic, equal, nor consensual by today's standards, but it was sensible, given that milieu. A growing body of work further argues that white, male sexual prerogative was normal throughout the Americas. If there was *plaçage* in French and Spanish colonies, why not in the United States? This research urges us to accept racial mixing as a core part of the American experience since the beginning. Sexual liaisons were going all directions, without necessarily being a problem, as they often were as the Civil War approached and in the decades that followed.[25]

In discussing Jefferson, I argue that the main reason why some people have denied his paternity is that a sexually active, interracially intimate Jefferson is dangerous to certain values that they look for in a national figure: intellectualism, chastity, and behavior consistent with written statements. The same is true for nonwhite figures as well—for example, Frederick Douglass. To admit Jefferson's baser urges is to acknowledge the array of power advantages between him, his wife, the Hemingses, and the other slaves. Acknowledging these complexities of gender, race, and class strain the hermetically sealed jar we display him under. Just as acknowledging interracial intimacy encourages us to employ these analytic lenses, it can also disrupt our understandings of them. Those who preserve Jefferson as intellectual, chaste, and straightforward also avoid the possibility that he was subject to compulsions, urges, and contradictions.

So we treat historical figures like texts, decoding and recoding them with our own ideologies. A text such as Thomas Jefferson also retains the meanings ascribed to him over the past two hundred years. He was tight-lipped about the matter, as were his descendants. Later, racial scientists followed his model, asserting that blacks were inferior and mixture was repugnant, even though their fellows engaged in interracial intimacy. Biographers positioned him far from these repugnant activities. The notion that Jefferson was father to Hemings's children has gained currency since the demise of Jim Crow, but it is still controversial. Instead, appreciation for his antislavery tendencies grew, rehabilitating his image rather than expanding it to include the less comfortable aspects. The more expansive historical work shows us that it is possible to value Jefferson and to critique him at the same time.[26]

During Jefferson's lifetime, the boldest challenge to his stance on mixture and slavery came from William Short, his "adoptive son" (see fig. 1.1). Also a native of Virginia, Short was born 1759 and graduated from William and Mary College. A relative of Martha Wayles Skelton by marriage, he helped settle her estate when John Wayles died. Jefferson was one of his examiners for the bar exam, as was George Wythe. Jefferson furthered the young lawyer's career in foreign affairs by appointing him as his secretary during his time as minister to France, 1786–1789. Upon Short's arrival, he immersed himself in the French language and explored agricultural industry in Italy. While managing Jefferson's agenda in France, Short proved himself a competent diplomat, at times acting as chargé d'affaires in Jefferson's absence. His command of French, his affability, and his youthful energy aided his work, placing him in some of Paris's leading salons. During this time, Short and Duchesse Rosalie de la Rochefoucauld, the young wife of an elder, pro-American nobleman, developed a romance. This influenced his decision to stay as the United States' representative when Jefferson departed in 1789. Short assumed the position of chargé, as well as the new nation's fiscal agent for all of Europe. At first, believing Jefferson would return, Short thought it would be a temporary post. When Jefferson indicated he was staying in America, Short hoped to rise to minister in France and then to obtain a higher position in the federal government. In the meanwhile, he became Jefferson's eyes and ears.[27]

Professional and romantic matters for Short turned out different from his expectations, but his extended stay in Europe gave him a distinctive perspective on international events. He continued to represent the United States to the court of Louis XVI, even as the National Assembly took charge of resolving France's financial crisis in May 1789. Although the legislative body represented the clergy, nobility, and bourgeoisie, the third dominated. They renamed it the National Constituent Assembly in July, and in August, they published the Declaration of Rights of Man, which drew from the same belief in natural, universal rights as the United States' Declaration of Independence. Since colonial productivity was central to economic recovery, the French Declaration stopped short of addressing slavery, but its principles did inspire opponents of slavery in France and beyond. In Paris, Jacques-Pierre Brissot founded the Society of the Friends of the Blacks in 1788, after seeing the work of the English abolitionist Thomas Clarkson and the London Society for the Abolition of the Slave Trade. He had visited the United States during the Philadelphia Constitutional Convention and returned there in 1789 to meet with leading American abolitionists. Brissot's organization consisted of elites who paid subscription fees and joined only through reference from an existing member. Its charter stipulated that it elect a new president every three months. Crèvecoeur and Short became members, but Jefferson,

Fig. 1.1. Portrait of William Short, by Rembrandt Peale, 1806

reflecting his abstinence from direct antislavery activity since 1782, declined the invitation to join, claiming that it would interfere with his status as an objective diplomat.[28]

The Society faced opposition from the Committee on Colonies, which supported the interests of big planters, protecting slavery and arguing that abolition would lead to catastrophe. If the mission of the National Assembly was to remedy the French economy, then abolition was counterproductive.

The Massaic Club, an organization of colonial planters who lived throughout France, published literature against abolition and attacked specific members of the Society. They cast them as subversives in cahoots with the British, as well as fomenters of violence on Saint-Domingue. Most of all, they emphasized the economic downfall that would come from emancipation. The island's revolution bound itself to the metropole's revolution. More importantly, if free people of color on Saint-Domingue could build a functional republic, then mixed people in France could be participants there. American leaders also observed these events, waiting for answers for their own questions about race, mixture, and equality.[29]

Unrest in Saint-Domingue brought French slavery to an end more quickly than did the efforts of the Society of the Friends of the Blacks. Its population consisted of four hundred thousand slaves, twenty-nine thousand whites, and twenty-nine thousand free people of color, who were mostly educated offspring of white elites and black slaves. Many of these aligned themselves with the whites in power and sought equality with them. Their efforts made the suitability of mixed people to hold citizenship relevant to the island, Paris, and, through Short's correspondence with Jefferson, the United States. In January 1790, the National Assembly refused to recognize land-owning free people of color who were arguing for voting rights. In March, the colony's local government decided to handle this domestic affair themselves. Vincent Ogé, one of the free people of color who had been in Paris, formed a militia of 250–300 of his class and initiated an uprising in October. Their primary concern was equality with whites for themselves, not the abolition of slavery. French forces overwhelmed them, and Ogé fled to the Spanish portion of the island. They returned the rebels to the French colonial government, which executed them in February.[30]

Regardless of the free men of color's position on slavery, the Society paid special attention to them, maintaining that giving them rights would quell the violence on Saint-Domingue. Together, their efforts gained more influence; even proslavery members of the Committee on Colonies saw that the free men of color could be instrumental in stabilizing the colony. In 1791, Abbé Henrí Grégoire, a priest and member of the Society, put forth the motion to give them rights, and the Assembly issued the May 15 Decree, which proclaimed that sons of free parents could vote. Colonial whites rejected this legislation, leading to more armed rebellion from the mulattoes in August. This time, they enlisted the black population, transforming the conflict into a slave rebellion.[31]

The French rescinded the May 15 Decree on September 24, but hoping to end the violence but still to maintain control over the colony, the Assembly passed the Law of April 4, 1792, granting equal rights to every free man of color. It also sent six thousand soldiers to quell the rebellion and commissioners to enforce this law. Léger-Félicité Sonthonax, a member of the Society, was one of the three men charged with this mission. Although he was an abolitionist, he also had a tempestuous, power-hungry side that encouraged him to centralize control. Ultimately, his goal was to save the colony for France, perhaps with himself as governor.[32]

In 1792, President Washington appointed Gouverneur Morris minister to France instead of Short, who was in the Netherlands negotiating loans that would settle Revolutionary War loans from France and Spain. Although Short held the same title for the country where he was currently conducting business, this news came as a disappointment, as he preferred to be closer to Rosalie. While apart, she corresponded with him by letters, professing her love, informing him of developments in France, and entertaining the possibility that the Rochefoucauld family would move to the United States. But when the hope for a constitutional monarchy fell that same year, moderates were arrested as enemies of the new republic. Rosalie's husband became one of many victims of the guillotine, which also decimated the Society. From The Hague, Short saved some of her property and assets by putting them in his name, with intentions to return them to her and to make her Mrs. Short.

The French declared war on the British in February 1793, thinning out their military resources. The war with Britain caused those in Saint-Domingue who were dissatisfied with the commissioners' mission to ally with the British, who offered asylum to the antiemancipation white colonists on Saint-Domingue at their own colony, Jamaica. In August 1793, Sonthonax took a desperate step that he hoped would fulfill his mission and remain true to his abolitionist principles; he freed all slaves in the northern province and then in the other two in September and October. Rather than recognize the new rights of the slave population, the mulattoes joined the whites' efforts to control the slaves and fought against Sonthonax. Knowing that his principal directive was to protect French control of the colony, the blacks did not trust him either, preferring total independence.

The National Assembly followed Sonthonax's model in 1794, declaring universal emancipation in all French colonies on February 4. Under the leadership of Toussaint Louverture, the black army on Saint-Domingue allied with the French, against the Spanish and British, two nations slower to end slavery. The colonial governor made him commander of the interracial black, mixed, and white army, which restabilized the island until Napoleon Bonaparte reinstated slavery on nearby Guadeloupe, indicating that he would do the same there. Then the Assembly called Sonthonax back to France to defend himself against charges of treason.

After a two-week visit with the widow Rochefoucauld, Short's began his next post, treaty negotiator in Spain, 1793–1795. Soon after he arrived, Spain allied with Britain in its war with France, stifling his efforts to build a treaty with the nation. He may have seen the *casta* (caste) paintings that titillated art collectors in Spain with images of mixture in the New World. These works depicted combinations of Spanish, indigenous, and African people in colonial Mexico. Instead of a dyad of white versus nonwhite, their system was more of a spectrum, appreciating many shades between white and black. Regardless, this pigmentocracy benefited those of greater white descent. Across eighteenth-century variations of this art, the heathen Indian was usually the lowest. Degrees of Spanish descent were a major preoccupation for the colonials, and those with more took great pride in that *calidad*, a term that translated as "quality." The term also referred to noble standing; these meanings were one and the same for the elites. Some host in Spain probably explained the labels for different kinds of mixture to Short, probably in terms that praised the successes of New Spain. In turn, Short possibly reflected on his home state, finding parallels with their colony. The more time he spent away from Virginia, learning the ways of other nations, the broader his perspective became. The impact of this exposure became clearer in 1798, when he challenged his mentor in matters of mixture and citizenship.[33]

Miscommunication gave the U.S. government the impression that Short was delaying negotiations, and it decided to replace him with Thomas Pinckney. In reality, he had nearly completed the business with the Spanish Court. With Short already anxious to return to Rosalie in France, this disappointment inspired him to resign from the foreign service. Lingering in Europe had already harmed his chances at advancing in Washington. Demotions from France to the Netherlands to Spain indicated that he had fallen out of favor in the diplomatic realm as well. He returned to France in November 1795 to live with Rosalie.

In 1798, Short wrote an extraordinary letter to his mentor, challenging him on matters of racial mixture, slavery, and emancipation. Many of Short's letters to Jefferson opened with salutations, a record of what correspondence was in transit or lost, and items of business. In this letter, he followed the greetings with his position on domestic matters of race, property, and citizenship, distancing himself from Jefferson in each of these. Short wished that his plot of land in Virginia, the Indian Camp, be rented out to tenant farmers who could produce crops and enough income to buy their own land somewhere. Even though selling the undesirable property would gain him a small amount more money, he wished to test the theory that "free people at their ease can be found to cultivate the lands of others, where they are able to purchase lands of their own."[34] Even though the tenants would be working someone else's land, the hope of obtaining their own homestead would make it less like the slavery they were accustomed to seeing. Short had come to the conclusion that real estate was the most stable investment in the United States, and it was better to own land and rent it, even if the immediate revenue was lower, than to sell it. He wished to make this plan for the Indian Camp come true as soon as he returned. But he was also communicating his position on land development, tenancy, and self-sufficiency. He preferred to contribute to the long-term expansion of self-sufficiency than to increase his own personal gain.[35]

The Indian Camp matter served as a foundation for the topics that followed. The first was Sierra Leone, which British philanthropists had established as a point of recolonization for blacks, whether the poor from London or those who had taken the British offer of freedom if they fought against the Americans in the Revolutionary War. At this point, the endeavor's success was a credit for British abolitionists. To Short, it indicated "the perfectability of the black race," hope of "improved, populous & extensive nations of the black color, formed into powerful societies who will par in every respect with whites under the same circumstances."[36] This idea clashed with Jefferson's position that blacks were incapable of creative genius. However, Short did predict that Sierra Leone would become merely a commercial enterprise, a new colony bound to England. Even though Short supported recolonization as an antislavery approach, he remained skeptical of its efficacy, preferring the tenant farming plan. Here, he differed with Jefferson, whose proposals for emancipation relied on recolonization.

Then Short posed that American blacks could enjoy citizenship in the United States. The success of Sierra Leone showed that recolonization could "insure the restoration of the rights of citizenship of those blacks who inhabit the U.S. if it be not sooner done, as it may be expected, by the gradual & beneficial operation of our own laws."[37] Knowing that Jefferson preferred recolonization, Short introduced that scheme as a way to abolish slavery. But he really wanted to discuss the possibility of black citizenship in the United States through a peaceful process, rather than an uprising.

But that was just a transition toward Short's audacious proposal: recognition of mixed offspring as a step toward emancipation without colonization. Even if Jefferson opposed the creation of a semifree class, that class existed. The simple solution would be to legitimize mixed offspring and to offer them citizenship within the United States. Short's membership in the Society and his experience in Spain surely influenced this view of free people of color. He acknowledged that even those who were "the least subjected to prejudice" had an aversion to racial mixing and asked, "If this be an evil, is it not the least that can take place under present circumstances?" Legitimate mixture and citizenship was better than segregation or recolonization. Episodes in European history showed how expulsion could backfire. He continued,

> [Mixture] is certainly less than keeping 700,000 people & their descendants in perpetual slavery even if it were possible—Is it not less also than having that number of free people living in the same country & separated from the rest of the community by a marked & impassable line?—Is it not less even than the expopulation of the U.S. of so great a number of their inhabitants by any possible means?

In other words, free mixture was minor in comparison to the subjugation of blacks, the mixture that was already going on, and the placement of "all of them in the state of degradation inseparable from the most mitigated degree of slavery."[38] Short denounced the one-drop rule that made all people of African descent slaves.

Short flattered "the most enlightened & virtuous minds" who happened to oppose mixture, but then he wielded the belief in environmentalism to defuse their concerns. Transporting blacks to a more temperate climate would lighten them, just as transporting whites to a warmer climate would darken them. In the southern states, this would lead to an intermediate shade, even without interracial intimacy. He cited the darker-complexioned Spaniards as one example of how this medium complexion was acceptable, and then he named prominent women from Virginia who were darker. "There is no sentiment arising from the contemplation of beauty that they would not be capable of inspiring equally with those who can boast the perfect mixture of the rose & the lilly."[39] Short was drawing attention to the effects of the environment on whites. If, even without interracial intimacy, whites were mutable, then how dangerous could the change be with racial mixture?

Transforming slaves into free citizens required "a penetrating genius capable of diving into the bosom of futurity," one with a utopian vision of the nation. As a first step, Short suggested that statesmen, philosophers, and philanthropists, "all who have any regard to the interests of their country or the rights of humanity," gather to address the issues.[40] Jefferson fit this description, as did Crèvecoeur. The second step involved abolitionist activism and state laws showing that it is in the interest of slave owners to reduce their dependence on chattel. Those owners would then transition their former bondspeople toward independence. This would reduce the odds of a violent uprising like that on Saint-Domingue. He returned to the case of renting lands as a profitable alternative to chattel. If the slave owners could learn this, then they would engage in wholesale emancipation. In the third step, organizations would work toward gradual emancipation by raising funds and purchasing slaves. The first priority would be the women, as their bodies produced new slaves. Freeing all the women at once could end the future generations of slaves. Besides, it would be less expensive than purchasing all the men. It is unlikely that Short knew of the Jefferson-Hemings liaison at this point, so he was not making insinuations against his mentor. Short's system, like European serfdom, bound laborers to the land, rather than to property owner. It also presaged the homesteading efforts of the Republican Party, as well as sharecropping agreements, since the laborers had to pay back their monetary worth. Short's was a fantastic scheme, but it did predict the tactics of the Civil War–era abolitionists.

William and Rosalie's plan of marrying and returning to the States never materialized. Although revolution had torn apart Rosalie's homeland, killing her husband and nearly bankrupting her, she preferred to stay there than to move to a new country. Short departed in 1802, remaining a bachelor for the rest of his life. Although he had inherited land in Virginia and had trained to be a lawyer, he chose to leave the state and to invest his capital in canals, railroads, and land along the frontier. He moved to Philadelphia and became a member of the American Philosophical Society. Later, in 1810, Rosalie married another aristocrat, the Marquis de Castellane, a widower with grown children, relatives in common, and an appointment from Napoleon.

During the last decades of the eighteenth century, the number of freed slaves in Virginia grew remarkably. Along with the ideals of the Revolutionary War, the work of antislavery Quakers and Methodists inspired a change of heart in some land owners. In 1782, the General Assembly made it easier to follow these urges with a revision of its manumission laws. Previously, masters needed special permission of the state's governing body, but afterward, they could do it by will or by presenting a deed to the county court. Across the states, the percentage of free blacks rose from 1% to more than 10% by 1810. In Virginia, the percentage nearly doubled, from 4.2% to 7.2%. During the same period, the state altered its laws regarding the leasing of slaves, increasing the mobility of skilled, black laborers.[41]

Still, Virginians had been watching the developments in Saint-Domingue with ill ease. With a slave population of 39.2% and high concentrations on plantations west of Richmond, they recognized the parallels between their home and the island, where the violence had targeted whites since 1791. In 1800, Gabriel, a literate, skilled slave, planned a revolt in the same region. Like other insurgents in northern and southern states, he was aware of the events in the Caribbean. He would lead slaves from the Tidewater into Richmond, but heavy rainfall postponed the revolt. Before he could regroup, two slaves informed their master of the plan. That landowner told the governor, James Monroe, who activated the state militia. The suppression was successful, Gabriel was captured, and he and twenty-five followers were hung. However, the prospect of slave uprising remained palpable for Virginians.[42]

Jefferson was inaugurated as the third president in 1801. That same year, at Monticello, Sally Hemings gave birth to a second daughter, named Harriet. The journalist James Callender, who had attacked Alexander Hamilton and the Federalist Party, left prison. He had served time for violations of the Sedition Act while attacking Jefferson's opponents and hoped for a political favor in return. When Jefferson declined to appoint him to his new cabinet, Callender attacked him personally, writing a series of articles in 1802 that insinuated that Jefferson had children by Sally Hemings. Many people considered the articles distasteful, whether they were aware of interracial master-slave relationships or naive. Around the same time, between 1802 and 1803, the Federalist weekly *Port Folio* published articles and songs about the Jefferson-Hemings affair, also hoping to damage his chances for reelection. Permissive reprinting and word of mouth spread the issue across the states, inspiring political cartoonist James Akin to produce "A Philosophic Cock" (see fig. 1.2). The engraving features Jefferson's head on top of a rooster's body, indirectly referring to the male genitals by presenting a more decent homonym still known for its sexual liberties around a chicken coop. Behind the Jefferson-rooster is a hen with a woman's head looking subservient toward him. Her complexion is darker, and she wears a turban, Akin's rough approximation of Sally Hemings's appearance and a slave woman's garb. The two figures are uncanny in appearance, bearing a strange mixture on their bodies. But they also hint at an illicit relationship between them. By this point in 1804, the notion of Jefferson having a sexual relationship with Hemings was popular enough for readers to recognize the illustration's premise.

An inscription, "Tis not a set of features or complexion or tincture of a skin that I admire," appears near the top, spoken by the Jefferson-rooster, alluding to his intellectual stature. This line comes from Joseph Addison's 1712 tragedy *Cato*, which dramatizes the conflict between Julius Caesar and Cato the Younger, who embodied republican values for many members of the Revolutionary generation. Ironically, Juba, Cato's Numidian ally, speaks these words early in the play, explaining his love for the protagonist's daughter. The prince admits to loving her despite her complexion, which is fairer than his usual tastes. Marcia's "inward greatness, unaffected wisdom, and sanctity of manners" are more important than her outward appearance. Akin

Fig. 1.2. "A Philosophic Cock," by James Akin, ca. 1804

thus transplanted an African man's statement of love triumphant over difference and put them in the mouth of a political adversary who would never have said such a thing in public. Out of context, Juba's statement resembles the antimixing protestations in *Notes on the State of Virginia*. The cartoonist could have been hinting that Jefferson actually loved Sally, but most likely he was juxtaposing Jefferson's words against his actions just as he juxtaposed his rational, human head against his licentious, animal body. Jefferson remained silent about the matter. He had already deplored Callender's behavior, and perhaps he knew his reputation could withstand it. But, within the context of the liberties that privileged white men possessed, the controversy was sure to disappear.[43]

In 1802, Jefferson reneged on the promise of the aid to quell the rebellions on Saint-Domingue that he had offered France as secretary of state. He learned that Napoleon hoped to use the colony as a launching point to fortify the territory past the Mississippi as permanently French, even though negotiations had begun for the Louisiana Purchase. Additionally, Jefferson hoped to obtain Florida from the Spanish, so he announced neutrality in regard to the rebellions. This allowed him to nurture plans for expansion. Meanwhile, U.S. merchants continued trading with the rebels, unofficially helping their cause.

The Haitian Revolution ended in 1804 with Jean-Jacques Dessalines, the new nation's first ruler, killing and exiling the remaining whites. He reached out to the United States to establish a diplomatic relationship, but this recent spree sealed the ill ease that the violence inspired there. Jefferson established a policy of nonrecognition of Haiti. The demonstration by the free people of color and blacks in the black republic convinced Jefferson that it was less suitable for democracy than were the era's two other revolutionary sites, the United States and France. The violence suggested that free, racially mixed people in the United States may similarly fail at republicanism.[44]

In response to Gabriel's revolt and others, Virginia ceased the education of slaves, closed down the leasing of skilled slaves, and required that freedpeople leave the state within a year of emancipation. However, interracial relationships and manumission persisted in Virginia, even among Jefferson's associates. George Wythe had freed many of his slaves when his wife died in 1787, making provisions for their independence. One of his former slaves, Lydia Broadnax, was likely his concubine, and her sixteen-year-old son, Michael Brown, their offspring. They stayed with Wythe, and he included them in his will. Wythe's other heir, George Sweeney, had accumulated gambling debts and resented sharing his great-uncle's inheritance. So, on May 25, 1806, he put arsenic in Broadnax's and Brown's food. But he also poisoned Wythe. Broadnax recovered, but Brown died within a week. Wythe died a week later, after discovering that Sweeney had forged checks against his bank account and revising his will to exclude the nephew. The previous version had left property to Broadnax and another former slave and had split bank stock between Brown and Sweeney. It also stipulated that Jefferson supervise the boy's education. It was ironic that an older man who was candid about his generosity to Broadnax and Brown charged a pupil, who had been secretive about his own lover and children, with executing part of his will that secured the future of his mixed son. Did he know about the private goings on at Monticello? Was he daring Jefferson to do the same? If Michael had lived, he may have had to leave the state. Depending on his physical appearance, he may have lived as white or black. Regardless, with an inheritance, he would have prospered. Jefferson had to navigate these choices for his own mixed offspring. The last of these, Eston, was born in 1808.[45]

In August of the same year, Abbé Henrí Grégoire, who had argued for the rights of free people of color in 1791, sent Jefferson a copy of his book *An Enquiry Concerning the Intellectual and Moral Faculties and Literature of Negroes*, refuting the supposed inferiority of blacks with examples of genius, including some from the United States, as direct challenges to *Notes on the State of Virginia*. Jefferson retired after his second term as president and replied to the bishop, revising his position from twenty-five years before. He hoped that blacks could be found equal with whites and said this about his past beliefs: "My doubts were the result of personal observation on the limited sphere of my own State, where the opportunities for the development of their genius were not favorable, and those of exercising it still less so. I expressed them therefore with great hesitation; but whatever be their degree of talent it is no measure of their rights." Jefferson admitted that he based generalizations on his limited experience. He still resisted calling them equal but offered Isaac Newton as an analogy; just because the scientist was very intelligent did not mean he should be master over blacks. Harking back to natural rights, Jefferson maintained that they could advance to "equal footing with the other colors of the human family."[46] His statements in retirement were too little, too late.

With a plan to return free blacks to Africa, the American Colonization Society resembled Jefferson's plan from 1778. Founded in 1816, the organization most successful at promoting this notion consisted of two kinds of antislavery activists: those who opposed slavery in principle, believing that Africa would be the most favorable locale for former slaves to live in liberty; and slaveholders who wanted to avoid more slave rebellions. The disparate positions on equality and freedom actually worked to the Society's benefit, making it appealing to a variety of Americans wishing to exclude the inferior race, hoping to subdue the dangers of slavery, or hoping for black equality— somewhere else.

The Society's first meeting was held in Washington, D.C., in 1816. Among its founders was Henry Clay, the congressman from Kentucky, Speaker of the House, and later architect of the Missouri Compromise and the Compromise of 1850. He was opposed to racial mixing, believing that physical differences between the races made it unnatural. Very early in the proceedings on December 21, Clay presented the question of free mixed people as the primary impetus for the founding of the Society:

> That class of the mixt population of our country was peculiarly situated; they neither enjoyed the immunities of freemen, nor were they subjected to the incapacities of slaves, but partook, in some degree, of the qualities of both. From their condition, and the unconquerable prejudices resulting from their colour, they never could amalgamate with the free whites of this country. It was desirable, therefore, as it respected them, and the residue of the population of the country, to drain them off.[47]

In other words, echoing Jefferson, mixture produced a middle category that threatened the racial order, and it should be removed. Clay echoed both of Jefferson's rhetorical modes—science and sentiment—showing how these tactics had already taken hold in American racial thinking. But mixture had always complicated the racial hierarchies. The development of the slave system in the Chesapeake colonies attested to this by establishing the first laws against intermarriage in the seventeenth century. The events that Thomas Jefferson, William Short, and Hector St. John de Crèvecoeur witnessed around the Atlantic confronted racial mixture, citizenship, and nation-building. At this moment, *amalgamation* was a term from metallurgy describing the creation of alloys by melting together different metals and resulting in a product stronger than the originals. Even though its associations were rarely with racial mixing at this point, the term established its place in the realm of race talk during the coming decades.

2

Wendell Phillips, Unapologetic Abolitionist,
Unreformed Amalgamationist

Upon the passage of the Missouri Compromise, Thomas Jefferson wrote John Holmes, a Massachusetts politician who had supported the legislation, reflecting on his life in retirement. The seventy-seven-year-old founder claimed to ignore public affairs and current events, but in regard to the 1820 act, he wrote, "But this momentous question, like a fire bell in the night, awakened and filled me with terror. I considered it at once as the knell of the Union. It is hushed indeed for the moment."[1] The Compromise admitted Maine, formerly part of Massachusetts, as a free state and Missouri as a slave state. It also attempted to establish the southern border of Missouri as the line deciding which new states would be free or slave. Jefferson was pessimistic that the agreement would settle the sectional differences, predicting that they would grow with "every new irritation." Political differences between federalism and republicanism were one thing, since they existed within each state, but a geographic line was irreconcilable. Jefferson regretted the institution of slavery, giving what comes across as lip service to its demise. His hope this late in his life was to spread slavery across a greater area, diffusing its effect. Those who remained slaves under those conditions were never fit for freedom.[2]

However, the most telling passage followed. "This certainly is the exclusive right of every state, which nothing in the constitution has taken from them and given to the general government. Could Congress, for example say that the non-freemen of Connecticut, shall be freemen," Jefferson asked, "or that they shall not emigrate into any other state?"[3] He sided with states' rights, including the right to categorize people. As this was before emancipation, the categorization also equated slavery with blackness. But he also questioned who could leave one state and enter another. If a slave could escape to a free state, then Jefferson was comfortable with his or her becoming free. During the winter of 1821–1822, the question of racial categorization, who was free and who could emigrate, whispered, rather than rang, at Monticello. Beverly, Sally Hemings and Jefferson's oldest surviving son, left in late 1821, and Harriet, Hemings and Jefferson's daughter born in 1801, left early in 1822. Jefferson made no effort to pursue either. Later, Madison claimed that they both moved to Washington, D.C., and lived as white people. Having changed their names, they have disappeared from the public record.[4]

Jefferson died in 1826, delegating his final answer to the question of mixture, freedom, and citizenship to Virginia laws and his creditors. Eston and Madison could remain free, but Sally and the others remained part of the estate, assets to resolve Jefferson's debts. Sally appeared on the 1830 census as a free white woman living in Charlottesville with her two free sons. On a special 1833 survey, Sally was a free person of color. The next year, she was "given her time" by Jefferson's daughter, which enabled her to retire around age sixty yet allowed her to stay within the state of Virginia. After Sally passed away in 1835, Madison settled in Ohio, and his descendants identified as black. Eston also went to Ohio, but he settled in Wisconsin, changing his name and living as white. They proved Henry Clay's statement at the founding of the American Colonization Society wrong; free people of color could amalgamate into society.

Loyal to white male privilege, Jefferson quit his antislavery work early in his career. Neither did he acknowledge the interracial intimacy he practiced. But his statement to John Holmes about escaping slavery, his nonchalance toward Harriet's and Beverly's departure, and Eston's and Madison's emancipation all suggest that he licensed claiming whiteness if one could. With enough white heritage, self-sufficiency, and a sense of self-making, a person of color could go free. Later, the trope of the "tragic mulatto" cast a pathological meaning on Beverly's, Harriet's, and Eston's choice, making it a denial of one's "true" identity with an inevitable punishment. But in reality it was very reasonable. If you had one black ancestor in eight, you appeared white, and you had what it takes to be self-sufficient, why not? If your community already recognized you as white, why not? If you lived during a time when slavery was common and manumission was rare, you might draw on whatever you could to secure your freedom. If you were going to leave your home state and family, never to return, you might also change your name.

A short period separated Jefferson's death and antebellum radicalism. In 1829, David Walker's *Appeal* critiqued Clay and colonization in general, arguing that African Americans belonged in America. He cited the Declaration of Independence, calling for inclusion and equality, but also described African Americans as a distinct group. Still heading the abolitionist newspaper the *Genius of Universal Emancipation*, William Lloyd Garrison called Walker's pamphlet "a most injudicious publication, yet warranted by the creed of an independent people."[5] At the same time, the editor was moving toward a more immediatist position than his employer, Benjamin Lundy, held. Soon after, in January 1831, he founded his own newspaper, the *Liberator*, which called for the immediate emancipation of all slaves.

Garrisonian abolitionism had from its beginning put interracial intimacy in the forefront. Followers undertook a campaign to repeal all laws in Massachusetts making distinctions of race, including the state's anti-intermarriage law, which had stood since 1705. This was one of Garrison's least popular campaigns, but for a while he persisted in defending intermarriage, a position that followed his belief in one human race, created by God. The editor declared, "As civilization, and knowledge, and republican feelings, and Christianity prevail in the world, the wider will matrimonial connexions extend; and finally people of every tribe and kindred and tongue will freely intermarry. By the blissful operation of this divine institution, the earth is evidently to become one neighborhood or family."[6] The promise of Christianity was central in Garrison's utopian vision and, in turn, the position of the *Liberator*. Rather than repugnant, intermarriage was only natural. He continued,

> If He has "made of one blood all nations of me for to dwell on all the face of the earth," then they are one species, and stand on a perfect equality: their marriage is neither unnatural nor repugnant to nature, but obviously proper and salutary; it being designed to unite people of different tribes and nations, and to break down those petty distinctions which are the effect of climate or locality of situation, and which lead to oppression, war and division among mankind.[7]

Garrison invoked Acts 17:26 to emphasize that God made all the people over the face of the earth his equal offspring. Against this higher authority, the distaste that proslavery scientists expressed toward mixing was misguided. Natural law, a singular family of man, and "the principles of the gospel" would prevail over their claims.

However, the most consistent defender of interracial marriage was the orator Wendell Phillips, who acted as counsel to the marriage-law campaign, wrote editorials, and delivered speeches from the 1830s onward. Wendell Phillips was born on November 29, 1811, to a prominent family that first came to America in 1630. His father, a corporate lawyer, was Boston's first mayor, and Wendell received the best education available, including Boston Latin School, Harvard University, and Harvard Law School. Most of his biographers attribute his coming to abolitionism to seeing Garrison barely escape an angry gang in 1835. But some put his courtship of Ann Greene, a young, zealous abolitionist, at the center of his conversion, portraying his early professional years as a period of finding himself and often clashing with his family. Through his genealogy and through his activism, it is easy to see him as a descendant of Puritan leaders, especially in his regard for private conscience. Post-Revolutionary reformers adopted the Puritan equation of industry with virtue, broad individualism under community, and the expansion of the region's covenant to the whole nation. Phillips and other New England abolitionists saw purging slavery as their responsibility, with the whole nation's downfall as the stakes. Extensive reform called for extensive positions. Fundamentally reforming the nation meant reshaping institutions taken for granted, including prohibitions on interracial marriage. The belief in one human race and equality broke down many social barriers. Even though most radical abolitionists kept mostly monoracial personal lives, this position did allow different relations in the future.[8]

As a follower of Garrison, Phillips contributed numerous articles to the *Liberator* and spoke at many antislavery gatherings. However, Phillips remained faithful to his position regarding interracial marriage throughout his career, while Garrison later qualified his statements before the campaign ended, saying that "the common sense of mankind and the usages of society will regulate this indispensable union."[9] This difference between Garrison and Phillips mirrors others between them. While both wanted immediate emancipation, critiqued political parties, and denounced the Constitution as a proslavery document, Phillips did examine institutional means for subverting slavery far more than Garrison did. He was a student of political economy, delving into topics such as India's cotton trade to better understand the interests that made slavery the labor system of choice. He regretted that, with no economic appeal, the abolitionists had no grounds to convince "that large class of men with whom dollars are always a weightier consideration than duties."[10] Lastly, he knew that it would take three or more generations to reeducate Americans regarding race relations, even with immediate emancipation.

A pair of essays from an April 1831 issue of the *Liberator* imagined two possible futures for the nation, both dreams of the author. The first described a society that had abolished slavery, bestowed equal rights to blacks and Indians, and succeeded at the "work of amalgamation and reconciliation."[11] The narrator has fallen asleep while reading and wakes to find himself in the future United States where blacks and whites interact "with perfect ease in social intercourse." The moral suasion of the abolitionists had been successful, bringing about "restoration to the rights and dignity of men" "upon principles of justice and humanity." Their reliance on the natural rights of humanity had won over their opponents. Once given opportunities, blacks rose to equality with whites within two generations. As one gentleman informs the visitor, "Our first black President was a man of such distinguished talents, that none chose to risk their own reputation for discernment by not acknowledging it, and African inferiority was heard of no more. In short, after the amalgamation was once begun," he continues, likely referring to social mixture rather than bodily mixture, "it is vain to attempt to enumerate all the circumstances that contributed to it." Within two generations, segregation became a thing of the past, along with distinctions of race beyond physical descriptions. Racial mixture had increased, tendering whites' natural pugnacious tendencies with blacks' natural musical talents. In romantic racialist terms of the time, each race brought their particular gifts to the creation of a united and equal country.

However, specific values prevail in this author's utopia: Christianity, masculinity, and upright social mores. The narrator encounters people who praise these values throughout his time travel. When they speak of rights, they refer to men only. Everyone he encounters is of the respectable upper classes, the paragon of black success, which affords this "passport to gentility." The narrator then has the opportunity to meet the president, "an intelligent looking black gentleman of most dignified aspect." Notably, this is a male figure rather than female, who embodies the values of the time. This black president was the first in a series of imaginary mixed figures deployed as a symbol of equality. As the abolitionist movement developed through the 1830s and '40s, the role of women became more active. However, male figures continued as political actors, while female figures mainly possessed physical beauty.[12]

This dream's counterpart follows immediately, on the same page, imagining retribution on a nation that has continued slavery. Instead of equality, peace, and the blending of each race's positive attributes, this dream features a violent uprising from the former slaves, the establishment of a black government in Charlestown, South Carolina, and the suggestion that whites (now laborers) be put to death. Both the promotion of freedom and the continuance of slavery have opposite outcomes for society. One brings unlimited potential for peace along with racial mixing, and the other brings a spiral violence recalling the Haitian Revolution.[13]

In the first year of the marriage-law campaign, John P. Bigelow, a Whig legislator, represented the effort to strike down the statute. Responding to accusations that he was promoting intermarriage, he voiced the sentiment of many in the movement, that his aim was to dismantle a law that denied that all men were free and equal. As the New England Anti-Slavery Society stated later in its Constitution,

> The objects of the Society shall be to endeavor, by all means sanctioned
> by the law, humanity and religion, to effect the Abolition of Slavery in the

United States, to improve the character and condition of the free people of color, to inform and correct public opinion in relation to their situation and rights, and obtain for them equal civil and political rights and privileges with the whites.[14]

Few members wished to intermarry, but they found the law onerous to civil rights more broadly. So like the sin of slavery, they had to remove it. They saw the commonwealth as a model of freedom for the nation, making the state a lab for the most controversial initiatives. Whether licensing, promoting, or simply paying lip service to marriage-law reform, their project was amalgamationist, bringing together blacks and whites, men and women, in a radical form of equality. When it came to the abolitionists' social interaction with African Americans, a variety of opinions existed. Some wanted no relations with blacks, advocating their deportation to Africa once slavery ended. Some accepted nominal contact but were more comfortable living segregated lives. For example, Bigelow emphasized the abolitionists' civil rights aims while calling interracial marriage "the gratification of a depraved taste," shying away from interracial intimacy while proposing social change.[15] Working for harmonious racial equality within the United States was, by definition, an interracial endeavor, even if the actors chose not to associate more closely with members of other racial groups. Others believed that blacks were simple yet spiritual, while whites were capable yet aggressive. Even in the more radical strands of the movement, rank-and-file abolitionists probably assembled an array of beliefs about racial differences.[16]

In August 1831, Nat Turner's Rebellion did what no other slave revolt had in the United States, killing fifty-five white people in Southampton County, Virginia. Turner was a literate slave who had run away once before. Deeply religious, he had visions that inspired his actions, and he ministered to black followers. Ironically, they had chosen July 4, Independence Day, as the date to strike but postponed until August 13. The violence ended after a few days, but white militias retaliated against blacks in the region, leading to nearly two hundred deaths. Some slaves in North Carolina were put to death for alleged connections to the revolt. Virginia executed fifty-five and introduced measures to limit education, assembly, and separate worship for both slave and free blacks. Across the South, Turner's terrorism inspired the strengthening of the slave system. For reformers, the revolt was an invigorating event; its cataclysm meshed with the evangelical cosmology that found sacred meaning in secular realms. As Garrison wrote,

For ourselves, we are horror-struck at the late tidings. We have exerted our utmost efforts to avert the calamity. We have warned our countrymen of the danger of persisting in their unrighteous conduct. We have preached to the slaves the pacific precepts of Jesus Christ. We have appealed to christians, philanthropists, and patriots, for their assistance to accomplish the great work of national redemption through the agency of moral power—of public opinion—of individual duty.[17]

He characterized the response to this appeal to conscience as hostile, even this early in the movement for immediate emancipation. However, certain of abolitionists' work to clear the nation of the sin of slavery, he called for continued dedication. So, while careful not to justify the actions of Turner and his followers, Garrison used their call to revolt as a call to action.

In November, Garrison called the meetings that began the New England Anti-Slavery Society. He, Theodore Weld, Arthur Tappan, and Lewis Tappan founded the American Anti-Slavery Society in 1833. With these organizations, abolitionism gained a national network, taking a more immediatist stance and often rejecting recolonization.

Amalgamationist became a cover-all epithet against any political stance that defended blacks, reflecting an association between civil rights and social rights, assuming that racial equality would lead to interracial intimacy. During the Massachusetts abolitionists' marriage-law campaign, the term gained close association with their transgressive mission. Newspapers such as the *New York Herald* tied that label with fanaticism, stoking suspicion of reformers with the threat of widespread racial mixing. Throughout this period, the *Herald* claimed neutrality while sensationalizing mixture. Southerners who defended slavery but disagreed with any portion of the proslavery argument had to deny that they were amalgamationists themselves. For example, proslavery scientists justified inequality between racial groups through the notion that each group had its own creation. Nearly as important as defending slavery was the task of denigrating the offspring from black and white unions. If various points of origin produced species of varying superiority, then interspecies mingling was naturally repugnant. Scientists such as Samuel Morton, George Gliddon, Josiah Nott, and Louis Agassiz held racial mixing as bad for whites, blacks, and the nation as a whole. This polygenesis stance found subscribers in both the North and the South.[18]

Hostility toward amalgamation became a central motivator for violence against abolitionists, making the connection more explicit, even if accusations of intimacy were unfounded. For example, in early June 1834, four nights of rioting in New York began after George Farren, the stage manager of the Bowery Theater and an English abolitionist, supposedly insulted white New Yorkers. The participants in this unrest, later called the Farren Riots or the Anti-Abolitionist Riots, sought out homes, businesses, and churches of antislavery activists and African Americans. They invoked amalgamation as the offense that inspired them, but their targets were any that emblematized interracial cooperation. On the night of the ninth, rioters stormed the Bowery Theater during a farewell event for Farren. They called for his apology, expressing antiblack sentiments. He attempted to quell the mob by waving an American flag, but it took a blackface performance by George Washington Dixon to settle them. The entertainer sang both "Yankee Doodle Dandy" and "Zip Coon," a song that lampooned northern, urban blacks.[19]

The English social theorist, feminist, and abolitionist Harriet Martineau encountered the pejorative use of *amalgamation* while traveling in the United States in 1834. Her memoir of the trip, *Society in America*, censured southerners who accused abolitionists of promoting interracial intimacy when they were the ones who profited from creating and selling mixed bodies. She had not yet met any American abolitionists when a woman she was visiting in Philadelphia asked whether she opposed "the marriage of a white person with a person of colour." Martineau already sensed this was a sensitive topic but decided to share her convictions: that she would never separate two people whom God had brought together and that "blacks were no more disposed to marry the whites than the whites to marry the blacks." The woman immediately labeled her an "amalgamationist," a term the visitor had never heard before. Word of her position spread around town, and some people even warned that the reputation of being an amalgamationist amplified the danger she faced as a spokesperson against slavery. Regardless, Martineau departed from Philadelphia, traveling farther south to see the slave system in action.[20]

The threat of violence in Philadelphia culminated in 1838 when mobs of white male workers burned down Pennsylvania Hall three days after its opening, in response to abolitionism, women's rights, and race mixing. The Pennsylvania Anti-Slavery Society had built the hall with its own fundraising, as a meeting place with offices, lecture halls, and meeting rooms. They founded a joint-stock company that sold twenty-dollar shares in the building. In addition to the $40,000 this raised, supporters donated material and labor to erect the civic center. It was also to be a space for other, allied causes, including women's suffrage. At the same time that the Society's anticipation for the hall's grand opening grew, so did antagonism to the project. Opponents posted flyers around the city, encouraging people to interfere, forcefully even, with the building's opening. These inspired the start of a crowd around the building, looking for gas pipes and other weaknesses in the construction.

Regardless, the abolitionists pressed forward with their plans to open the facility on May 14. The dedication ceremony featured speeches by William Lloyd Garrison, Maria W. Chapman, and Angelina Grimké Weld. In addition to antislavery, they addressed topics such as women's rights, temperance, and the treatment of Indians. They read letters from Gerrit Smith, Theodore Weld, and former president John Quincy Adams to nearly three thousand people in attendance. The interracial gathering of men and women celebrating radical causes excited the mob, who threw rocks through windows and at the participants.

The building's executive committee knew that they could not defend themselves, so they met with the mayor, who knew that public opinion outweighed their interests. He suggested that they surrender the keys and cancel the rest of the meetings, including those of the Anti-Slavery Convention of American Women. On the evening of May 17, the mayor locked the doors and urged the crowd outside to disperse. This met with approval from the crowd, but some people still broke in and set fire to the building. Firefighters arriving at the scene showed their antipathy toward the cause by spraying the neighboring buildings only. When one unit did water the hall, others turned their hoses on those men. On the night of May 18, just three days after Pennsylvania Hall opened, it burned to the ground (see fig. 2.1).[21]

While the New England Anti-Slavery Society deemphasized its marriage-law campaign between 1833 and 1838, the organization did grow in membership, emphasizing the mission of defeating all laws referring to race. Local chapters increased in number and realized that integrating their activities was part and parcel of their mission. Then, at Garrison's prompting, a group of ladies in Lynn, Massachusetts, resubmitted the petition to repeal the marriage law. The new effort reflected a change in the movement; over the previous years, the New England Anti-Slavery Society had resolved that blacks could join its societies and had rededicated itself to ending all prejudice. It remained ambivalent to actual intermarriage but fortified the belief that its region was the starting point for its mission to bring equal rights to blacks. As the constitution of the New England Anti-Slavery Society stated, "Before New England can go forward boldly and efficiently in the cause of emancipation, she must elevate her colored population, and rank them with the rest of her children. Reform, not partial but entire—not in the letter but the spirit— must first commence at home."[22] Phillips best communicated this sense of New England exceptionalism later, in a speech addressing the Fugitive Slave Laws, claiming, "While the others have been gathering into rich laps the harvests of the material world, the brain of New England has gone sounding on and on in the pathless voyage of discovery, and working out for the empire

Fig. 2.1. Destruction by fire of Pennsylvania Hall, the new building of the Abolition Society, on the night of May 17, 1838 (Print by J. T. Bowen)

its noblest title to lead the van of progress in the nineteenth century."[23] The Society would set an example for the rest of the nation by curing Massachusetts of licentiousness, bastardy, and family desertion, three ills of slavery.

That year's marriage-law campaign was unsuccessful, but in 1839, more than thirteen hundred women from Lynn, Brookfield, Dorchester, and Plymouth petitioned the legislature once again to repeal the marriage law, receiving abuse from their townsmen, who cursed them to "embrace some *gay Othello*."[24] State Representative Greenleaf, of Bradford, suggested that the women undertook the project in ignorance. Another representative, Colonel Minot Thayer, unleashed the greatest condemnation, implying that there was not "a virtuous woman among them."[25] The Committee on the Judiciary reviewed the petition for repeal, along with another for retaining the law, ultimately defending the state's right to regulate marriage and denying that the standing law implied racial inequality. Furthermore, the committee reported that children had signed the petition and that many of the Brookfield signatures were by one person. Lastly, the committee appointed Minot Thayer to head a task force to investigate the possibly fraudulent petition. The Thayer Committee reached many of the same conclusions as the state, declaring that it was immodest for "a virtuous woman to solicit the repeal of laws restraining the union of the white and black races in marriage."[26] A speech of Phillips's at Boston's Marlboro Church, after he became the group's counsel in the 1838 Thayer Committee hearings, rebuked the legislature and the governor for their attitude toward the petition. The speech was not recorded, but those who were present described how he "tore the legislature all to pieces."[27] Minot Thayer was among his targets, even though he and Phillips were acquaintances. Later, Thayer complained to the abolitionist about the "severe and unjust sarcasm against [his] character" that the speech deployed.[28]

In February 1839, the *Hampshire Republican*, a rural weekly in Springfield, Massachusetts, printed an editorial that supported the ideals of liberty, sympathy, and equality but denounced intermarriage. Willing to split ways with the abolitionist movement, the newspaper warned that slavery was evil but that amalgamation was no remedy for it. "If the abolitionists, as a party, sanction the course of the FAIR petitioners in Lynn, we eschew them as too filthy and loathsome for a free New Englander to act with."[29] In response, Garrison abandoned the topic, writing in the *Liberator*, "At the present time, mixed marriages would be in bad taste," maintaining that common sense, societal mores, and the principles of the gospel would regulate people's marital choices.[30] So great was the antagonism toward interracial marriage that leaders who defended it would recant within the pages of their own publications. However, some others in Massachusetts had come to accept the possibility of interracial relationships, even outdoing the *Liberator*. An editorial in the nonabolitionist *Lowell Journal* supported them, writing, "We have no hesitation in saying, that the law ought to be struck from the statute book, nor are we haunted with any apprehensions of seeing, in consequence thereof, a new race spring up in our commonwealth, bearing the distinctive marks of the Anglo-Saxon mingled with those of the African." Rather than the transformation of all into a new, mixed race, the editor imagined that a number of mixed people would appear. The *Journal* maintained that marriage was a private choice, something that the state should not interfere in. Even if the writer doubted that the number of interracial marriages would increase, he maintained that "if, perchance, they should occasionally happen, no very great evils would result therefrom."[31]

Between 1839 and 1841, Wendell and Ann Phillips toured England, France, and Italy, hoping to find a more suitable climate for her health and to meet with British abolitionists. Their first time overseas, the experience broadened his perspective on race relations in the United States. In Rome, he found black priests leading Catholic services without recoil from the parishioners. In Paris, he encountered "half a dozen couples, black and white, parading the Boulevard," a sight so different from the States that it made him "turn around and stare."[32] At the same time, he witnessed great poverty and gender inequality in Europe that kindled his sensitivity toward those issues. He was willing to praise these countries for their racial integration, but he believed that America, as a republican, Protestant nation, could better give its people their rights.[33]

In 1840, the women tried the petition again, making sure to conduct it more legitimately. The American Anti-Slavery Society split in 1840, with Lewis Tappan and others who disagreed with Garrison's abhorrence of politics and acceptance of the role of women leaving the organization. Believing that electoral politics could bring the end of the slave system, they formed the Liberty Party. Their candidate in that year's presidential election, James Birney, received sixty-two thousand votes out of more than two and a half million.[34] This small number split the vote for the Whig Party, which traditionally did receive abolitionist support, and contributed to a victory for James Polk, the Democratic candidate. By the start of the next year, the *Harrisburg Keystone* encouraged its readers to vote against abolitionists, questioning the marriage-law campaign. Writing from Pennsylvania, the editors asked if the petitioners were "in favor of putting negroes on an equality with whites, . . . making them officers, jurymen, judges, sons-in-law, . . . and equals of yourselves and your posterity."[35] Along with the usual equation of social equality with interracial intimacy, the *Keystone* objected to votes for Whigs or Liberty Party candidates.

However, the Massachusetts legislature finally repealed the law in 1843, providing a major victory for the abolitionists. In part, this success came from the ascent of sympathetic, northern Democrats in the 1842 elections. Among these was the new governor, Marcus Morton, whose opposition to slavery made him the target of southern partymates. While he never joined the abolitionist movement, he set an example of how antislavery had broad, popular support in Massachusetts at the time. Later, in 1863, Phillips referred to the campaign as part of a social movement, recounting, "In the first place men said, If you repeal the law that white men and colored women shall not marry, we shall have amalgamation throughout the Commonwealth. Half the legislators, for a dozen years, were afraid to act. Finally, after as many years as the Greeks spent in taking Troy, the statute was erased from the statute book, and no one has heard of it since."[36]

Frederick Douglass, another famous orator in the movement, had three notable relationships with white women since 1848. Douglass was racially mixed himself, the son of an anonymous white man and a slave. He had always felt estranged from his white parentage, and he developed a strong sense of racial awareness. However, a universal humanism superseded that, as did his sense of American nationality. Unlike Martin Delany and other separatist, black contemporaries, Douglass promoted integration and assimilation to create a diverse America with liberal, secular values.[37]

In 1847, Douglass moved to Rochester, New York, to start his own newspaper. The next year, he met Julia Griffiths in England and brought her back to Rochester to be a tutor to his children and wife. She also became his business manager and companion. The residents in Rochester became accustomed to seeing them together, but in New York City, thugs attacked Douglass, Griffiths, and her sister. From 1850 to 1855, Griffiths helped organize the finances of Douglass's antislavery newspaper the *North Star*, through her administrative skills. She was also a cofounder of the Rochester Ladies' Anti-Slavery and Sewing Society, which held bazaars, published Autographs for Freedom, and sponsored a lecture series. Much of the Society's proceeds supported the *North Star*, along with supporting a school for freedmen in Kansas, the Underground Railroad, and the distribution of literature in Kentucky. Because of the mounting scandal around Douglass and Griffiths's relationship, propagated in part by William Lloyd Garrison, Griffiths moved out of the Douglass household in 1852, returning to England in 1855.

The same year, Douglass met Ottilie Assing, a German-Jewish journalist who traveled to Rochester to interview him. A privileged, educated, radical-leaning woman, Assing had strong abolitionist sympathies, and she undertook a German translation of Douglass's autobiography *My Bondage and My Freedom*. Although familiar with prejudice through the anti-Semitic sentiments of her home country, she also maintained romantic racialist beliefs about the simplicity of black culture. Still, she wished to present Douglass's work in the most positive light possible to German readers. For the next twenty-two years, Assing traveled to the United States to spend summers with Douglass, and they corresponded weekly in between. When John Brown and his followers raided the federal armory at Harper's Ferry in 1859 and the government suspected that Douglass aided him, he fled the country and met with Assing. He undertook a European lecture tour until he learned of his daughter Annie's death the next year. This is another illicit story, like that of Thomas Jefferson's relationship with Sally Hemings, that would be easy to deny in the name of protecting Douglass's upstanding reputation. On one hand, the majority of the letters between the two are missing, making the reconstruction of their exchanges a labor of imaginative historiography. On the other hand, Douglass likely had an intimate, interracial affair with Julia Griffiths and another with Ottilie Assing, and he was to have another later in his life. Reactions to these relationships reflect the comfort levels of Douglass's associates and family. They accepted him as the outstanding black orator and acknowledged that he was an attractive man. But they chastised him when he seemed to participate in an inappropriate interracial affair. In a way, this pattern from his life proved those who conflated social equality and amalgamation correct; integration would lead to interracial mixture. More specifically, it would lead to mixture between literate black men who traveled in circles committed to transgressive causes and white women of like minds, a configuration at the opposite end of that involving white masters and black chattel. In this, Douglass's affairs serve as counterpoints to Thomas Jefferson's, but they both illustrate how great men were sexual beings. Both held some sway over the women around them, and both made choices that contradict their images as chaste.[38]

The antebellum period saw the birth of ideas about racially mixed people that persist to this day. American authors had begun employing the character trope that became the "tragic mulatto." In 1842, Lydia Maria Child published a short story, "The Quadroons," featuring a white woman who learned that she had a black mother. The lady became part of her father's estate upon his death, losing her white fiancé and entering into slavery. Her upbringing, her manners, and her beauty shrank before the fact of her mixture. This story decried the sexual exploitation women experienced under slavery. However, the trope grew in popularity, becoming a favorite of those who were warning against the ills of intermarriage, performers of blackface minstrelsy, and indifferent white readers identifying with the more flattering characteristics. The tragic mulatto helped naturalize the notion that racially mixed people were confused, marginal, and doomed.[39]

Since determining the status of mixed offspring protected the inheritance of servitude, the natural sciences fixated on racial mixture as much as it did on slavery in general. Antislavery scientists argued for the unity and equality of the human race. Some proslavery scientists believed in the unity but not the equality. They believed in monogenesis, recalling one creation by God in the first book of the Bible. A third faction argued for polygenesis, or multiple starting points for the human race, and placed each human variety in a hierarchy. This made it easy to argue for black inferiority and the supposed "natural repugnance" of interracial intimacy. Samuel Morton, leader of the polygenesists, passed away in 1851, but they soon began codifying their proslavery work into one opus that would debunk the King James Bible's chronology, provide physical evidence that species of plants and animals were exclusive to their own continents, and convince the public that different varieties of humans were different species.

The result, *Types of Mankind*, contained eight hundred pages, with contributions by Louis Agassiz and other natural scientists. The one thousand subscribers from the North and the South paid $7.50 for it and saw their name in print within the acknowledgments. Others paid the full price of $8.00. By the end of the nineteenth century, it went through nine editions. Its success elevated polygenesis to common sense. It also provided a vocabulary for talking about racial mixing as a threat to society as a whole. Just as social Darwinism later rationalized poverty and eugenics later bolstered institutionalization, these American ethnologists were central in supporting slavery. To this day, even with slavery moot, *Types of Mankind* echoes in misinformed statements about racial character.

The *National Era*, an abolitionist weekly founded in 1847 with the aim of providing a "complete discussion of the Question of Slavery, and an exhibition of the Duties of the Citizen in relation to it," was the first to serialize Harriet Beecher Stowe's *Uncle Tom's Cabin* in June 1851. The novel spanned forty-one issues, and its popularity expanded the number of subscribers by 25% by April 1852. Known as a major help to the abolitionist cause, it dramatized the effects of slavery on the black family. Toward this end, Stowe employed romantic racialist ideas, casting whites as lecherous, ambitious, and violent and blacks as pious, generous, and passive. Much of the story's drama relies on this characterization. However, *Uncle Tom's Cabin* also presents Stowe's position on racially mixed people. The character Cassy, who is concubine to Simon Legree, Tom's new, cruel master, draws on the figure of the tragic mulatto. Her father is a white, wealthy man from New Orleans. When he dies, she is sold to another man, and this begins a series of misfortunes with other masters, lost love, and infanticide. However, Cassy's willfulness moves her to escape, and Tom's secrecy over her whereabouts leads to his death. Two other mixed characters, George and Eliza Harris, show a more desirable outcome within the familiar tropes. George's white blood dominates his personality, making him brilliant, restless, and combative. Eliza, who turns out to be Cassy's daughter, is the ideal wife and mother, loyal, sacrificing, and courageous. In Hammatt Billings's illustrations to the first edition, these characters have white-appearing skin, features, and hair, a convention applied to mulatto characters to make them more sympathetic to readers of literature and viewers of plays. These were qualities white readers could admire. The young family escapes to Canada and then to France, where George receives an education. At that point, there were many options for these characters. Abroad, they could have stayed in France as free people of color or returned to Canada. Within the United States, they could have settled in a northern state or racially passed as white in a number of locales. Instead, Stowe has them immigrate to Liberia, reflecting her support for colonization (see fig. 2.2). Years later, she believed that mulattoes would die out.[40]

THE FUGITIVES ARE SAFE IN A FREE LAND. Page 238.

Fig. 2.2. The fugitives are safe in a free land; Hammatt Billings's illustration to *Uncle Tom's Cabin*, 1852

Stowe's literary work offers several juxtapositions to the scientific position of the American School ethnologists, who were proslavery and antimixture. She was antislavery, but she believed in hybrid degeneracy, the notion that mixture creates weaker offspring. She supported immediate emancipation but also suggested colonization as the solution for a biracial society. She never supported interracial marriage but did believe mixed people, like all others, could receive redemption through Christianity. So her vision of the United States was all white and unmixed, perhaps very similar to the nation that many nonabolitionists wanted. These contradictions show the variety of ideas circulating at the time, as well as the combinations of racial thought that many people assembled.

The *National Era* also provided the inspiration for this book's title, printing "The United States of the United Races," an extraordinary essay by Wendell Phillips that was neither his first public defense of racial mixing nor his last. In the summer of 1852, he moved from Boston to Florence, Massachusetts, in hopes of alleviating his wife's weak health at Dr. Munde's Water Cure Establishment. Until fall 1853, that involved sitting by her bedside in a dark room and assisting in her treatments. Ann Phillips had been part of his motivation to join the movement, and the two were constant companions. Phillips's speaking engagements reduced to just a few, and he was absent from meetings and events. In many ways, 1853 was an interim year for him, just as it was a less dramatic part of the continuum on the national level.[41]

Phillips probably wrote "The United States of the United Races," one of his most outstanding statements defending racial mixture, in Florence. It appeared in the September 15 issue of *National Era*. After listing the diverse peoples in the United States, Phillips declared, "Whether the varieties of the race began in one family or not, they are destined to meet in one family of people at last," providing destiny as the answer to scientists' monogenesis-polygenesis debate. Creating a diverse republic was one of Phillips's concerns in the 1850s, and rather than suggest any limitations, he imagined a future America that was fully integrated and mixed. In fact, "The United States of the United Races" maintained that such as future was inevitable. The path of progress from Christ's mission to Roman Catholicism united all under one faith. Protestantism and republicanism would complete the process. As he predicted, "It is coming, and must come. America has every variety of climate and soil, with all the accommodations of political and religious institutions, and room enough, besides, for the wide world's widest range of wants, and the happiest conditions for the furtherance of its welfare."[42] In this schema, America stood as the fulfillment of this vision, and its varied lands, climates, and institutions would be the home of a diverse, democratic, and equal people.

Rather than slavery, this essay mainly addressed the inclusion of Asians, referring to the Chinese coming to California and the East Indians coming through Jamaica, Cuba, and Guiana. Phillips asked, "What if they were to apply for naturalization?" He acknowledged that they are not white, as the 1790 naturalization law required, but he asserted that kinship in Christ, not color, would settle the question of their citizenship. As he predicted,

> In short, the doctrine of despotism, ecclesiastical and political, which has served you so well and so long in the extreme cases to which it has been applied, is going to be gradually dissolved in the intermediate shades of coloring to which it will be exposed, so that you will not be able to tell black from white, for any purpose that you now make the distinction. Reason, religion, and republicanism, have all failed with you; but now Providence is about to take you in hand, and you are as good as done for.[43]

Equal rights will lead to racial mixture and the fulfillment of America's destiny. The inability to tell "black from white" seemed to hint at ambiguous physical appearances. However, this sentence primarily targeted the purposes of distinction. Rather than a wish for race to disappear, Phillips was condemning the uses of racial categorization—in other words, racism. In the next sentence, the nation of "intermediate shades" described the future, racially mixed people who will dissolve racial inequality.

As Phillips suggested, if Chinese immigrants could learn Christianity and American ways, then they could be one with all the other Americans. The last stage would feature their intermarrying into American families: "If Fum Hoam can learn Christianity as well as silk-weaving and card-painting, he can substitute phonography for his alphabet of three thousand characters; and, after calling you brother for a generation or so, in good Yankee, he will marry your cousin, and then, how will you keep him out of Congress?"[44] Sociologists later called this process assimilation, but even at this time, Phillips placed intermarriage at the center of it. Learning to speak "good Yankee" English, adopting the dominant religion, and marrying into native families were indicators of integration to Phillips, just as they were to be for social scientists dealing with racial intermarriage through the twentieth century.

Beginning in 1859, Phillips described the republic he wished for. At that year's First of August celebration, which commemorated the British abolition of slavery in 1833, Phillips defined a republic as "a government where the rulers are initiated by the votes of a majority of the people. A Republic is an educated community, where ideas govern;—ideas stamped into laws by the majority, and submitted to by the minority."[45] New York fell short of this standard because of the martial law there, as did Kansas for its rule of violence and the entire South for the retaliation against those who questioned slavery and its sway over President Buchanan. Phillips praised New England as the closest approximation, a land that conferred freedom on its inhabitants, but he also warned against complacency.

Two months later, Phillips expanded on his vision, saying, "My idea of American nationality makes it the last, best growth of the thoughtful mind of the century, treading under foot sex and race, caste and condition, and collecting on the broad bosom of what deserves the name of an Empire, under the shelter of noble, just, and equal law, all races, all customs, all religions, all languages, all literature, and all ideas."[46] He told the story of a man in Milwaukee whose Asian wife had passed away and who wished for the cremation of her body. The sheriff led a mob to retrieve the body for Christian burial. Rather than such forced conformity, Phillips envisioned a multicultural society like ancient Rome, as symbolized by Trajan's column, which illustrated that emperor's return to the city, "leading all nations, all tongues, all customs, all races, in the retinue of his conquest." Phillips idealized the diversity of Rome, overlooking its slave system, as well as its urge to conquer, but this analogy emphasized how the empire included people of many origins. "Just such is my idea of the Empire," Phillips wished for the United States, "broad enough and brave enough to admit both sexes, all creeds, and all tongues in the triumphal procession of this great daughter of the west of the Atlantic."[47] As opposed to his comments about his imaginary Chinese citizen in 1853, this conception of nationality carried fewer stipulations in regard to religion and language. (See Fig. 2.3.)

Phillips's statements on racial mixing became more explicit in the 1860s. At the annual meeting of the Massachusetts Anti-Slavery Society on February 10, 1860, he said, "I never did dread that terrible word amalgamation. I hold it to be the secret of almost all progress, viewed from the point of race." Phillips employed a meaning of race that was biological, discerning between whites, blacks, Indians, and Asians. In this speech, he also used the term to denote national origin, continuing, "We Saxons were nothing while we were pure Saxons. I hold the German race, at a sad discount, on many points, and the English race superior to it in those very respects, because the English race adopted the principle of amalgamation."[48] Phillips referred to Germans as a distinct race and claimed that the English were less developed until they mixed with other groups in the North Atlantic. This interaction had carried on with England's colonial successes and ultimately the mixture of people in the United States. Meanwhile, the Germans had no such expansion and are called inferior because of it. Phillips continues in his description of "English blood":

> And I believe, with Mr. [John Sella] Martin, that, as far as our eyes can divine the future of Providence, it means that the next chapter of the progress of race shall be another mixture of that English blood, that our thirty States are probably to receive the finish and complement of civilization by the melting of the negro into the various races that congregate on this continent, and that the historian of a hundred years hence will view with utter incredulity the popular nightmare of amalgamation, and will trace some of the brightest features of that American character which is to take its place in the catalogue of the world's great races, to the root of this black race, mingling with the others that stand around them. Undoubtedly, to every thoughtful mind, that is the ultimate solution of the problem which is working out in these States.[49]

Phillips gave a vision of the future America where, first of all, fear of racial mixing will become an oddity of the past. Second, mixture will distribute the

Fig. 2.3. Wendell Phillips, ca. 1855–1865 (Photograph by Mathew Brady)

best qualities of its inhabitants. Third, interracial intimacy will bring peace instead of the threat of war at that moment. His mention of "the others" indicated that he was talking about more than just blacks and whites but rather all the races present in the United States. While slavery was the prominent issue of the time, Phillips was talking about more than just blacks and whites. Here, and at many moments throughout this study, speakers had universal racial equality in mind, even when they addressed one variety of racism in particular.

Reactions to Phillips's statements show how racial mixing connected to the issues of the time. For example, soon after this speech, the *Vermont Patriot* printed a letter titled "Democracy and Black Republicanism" that insinuated that the abolitionists had inserted amalgamation into the party's platform. This letter appeared alongside the paper's endorsement of Stephen A. Douglas's 1860 presidential bid. The author called Phillips a monomaniac, attacking women's rights, integration, and the repeal of Massachusetts's marriage law. "Think, also, of his gravely recommending in a mixed audience of whites and blacks of both sexes in the same city, as the only effectual mode to do away with the prejudice of the whites against the colored race, free intermarriage between the negro and Caucasian!"[50] Like the Philadelphia mob, the Massachusetts legislature, and the New York rioters, the *Patriot* objected to both integration and intermarriage and bound both together.

The *New York Herald*, continuing in its supposedly moderate position, printed a letter from its Alabama correspondent explaining why the state had recently seceded:

> We desire a separation from the North, not because we hate you, but because you have fanatics in your midst, who, regardless of the good old rule of minding their own business, will meddle with us and our negroes, and endeavor to incite insurrection, &c., among our domestics. It is true this is a minority; but the majority are equally to blame because of their apathy, which allows such men to promulge their mad views, instead of putting them down.[51]

The correspondent accused abolitionists of ruining the relationship between the North and the South and hoped that northerners would forcibly silence them.

The Emancipation Proclamation went into effect January 1, 1863, announcing the freedom of slaves in Confederate states not under Union control. This made the plan for postwar society more urgent, and Phillips sharpened his statements about racial mixture. At the May anniversary of the American

Anti-Slavery Society, Phillips expressed his distaste for racial homogeneity: "I despise an empire resting its claims on the blood of a single race. My pride in the future is in the banner that welcomes every race and every blood, and under whose shelter all races stand up equal. I hope the negro never will die out. God grant he may figure on the monuments of America a thousand years hence, a symbol of the breadth of our nationality!"[52] These public edifices, like Trajan's column, were static. However, bestowing equality on all and casting them in close association implied that there will be little social distance between them, that they will participate in American democracy, and that they will intermarry at will. Phillips did not wish for the end of race altogether or for the end of racial identification. Instead, he described a future where equality would allow all racial groups and identities to flourish together.

Phillips continued, in language that poked fun at racial science's obsession with the black man's physical proportions: "I do not care for his race, whether it is first, second, or third. I don't care for his brains, whether they weigh much or little." Having brains enough to vote, to stand trial, or to follow the law was enough to deserve equality in education and employment. Phillips's focus on participation in civic institutions as the best indicator of citizenship echoed Crèvecoeur. It became a precursor to the concept of color-blind citizenship held by the legal team arguing against segregation in the *Plessy v. Ferguson* case. Phillips also presaged Martin Luther King, Jr.'s "content of his character," emphasizing one's "worthiness by character, ability and success." However, even if he dismissed racial hierarchies, hoping for the day when "there is nothing in the heart of the American which recognizes races," he still believed in races, as shown by his consistent reference to racial groups. But in his optimistic view of American nationality, each race made its own contribution to the American race more broadly. Phillips hoped that, after true emancipation and suffrage, nationality would trump race as a measure of inclusion. In regard to giving blacks equality, he estimated, "It will take all our thirty years to learn it. I do not expect this nation can come out of its chrysalis in less than a generation."[53]

On May 11, 1863, at the Sixteenth Ward Republican Association meeting, Phillips did something different than he had ever done before, presenting a mixed child as a symbol of reunion with the South. Following a reminder that he had no faith in political parties and a call for "death to the system and death to the master," Phillips summoned a light-skinned, mixed black-and-white girl to demonstrate his vision of the South after the end of the Civil War, calling her the representative of "the party for whom I have conciliation." He continued,

In the veins that beat now in my right hand runs the best blood in Virginia's white races, and the better blood of the black race of the Old Dominion—a united race, to whom, in its virtue, belongs in the future a country, which the toil and labor of its ancestors redeemed from nature, and gave to civilization and the nineteenth century. . . . This blood represents them all—the repentant master, when he sees matters in their true light, the slave restored to his rights, when at last for the first time in her history, Virginia has a government, and is not a horde of pirates masquerading as a government.[54]

This was a rare statement from the Civil War era that explicitly tied racially mixed people to progress, racial improvement, and utopia. Other abolitionists had begun using fair, mixed children born into slavery to gain sympathy for their cause. Leaders such as Henry Ward Beecher held antislavery auctions to buy the freedom for such children as early as 1848. *Harper's Weekly* featured photographs of white-looking slave children to evoke "sympathy, speculation, voyeurism, and moral outrage."[55] More often than not, the subject's white appearance, and its associations with purity, innocence, and femininity, made these photo cards effective. The vignettes decried the maltreatment of children, the splitting of families, and the sexual exploitation that a light-skinned slave girl would face in the "fancy trade." Most likely, Phillips's guest onstage was Fannie Virginia Casseopia Lawrence, a model for many of these portraits, whom Beecher baptized the same month (see fig. 2.4). However, for Phillips, the mixed child was the avatar of racial harmony and peace. She symbolized a future after the Civil War, free of slavery, with the Union intact and rights conferred on all. Hopeful that the nation would overcome such inequality, Phillips suggested that the newfound equality would absolve the sins of the past, including the power and gender relations between white men and black women that brought the child into being.

If the Lincoln administration declared its position on slavery through the Emancipation Proclamation, then Montgomery Blair, postmaster-general, delivered the Cabinet's opinion on the amalgamation matter at the Union Convention in Concord, New Hampshire, June 17, 1863. Blair was from Kentucky, a border state, and he opposed the expansion of slavery. As a conservative Republican, he delighted in challenging other members of the Cabinet. During the war years, he grew more uncomfortable with the radical branches of the party and spoke out against them. As the keynote speaker, he denounced the "two knots of conspiring politicians, at opposite ends of the Union, that make slavery a fulcrum, on which they would play see-saw with the government." He named one of these "knots" after Senator John

A Virginia Slave Child in 1863.

Entered according to act of Congress in the year 1863, by T. C. FANNING, in the Clerk's office of the District Court of the United States for the Southern District of New York.

Fig. 2.4. A Virginia slave child in 1863 (Photograph by Van Dorn)

Calhoun and the other after Phillips, who had never held an elected position. Understanding that theirs were political stances as well as social ones, he characterized one as proslavery and the other as proamalgamation. Proslavery arguments were moot after the Emancipation Proclamation, which conferred, in Blair's opinion, ample rights on the free blacks, but mixture of the races was unacceptable. Speaking of Haiti and Mexico, Blair declared the results of amalgamation apparent in "the degradation of both races, and in the instability of their governments." In response to Phillips's statements at the Sixteenth Ward Republican Association meeting, Blair suggested that the abolitionists wished for compulsory amalgamation in the South: "But the Phillipeans probably do not expect the amalgamation, liberty, equality and fraternity theory to be acceptable to the present ruling class, but intend that the northern white man, while rejecting it for himself, shall enforce it on the southern white man."[56] This scenario was as unacceptable as the continuance of slavery. Instead, he offered a plan in which the government administered services to free blacks and transitioned them toward colonization in Africa. Just as the *Herald* appealed to the reasonable middle ground, so did Blair.

A week later, the *Liberator* objected to making Phillips analogous to Calhoun. The problem was "licentious amalgamation," which produced illegitimate mulattoes in the slave states and showed how hypocritical it was for defenders of slavery to decry amalgamation if the creation of new slaves relied on it. The newspaper's response to Blair's speech critiqued his version of racial history, once again invoking Acts 17:26: "Mr. Blair speaks contemptuously of 'mongrel races.' Those races constitute but one human race, created by the same God, amenable to the same divine tribunal, under the same eternal law, and endowed with the same immortality. Is diversity of complexion or condition a warrant for pride and oppression on the one hand, or for abasement and servitude on the other?"[57] Nationality, physical appearance, and status were moot to the Garrisonians, but Blair focused on racial differences. Blair's version of U.S. history, which he summarized in his speech, revealed that he had little concern for blacks and Indians, who were "extruded" from their lands, "introduced" to kidnapping, and "accommodated" to slavery.[58] Blair privileged the white man as the primary historical actor, with others as victims. This was all the administration had to say about mixing, even if Democrats, southerners, and antiabolitionists continued to claim there was a connection between it and Republican plans.

Just a month later, Phillips provided his most unequivocal endorsement of amalgamation at his July Fourth address in Framingham, Massachusetts. Here he repeated his position from "The United States of the United Races" that it was America's destiny to become multiracial and mixed. "This country has no value, except as the home of all races. That is the idea underlying all our history," Phillips said. He gave examples of ethnic groups that would never "lie down together" in their home lands—the English and the Irish, the French and the English, and other European nationalities with centuries of hostility between them. In the United States, "their children are at the same schools, worshipping at the same altars, fighting under the same flag, dying for the same idea, mingling their blood in the same channel." Then Phillips posed a question that many people avoided: "By what logic is it made out that the black race is an exception to the law which governs all others?" Rather than question minorities' worthiness, he included all races:

> Remember this, the youngest of you: that on the 4th day of July, 1863, you heard a man say, that in the light of all history, in virtue of every page he ever read, he was an amalgamationist to the utmost extent. I have no hope for the future, as this country has no past, and Europe has no past, but in that sublime mingling of races which is God's own method of civilizing and elevating the world. Not the amalgamation of licentiousness, born of slavery—and the ruin of both races—but that gradual and harmonizing union, in honorable marriage, which has mingled all other races, and from which springs the present phase of European and Northern civilization.[59]

Beyond the universal distaste from his opponents, direct responses to Phillips's statements on amalgamation remain hidden. So, it is possible that many followers were uncomfortable with Phillips's statements on racial mixing, even if the *Liberator* reported "loud applause." After all, many of the abolitionists wanted equality for blacks in an abstract way but were uncomfortable with actual social interaction.

The *Herald* reproduced Phillips' speech in full and declared that amalgamation was the "new code of the abolition party."[60] The paper further suggested that the abolitionists wanted separation and war all along and were now rejecting Lincoln's plan of emancipation and colonization. They wanted "to violate the laws of nature and of God by producing a hybrid, deteriorated race, fit only to be ruled by despotism; and it is to this very point the whole base, brutal and bloody policy of the radicals tends."[61]

The *Baltimore American* also critiqued the abolitionists for furthering division rather than letting the president, the Republicans, and the Constitution dismantle slavery. Its July 29 response to Phillips's speech defended colonization, suggesting that emancipation and northern victory without equal rights would lead to continued oppression of blacks. However, equal rights for southern blacks would lead to the subjugation of southern whites.

Amalgamation would lead to unrest and violence, as did the Spanish Inquisition and the removal of Indians from the eastern states. Echoing Jefferson, the removal of free blacks was the only solution.[62]

If imitation is the greatest flattery, then *Miscegenation: The Theory of the Blending of the Races, Applied to the American White Man and Negro*, which seemed to be an iconoclastic promotion of interracial relationships in the United States, was a medal of honor for Phillips. This pamphlet appeared December 1863, its title combining the Latin words for "mixing" and "kinds," as a label for the interracial intimacy that alleged amalgamationists defended. It claimed, "[C]hristianity, democracy, and science, are stronger than the timidity, prejudice, and pride of short-sighted men; and they teach that a people, to become great, must become composite."[63]

In truth, *Miscegenation* was a hoax, a piece of anti-Republican propaganda written by two New York journalists, David Goodman Croly and his junior, George Wakeman. Croly was managing editor of the *New York World*, "the ablest and most influential Democratic journal in the country, the organ of the high-toned Democrats of New York City and State."[64] The two wrote the booklet in their spare time, and Croly bankrolled its printing. As historian Sidney Kaplan explained, "This pamphlet, a curious hash of quarter-truths and pseudo-learned oddities, was to give a new word to the language and a refurbished issue to the Democratic Party—although its anonymous author, for good reason perhaps, never came forward to claim his honors."[65] Many of the pamphlet's assertions were extreme, especially its claim of a secret love that whites have for blacks, the conjoined future of the Irish and the blacks, and the benefits of social intercourse between blacks and whites in the South. However, its reliance on "irrefutable facts" was similar to scientific racialist writing of the time. Its convenient rejection of theories contrary to its apparent aim made it similar in tone to ethnological works such as *Types of Mankind*. Taken at face value, *Miscegenation* cast itself as thoroughly earnest in its claims, and its chapters addressed topics such as the "Physiological Equality of the White and Colored Races," the "Superiority of Mixed Races," and "The Blending of Diverse Bloods Essential to American Progress." After supporting the physiological equality of all races, it argued, "If any fact is well established in history, it is that the miscegenetic or mixed races are much superior, mentally, physically, and morally, to those pure or unmixed."[66] The author went on to attribute the success of certain nations to their varied racial makeup and the decline of others to increased in-marriage since their more successful days.

A true interdisciplinary text, *Miscegenation* cited texts by abolitionists such as Theodore Tilton, scientists such as James Pritchard, and an occasional passage from Tennyson, Shakespeare, and Lowell praising mulatto women. Elise Lemire suggests that the pamphlet's main accomplishment was to combine antiamalgamation rhetoric from different fields all in one place, offering something very familiar for its readers. The pamphlet was a sort of clearinghouse of Civil War–era thought on race mixing. The similarity between Croly's writing and Wendell Phillips's statements on amalgamation are apparent when comparing the pamphlet's positions to his. First, as Phillips joined Christianity with republican values to produce "Liberty, Equality, and Fraternity," *Miscegenation* claimed that "Christianity, democracy, and science, are stronger than the timidity, prejudice, and pride of short-sighted men." The introduction continued, suggesting that these values lead to the same results as Phillips's "United States of the United Races." Echoing Phillips's praise of the English from 1860, Croly credited their success to the mixture of their people, writing, "Whatever of power and vitality there is in the American race is derived, not from its Anglo-Saxon progenitors, but from all the different nationalities which go to make up this people. All that is needed to make us the finest race on earth is to engraft upon our stock the negro element which providence has placed by our side on this continent."[67] The invocation of national destiny was similar to Phillips's in "The United States of the United Races," as well as to his 1860 speech. Lastly, just as Phillips imagines monuments of the future, *Miscegenation* portrays travelers approaching Washington, D.C., from a distance, admiring the bronze statue on the dome of the Capitol:

> When the traveler approaches the city of magnificent distances, the seat of what is destined to be the greatest and most beneficent power on earth, the first object that will strike his eye will be the figure of Liberty surmounting the capitol; not white, symbolizing but one race, nor black typifying another, but a statue representing the composite race, whose sway will extend from the Atlantic to the Pacific ocean, from the Equator to the North Pole—the Miscegens of the Future.[68]

The pamphlet's vision of the future echoed Phillips's, although it lacked any deeper conception of the characteristics of a republic, the means by which citizens will assimilate, or any correlation to ancient Rome.

Later chapters claimed that the *miscegen*, or ideal, racially mixed person, will combine "all that is passionate and emotional in the darker races, all that is imaginative and spiritual in the Asiatic races, and all that is intellectual and perceptive in the white races." He will have brown skin, with dark, wavy hair and full features, much like the biblical Adam. In the end, the text maintained that "the bloods of all nations find their level" and that the future will have "no white, no black."[69] This echoed Phillips's prediction in "The United States of the United Races." It is easy to imagine Croly and Goodman working from transcripts of their opponents' speeches. In fact, the authors used Phillips's name throughout. For example, they named him as an example of how humans were attracted to their opposites.

> The same is true of Mr. Wendell Phillips. He, too, is the very opposite of the negro. His complexion is reddish and sanguine; his hair in younger days was light; he is, in short, one of the sharpest possible contrasts to the pure Negro. . . . The sympathy Mr. Greeley, Mr. Phillips, and Mr. Tilton feel for the negro is the love which the blonde bears for the black; it is a love of race, a sympathy stronger to them than the love they bear to woman.[70]

The pamphlet claimed that this attraction is "natural law," but in reality the assertion was a slur, questioning their tastes and their sexuality.

Believing the ruse, even the *Liberator* dedicated advertising space for the pamphlet on two occasions. The *Newark Advocate* called amalgamation "a terrible thing" from Phillips but accepted it as "the possible destiny of the races on this continent" from a scientific text.[71] The *San Francisco Evening Bulletin* reported the notoriety that the "new doctrine of miscegenation" was receiving on the East Coast. The paper acknowledged the discomfort the theory caused and argued that "no man of eminence or education appears to have confessed himself a believer in or an advocate" for it.[72] Still, the editors reproduced excerpts from the pamphlet on its front pages on May 7, 1864.

As the controversy around the pamphlet mounted, some people began to attribute authorship to various figures. This finger-pointing mainly took place in the newspapers, with accusations that Horace Greeley, antislavery editor of the *New York Tribune*, was its author, which he quickly denied in the *National Antislavery Standard*. The reputation of the pamphlet provided antiabolitionists opportunities to use its anonymous source in their favor. For example, the mere distribution of flyers advertising it during a speech could lead to people attributing its authorship to whoever was speaking. This is how one abolitionist speaker, Anna Dickinson, came to be one of the suspects for its authorship. Needless to say, Phillips became one as well. After all, most of the language was his. Phillips did not reply to the copy sent to him, and his copy ended up in the Boston Public Library.[73]

In the reactions to this hoax, we can see a variety of pro- and antislavery attitudes toward racial mixing. Of the abolitionists whom Croly solicited for endorsement, Lucretia Mott was most cautious, admitting little familiarity with the scientific theories and calling the conclusions untenable. Writing back, she shied away from considering a miscegenation plank in the antislavery platform and clarified that the Massachusetts campaign was to remove civil and social disabilities rather than to advocate racial intermarriage. Sarah and Angelina Grimké enjoyed the liberality of the document but disagreed with some of its flamboyant claims, especially the attraction of opposites. They admitted feeling weary with the United States' caste system, but in the end, they thought it rash to publish such a pamphlet, warning that the opposition to amalgamation could retard the greater work of gaining justice and equality for blacks. After all, they had witnessed the violent backlash at Philadelphia Hall in 1838. Parker Pillsbury was far more enthusiastic, agreeing with the ideas but reserving any public endorsement. Albert Brisbane saw the pamphlet *as a sign of the times, rather than a solution for a great problem.*[74]

Samuel Cox, Democratic congressman from Ohio, brought the topic to the Capitol floor, warning that miscegenation was a central platform of the Republican Party: "The senate of the United States is discussing African equality in street cars. All these things . . . culminating in this grand plunder scheme of a department of freedmen, ought to convince us that the party is moving steadily forward to perfect social equality of black and white, and can only end in this detestable doctrine of—Miscegenation!"[75] Cox's equation of social intercourse with sexual intercourse received some heckling while he delivered his speech, but it also received wide circulation in the Democratic press of the country. John Van Evrie, editor of the *New York Weekly Day-Book Caucasian* and author of the proslavery book *Negroes and Negro "Slavery": The First an Inferior Race; the Latter Its Normal Condition*, even lambasted Cox for taking too favorable a stance toward abolition. For Van Evrie, one had to support slavery or else be in support of racial mixing. As he claimed, "Every man, therefore, opposed to 'slavery' is in necessity for amalgamating with negroes."[76] The pamphlet became an item of debate up and down the East Coast, forcing the Republicans to make explicit the difference between amalgamation and emancipation. Croly took out more advertising space for the pamphlet yet avoided the topic in the *World*, protecting its true authorship from the public. Some people, like Cox, accepted "the genuineness and seriousness of the document," while others, like the *National Antislavery Standard*, reported that it was a burlesque, satire, or jest. The abolitionist paper suggested that the Democrats gained nothing from the controversy.[77]

A political cartoon from 1864 condensed these themes into one tableau. "Miscegenation or the Millennium of Abolitionism" imagines a future with the abolitionists victorious (see fig. 2.5). However, the message is the reverse of the *Liberator*'s two anonymous essays from 1831. Its garden of delights includes white men consorting with unmarried black women. The white men include Horace Greeley, Henry Ward Beecher, and Theodore Tilton, the same names Croly and Wakeman cited in *Miscegenation*. White women embrace black men, asking for reassurance that they will be married or that the man will support their public speaking engagements. These interactions relied on the quick association between social equality and interracial intimacy, the characterization of black men and women as sexual and bestial, and the casting of reformer women as morally wanton and misguided about their role in the public sphere. However, Bromley & Co.'s garden scene also incorporates the political anxiety around the defense of interracial marriage, mainly that social equality would lead to a complete reversal of political power. Near the center, a privileged black party approves of Charles Sumner, consenting that he may continue his work. Three white men attend to their carriage, just as black slaves did for wealthy whites. Lastly, Abraham Lincoln appears at the opening of this scene, bowing to one of the interracial couples. He has executed the abolitionists' political agenda, binding miscegenation, the Republican platform, and emancipation into a dystopia repugnant to opponents of any of these.

Still, the challenging party harped on the miscegenation issue up to the last minutes of the 1864 presidential campaign. However, radical Republican John C. Frémont withdrew from the race in September 1864, in exchange for the removal of Montgomery Blair, the conservative, from the Cabinet. Victories by Sherman in Atlanta and Farragut at Mobile Bay drastically reversed the Democratic Party's fortunes. In the end, the truth behind the pamphlet came out in England, via a dispatch by the New York correspondent from the *London Morning Herald*. The article that appeared on November 1, 1864, revealed that "two young gentlemen connected with the newspaper press of New York, both of whom are obstinate Democrats in politics," had written and distributed the pamphlet, but it did not reveal their names. Croly never accepted responsibility for the hoax, although his wife credited him with coining the term *miscegenation*. Since then, many readers have believed its conceit. For example, a column from 1999 imagined that Croly was "a Northern White abolitionist, a Republican, and an integrationist."[78]

On December 18, 1865, the Thirteenth Amendment abolished slavery in the United States. William Lloyd Garrison had resigned as president of the American Anti-Slavery Society in May, and he concluded publishing the *Liberator* at the end of the year. To him, the end of slavery meant that the organization had reached its goal, and it was time to dissolve it. Others, including

Fig. 2.5. Political caricature, No. 2, "Miscegenation or the Millennium of Abolitionism,"
Bromley & Co., 1864

Wendell Phillips, believed the work remained until political and civil equality was secure for blacks in the South. With a vote of 118 to 48, the majority of the Society defeated Garrison's resolution to dissolve the organization. He carried through with his resignation, letting the others continue without him. The coming years proved the greater portion of these voters correct. Questions of race, citizenship, and equality persisted throughout the Reconstruction era. Radical Republicans pushed legislation to bring equality to the freedpeople. But new forms of white supremacy resisted these changes. Antagonism to interracial intimacy continued, with violent turns that reflected antagonism to black political participation. Indian wars, expansion into the Southwest, and resentful laborers brought white supremacy to American Indians, former Mexicans, and Chinese immigrants. In all these arenas, mixture was at the center of deciding who to exclude from equality and citizenship. At the same time, some antiracists wielded mixture as a weapon against white supremacy and racial classification as a whole.

3

Plessy v. Racism

Throughout the nineteenth century, the United States' acquisition of territory incorporated more types of people, complicating the master narrative of white supremacy that the Atlantic colonies established. Interracial encounters occurred in various paradigms, showing that mixture was relevant to more than just blacks and whites. Interracial intimacy with Hispanics, Indians, and Asians tested the borders of inclusion in different ways in the context of white supremacy, just as they do today. Even though the Civil War had ended, legal battles over the meanings of citizenship erupted throughout the Reconstruction era. These proved relevant to all racial minorities, even though the question of emancipation focused primarily on African Americans. Those who argued for an expansion of citizenship for minorities faced a grave defeat with *Plessy v. Ferguson*, in which the Supreme Court decided the legality of racial segregation in 1896.

Set in Louisiana, the principals in this case were people of color with a high degree of mixture in their backgrounds. Because of the state's French and Spanish colonial past, Louisiana had a different perspective on racial mixing than did most of the United States. The British colonies on the East Coast protected white racial purity by punishing interracial marriage and leaving white male sexual privilege alone. They also promoted endogamy by bringing British women to the colonies soon after their establishment. On the other hand, the French settling Louisiana (much like the Spanish settling Mexico) accepted racial mixing as part of their colonial identity. It took much longer for marriage-able women to arrive, so the original settlers took black and Indian mates. They also privileged white male sexual privilege, but they set up practices that let the existence of their mixed population be more public. Some of their offspring were slaves, but some were free people of color who owned property, enjoyed a higher standard of living, and identified as Francophone just as the French did. This is how the term *Creole*, which in its strict sense referred to European settlers born in the colonies, came to refer to the polyglot of European, African, and indigenous descent in New Orleans. Since the nineteenth century, Louisianians concealing the racial mixture in the region's past have inscribed a white-only meaning to the term *Creole*, attempting to make its meaning refer only to the French and Spanish settlers in Louisiana. But, as in colonial Mexico, those Europeans immediately began mixing with the black and Indian women around them, and *Creole* implied mixture by definition. The free people of color acknowledged their mixture, considering themselves a separate, mixed group rather than black or white.[1]

One way colonial Louisiana flaunted its widespread racial mixture was through the eighteenth-century practice of *plaçage*, or "placement." At quadroon balls, free women of color presented their young daughters to white men, hoping to secure a commitment to house them, clothe them, and provide for any offspring. This system offered less protection than marriage, but it often resulted in lifetime relationships. However, concubines had no legal claim to the man's estate. The women were dependent on the fortunes of the white men. So the most affluent men could offer the most secure arrangements and choose from the most desirable young women. The shadow families these relationships produced stayed in the community of free people of color. They were semisecret and well known but also illegitimate.

With the American ascendancy that came with the Louisiana Purchase came meanings of race more dyadic than the French (and, for a short time, the Spanish) employed. However, racial mixture was part of the identities of the free people of color, so they were hesitant to identify as white. The mixture was also a public fact, making it hard to claim pure whiteness. Reflecting a nationwide fixation on determining who was white and who was black, Americans attempted to organize Creoles of color under this schema. Still, Creoles of color resisted the assumptions about both whiteness and blackness.[2]

In Louisiana, the work of Reconstruction had begun since the Union had assumed control in 1863. Descendants of refugees from the Haitian Revolution, including free people of color who brought a conception of freedom bound with racial equality, joined the Republicans in establishing racial equality in the state. From 1863 to 1868, radical Creoles of color influenced lawmaking in Louisiana, resulting in a state constitution that unified social and political rights into one rubric, public rights. Even after the Louisiana Purchase, they were hesitant to embrace whiteness. Knowing that limitations on the less fortunate, more black members of society set the way for widespread practices of white supremacy, the radicals among them wanted public rights for all. Because of the recent emancipation of slaves, the prominent issue was black equality. The status of the Creoles of color in regard to both whiteness and blackness expanded the meanings of the civil rights struggles they undertook, making public rights relevant to racial equality in general.

In 1890, when a more conservative state legislature passed the Separate Car Act, these former radicals deployed their sense of public rights to protest racial segregation. The Comité des Citoyens, the Creole-of-color group developing the test case, ultimately retained Albion Tourgée, Civil War veteran, Reconstruction federal judge, and author, as lead counsel in their campaign. Many historians assume that the Creoles of color undertook this legal action to protect their own privileged status. Some have interpreted their work as relevant to the segregation of African Americans only. Others have cast it as a lost cause, a legal folly but a moral victory. To the contrary, the effort was part of a utopian vision that they believed in. The *Plessy* campaign attempted to transform society as a whole, not just to address one issue, and racial mixture was at the center of this effort. While many of these Creoles of color appeared white, they knew that their mixture excluded them from whiteness in the predominant American sense. So they undertook this test case to challenge racial classification altogether, for all minority groups. Just as Wendell Phillips knew that other minority groups were relevant to the debates about racism, equality, and mixture in 1853, these activists knew that their success would affect all. Central in their strategy was the use of mixture to challenge racial categorization.[3]

In this chapter, I present three other paradigms of mixture to show the relevance of the *Plessy* drama to the rights of many minority groups, mixed or not. Bringing these understandings together shows how the legal team revised the positive visions of racial mixture before them, whether that of William Short, Hector St. John de Crèvecoeur, or Wendell Phillips. It also connects the *Plessy v. Ferguson* case to every progressive use of mixed race that followed. Israel Zangwill's melting pot called for the absolution of past animosities and the creation of interethnic families. The Multiracial Movement believed that mixed race would sabotage traditional racial categorization, leading to its dissolution. Mixed-race public figures in entertainment, sports, and politics indicate the arrival of a postracial state where their successes prove that racism has failed.

Even before Americans moved from east to west, the Spanish had been settling the continent from the southwest, hoping to continue the successes of New Spain. This brought under colonial control regions that were to become California, New Mexico, Arizona, and Texas. In time, the sense of distinctiveness among the mixed people of Mexico led to a war for independence from 1810 to 1821. The new republic's Colonization Law offered land and temporary tax exemption to foreign settlers, a proposition that attracted American impresarios. In central Texas, future heroes of the Texas Revolution joined in marital and business unions with the Tejanos. New Mexico and California had more sparse populations, and trapping and trading predominated instead of agriculture. But Anglo men still married into Mexican families, some common and some elite. Closer to the southern American states, this intermarriage was more rare. Because it helped secure land, assimilate into Mexican society, and further business ventures, this intermarriage contributed to American success in the Southwest and, in turn, to white supremacy.[4]

Texas became an independent republic in 1836 after its coalition of Anglos and Tejanos defeated Mexico's General Santa Anna. Its leaders favored annexation to the United States to become a state. Since this plan would expand slavery and spark a war with Mexico, it was delayed until 1845, when popular opinion, Congress, and expansionist President James Polk made it a reality. The ensuing Mexican-American War resulted in the gain of the whole Southwest in 1848, including 947,570 square miles of land, or half of Mexico's territory. Conquest of all of Mexico would have been possible, but that would have brought eight million Mexicans under American rule, possibly creating new states full of what Senator John Calhoun labeled "Aztecs, Creoles, Half-breeds, Quadroons, Samboes, and I know not what else" who would usurp the power if given the vote. Instead, the Rio Grande became the southern border, bringing the most land and the least of that "mongrel race."[5]

The Treaty of Guadalupe Hidalgo defined the terms of victory for the United States, including the monetary compensation, the gain of land, and the military occupation of Mexico City. However, it also governed the status of one hundred thousand Spanish-speaking inhabitants of the land that was now American. The document had originally promised to honor all land grants to citizens of Spain and Mexico, but the Senate deleted this provision. Article VIII guaranteed U.S. citizenship to Mexicans remaining in the ceded lands for more than a year, a promise that disrupted the stipulation from the Naturalization Act of 1790 that offered citizenship only to any "free white person," by including populations who pushed the limits of whiteness. This article remained in the final treaty, under the jurisdiction of Article IX, which originally promised to offer "the enjoyment of all the rights of citizens of the United States" to all who wanted. The text promised to respect their property, civil rights, and religious practices. Their admission was to happen "as soon as possible."[6] The Senate shortened this passage from three paragraphs to just one. Those who wanted American citizenship would "be admitted at the proper time (to be judged of by the Congress of the United States) to the enjoyment of all the rights of citizens of the United States, according to the principles of the Constitution."[7]

In areas where Americans outnumbered Mexicans, such as East Texas, they had already made white supremacy the norm and intermarriage a rarity. The Mexican-American War had stoked feelings of racial superiority across the country. The hesitant language of the treaty continued the unlikely prospects for racial equality in the Southwest. The protection of Mexicans depended on their racial status, with a higher degree of European descent a shield against the emergent brand of white supremacy. Still, Americans dismantled the rights of the Mexicans throughout the region, stripping away property, intimidating laborers, and coercing both migrant workers and long-time residents into a lower status. Intermarriage with Americans dipped in the 1850s and '60s and increased afterward. However, now Americans in such relationships felt no compulsion to assimilate into Mexican society; the adjustment went the other direction. This internal colonization set the model for treatment of Hispanics and Latinos well into the future.[8]

Chinese men, mostly sailors and laborers, began immigrating to the United States as early as the 1830s, sailing from plantations in the West Indies and disembarking in New York City. Chinese merchants arrived in California in the 1840s and '50s with their wives and children. After the Civil War, planters in Mississippi and Louisiana explored the possibility of using Chinese as cheap agricultural labor. This plan failed, but a number of Chinese laborers remained in the region. In Mississippi, they discerned the dominant position of the whites and the lowly position of the blacks, aligning with the more advantageous group. However, even though they formed an enclave that rarely married out, some did form unions with blacks and whites. On the other hand, in Louisiana, the remnant Chinese did intermarry with those around them. The state had no prohibition against Chinese intermarriage, whether to blacks, whites, or Indians. The number of Chinese was so low that an enclave was impossible. Louisiana's racial tradition appreciated in-between racial groups more readily. With fewer disincentives to intermarriage in that state, the Chinese blended into the population more readily.

Only when Chinese became a supposed threat to public health, free labor, or cultural norms did whites consider them negatively. Even then, only the most radical whites opposed their integration into American society. They feared that unmarried Chinese men who were allowed to stay too long in the country would seek white women as mates. Thanks to an economic downturn after the Civil War, antipathy toward the Chinese spread, often with violent repercussions. Both white workers and politicians saw them as a scapegoat, and the Chinese Exclusion Act passed through Congress in 1882, bringing immigration from China to a near halt, considering many Asians ineligible for citizenship, and making reentry into the United States impossible. Some Asian men formed unions with American women, but these contradicted the image of them as deviant, nearly asexual. Their demographic

rarity reinforced conceptions of them as alien, a peril to society, and pollutants to the normative family.[9]

Westward expansion led to wars with Indian tribes in nearly every territory past the Mississippi River. As with Indian Removal along the East Coast,
this involved coercing Native Americans to sign away their lands so that
Americans could colonize more of the continent. When that failed, military
engagement reduced Indians numbers, facilitating their relocation to res-
ervations. As settlement consumed more land, it became clear that Indians
were no longer outside American territory but rather were part of the country, even if tribes were sovereign. This called for a shift in policymaking, and
the resulting Dawes Act of 1887 exhibited the change in relationship between
the United States and American Indians by initiating the granting of citizenship, with guidelines that pushed Indians toward adopting American ways.
Legislators and philanthropists hoped that Indians would adjust to a station-
ary, agricultural, life that revolved around family units. Individuals could
receive a private agricultural life allotment of land in exchange for a promise to quit their wandering, hunting, communal ways. Only after twenty-five
years could one sell or lease one's lot; in the meantime, the federal government held it in trust.[10]

The Dawes Act continued to treat Indians as second class by defining their racial difference. Although standards of blood quantum were not
the only criteria, they helped in this definition, setting guidelines for how
much Indian parentage one needed to qualify for land allotment. Measuring descent by halves, quarters, and eighths had always been inconsistent,
yet both the government and tribes themselves employed various blood
quantum standards to define membership. Those with too little Indian blood
could not receive an allotment. This produced a surplus of land that the
government reabsorbed and sold to white Americans. This process of taking Indian land and bestowing it back to a few whites resulted in the loss of
two-thirds of Indians' land base from 1887, or ninety million acres over the
forty-seven years of the act's prevalence. Blood quantum remained one of
the principal tools in defining membership in Native American tribes, and
thus access to resources. However, unlike the one-drop rule, which defined
blackness, blood quantum was more like an X-drop rule, where X equaled
the agreed-on number of drops. For official purposes, the standard considered mixed Native Americans as monoracial, just as the one-drop rule did
to mixed African Americans. But too much mixture could strip one of full
Indian identity, whereas too little blackness rarely did.[11]

These cases of Creoles of color, former Mexicans, Asians in America,
and mixed American Indians show that definitions of race continued to be

inconsistent at the end of the nineteenth century. Likewise, racial mixture compounded these inconsistencies in various arenas across the country. Still, definitions of mixture remained tools for exclusion through this period. However, the defense team for the *Plessy v. Ferguson* case used mixture to disqualify racial classification as a practice, providing an example of how mixture could be used for racial equality.

The Louisiana context intersected with the white American context through the non-Creole sojourners there. The most notable of these was Albion Tourgée. Born in 1805, the lawyer grew up in Williamsfield, Ohio, located in what had been the Western Reserve, land Connecticut possessed in the Northwest Territory. Even after the eastern state gave up its claims in exchange for federal assumption of its Revolutionary War debt in 1786, it held on to more than three million acres in the northeast corner of Ohio. Settlements that were to become Cleveland, Youngstown, and Warren began at this time. Connecticut relinquished the land in 1800, but the label "Western Reserve" remained.[12]

Tourgée's mother died when he was five, leaving the boy and his father alone. Even though his father remarried, neither of them gained the same sense of fulfillment with the new family. During this time, the Western Reserve featured radical individualism common to New England. However, it lacked the Puritan colonies' social hierarchy. Religious revivalism thrived, resulting in a belief in individual conscience similar to that which influenced Phillips. All political parties present in the region opposed slavery in principle in the 1840s, even if they differed on how to handle it. Tourgée's father was a Whig, but the younger found inspiration in the abolitionist work of Ohio congressmen Joshua Giddings and Benjamin Wade.

Because the Fugitive Slave Act of 1850 required citizens to act against their conscience, it amplified the antislavery sentiment in Ohio and elsewhere. Already having legislated against a similar act in 1793, Ohioans opposed the new one. The Ohio River, which separated free and slave states, was the destination for many blacks on the Underground Railroad. However, even amid the work of slave rescue, Tourgée was rather apolitical. In his journals, he acknowledged the advantages of being white, young, and male. Years later, he took great pride in the region's antislavery activism.[13]

Tourgée met Emma Kilbourne, another Western Reserve native with even greater abolitionist convictions, at age nineteen. He graduated from Kingsville Academy in 1857 and pursued his goal of attending Harvard University. But the expense was too great for him and his father to handle, so he attended the University of Rochester, engaging in a long-distance relationship with Emma. By time the southern states ratified their constitution in

1861, Tourgée, like many Americans, accepted that a war was inevitable, and he was ready to enlist. He suffered a back injury at the First Battle of Bull Run, July 21, 1861. Although he recuperated well enough to return to action, the pain afflicted him for the rest of his life. In July, he reenlisted in the 105th Ohio Volunteer Infantry as a first lieutenant, participating in the Battle of Perryville on October 8, 1862. There he injured his back again but returned to duty again by January, when he was captured at the Battle of Stones River, near Murfreesboro, Tennessee. Confederates held him as a prisoner of war until a hostage exchange in May, and he returned to Ohio to marry Emma.

After the war ended, the Tourgées moved to Greensboro, North Carolina. The warmer climate would be better for his injuries, and he could actively participate in the reconstruction of the southern state as a lawyer and editor. He represented Guilford County in the state's constitutional convention in 1868, helping pass measures to expand rights to all. He and his fellow car-petbaggers ended property-holding requirements for jury duty and office-holding, established elections for all state officers, and instituted free public education for all.[14]

Between 1865 and 1866, Wendell Phillips, now president of the American Anti-Slavery Society, lobbied for a version of the Fourteenth Amendment that would have prohibited making "any distinction in civil rights" based on "race, color, or descent." This echoed the 1833 constitution of the New England Anti-Slavery Society. It also recalled his assertion in the *National Era* that future racial mixing would make racial distinctions impossible. In 1853, he hinted at the difficulty of categorization. In his version of the constitutional amendment, he announced that the purposes had become obsolete. Tourgée read the *National Anti-Slavery Standard* regularly, absorbing the Bostonian's rhetoric. Phillips's influence was most apparent in Tourgée's conception of "color-blind justice."[15]

As a superior court judge from 1868 to 1874, Tourgée had to enforce these reforms, and he met with resistance from former Confederates who were active in the early Ku Klux Klan. Rather than pinpoint the beginning of Jim Crow later, I place it here with the South's maladjustment to the end of slavery. Rather than evaluate this vigilantism as private acts of aggression, I argue that this intimidation was political action. And rather than argue that lynching was a reaction to black sexual predation, I concur with Ida B. Wells in pointing out the root cause: black political empowerment. The antiblack, anti-Republican violence of the early Reconstruction era was the beginning point for the Jim Crow system prominent through most of the twentieth century. The presence of federal troops, the fervor of radical Republicans in Washington, D.C., and the labors of local reformers held the full-blown Jim

Crow order at bay. But Tourgée's challenges show that Reconstruction had opponents from its beginning.[16]

In Greensboro, Tourgée received hostility for his public reforms, as well as for his lifestyle. The family made a conscious effort to live without prejudice. They associated with poor whites such as John Walter Stephens, an uneducated Republican with a reputation for allegedly stealing chickens. The judge personally tutored him to become a justice, and both men faced marginalization from the North Carolina State Bar Association. The Tourgées also made a point of living in an integrated area, attending black political meetings, and entertaining black and white guests. This made them the target of gossip throughout the area, including suggestions that they were participating in voodoo rituals.

They continued to flout social norms when they adopted Adaline Patillo, a thirteen-year-old, racially mixed girl with a near-white complexion, in 1868, shortly after their second child died in infancy. Along with legally adopting Ada, they also brought her mother and sister into the household (see figure 3.1). The local press responded by suggesting that Ada was Albion's illegitimate child, even though she was born years before the Tourgées had arrived. However, the Tourgées treated Ada as their own, perhaps transferring some of the affection for their lost child to her. Through Ada's adoption, they provided an example of how life could turn out for the white-appearing girls in the postcards that abolitionists sold to support their cause. Her background was similar to that of the girl Wendell Phillips presented at the 1863 Sixteenth Ward Republican Association meeting. The Tourgées made their own family interracial, a microcosm of their hopes for the nation.

At some point, the family took Ada to their white church, consciously violating the segregated seating policy. After a committee of members confronted Albion, he decided that they would never return to the congregation. Preferring a Methodist or Baptist church, the Tourgées were now without a place to worship, dealing with the constant threat of violence, and isolated without extended family. Emma had always been supportive of Albion, proving to be his peer at intellectual repartee and his ally in working for racial justice. But she retreated from these pressures to her sister's home in Erie, New York, in 1870. Albion convinced her to return a few months later, but she left North Carolina for good in 1878.

Albion and Emma gave Ada the best education they could, sending her to Hampton Institute in 1871. The Tourgées acted on the hope that Radical Reconstruction would be a success. At that time, Hampton was a boarding school with the goal of training black teachers who would educate blacks across the South. Albion's choices set Ada toward contributing to racial uplift

Fig. 3.1. Adaline and Mary Patillo, ca. 1873

of blacks. She subscribed to the "politics of respectability" that had transformed since emancipation into a code of expectations for the educated to
purvey. The Tourgées urged Ada to develop intellectually just as they did
their biological daughter, Aimee, who was born eighteen months later and
went on to become a writer and artist who traveled throughout Europe. They
wanted Ada to follow creative and intellectual pursuits as well. With distinctions based on race obsolete, nothing could stop Ada from achieving these

goals. The Tourgées' actions suggest that they believed in fostering interracial families, creating a nation of equal opportunity, and the viability of mixed people. But Ada followed a different path than Aimee. Perhaps she encountered a glass ceiling, preventing her from pursuing similar goals. Or maybe prejudice barred her. Most likely, her minority identity led her toward racial uplift rather than personal edification. This collective imperative existed before and continued after this period, but emancipation did amplify the notion that a respectable, educated, black middle class could improve the lives of common freedpeople.

In Louisiana's 1867–68 constitutional convention, nearly as many black and Creole-of-color men participated as white men, who had traditionally shaped the state's laws. Among these were P. B. S. Pinchback, who later became the first nonwhite governor of a state and grandfather to the novelist Jean Toomer; Louis A. Martinet, editor of a weekly, the *Crusader*, dedicated to racial equality; and Rodolphe Desdunes, a contributor of Haitian descent to Martinet's paper and later author of *Nos Hommes et Notre Histoire*, a history of Louisiana's Creoles of color. These men enacted a sense of public rights that covered the whole public sphere. Their 1868 bill of rights guaranteed equal treatment and equal access to public services:

> All persons shall enjoy equal rights and privileges upon any conveyance of a public character; and all places of business or of public resort, or for which a license is required by either state, parish, or municipal authority, shall be deemed places of a public character, and shall be open to the accommodation and patronage of all persons, without distinction or discrimination on account of race or color.[17]

This defined a public place as any with a license from any level of state government, but it also included places that may become public in the future. It prohibited the practice of discrimination, as well as the enforcement of racial distinctions. There would be equal treatment, free of racial classification. This would protect the participation by all in all aspects of public life. Similar to the Massachusetts abolitionists, champions of Radical Reconstruction defended political equality. Louisiana's 1868 Article XIII echoed this principle.[18]

The legislation of the early Reconstruction period increased blacks' voting and officeholding. It seemed that the Thirteenth and Fourteenth Amendments, plus the Union army, had set the basis for freedpeople's equality. However, later Reconstruction legislation reined in the power of these acts even as it refined them. The Fifteenth Amendment explicated the voting rights of citizens regardless of "race, color, or previous condition of servitude," but carpetbaggers' wish to retain loyalty tests to limit the influence of ex-Confederates, northern Republicans' antipathy toward newcomers, and westerners' efforts to exclude Chinese undermined the possibility of universal male suffrage. Because of these double-standards, the Fifteenth Amendment only did part of what it could have done. Blacks' voting rights were vulnerable as long as others' were. The amendment also narrowed the focus to race while there were several classes of people who needed protection.[19]

The first opportunity for the Supreme Court to interpret the Fourteenth Amendment came from Louisiana. During much of the nineteenth century, the meat-processing industry in that state had its base a mile and a half upstream from New Orleans. The remains from slaughtered animals entered the city's drinking water, spreading cholera. Similarly, mosquitoes fed on the scraps, spreading yellow fever. Even though this industry took place outside the city, the state legislature allowed the city to create the Crescent City Live-Stock Landing and Slaughter-House Company, a private corporation consolidating meat processing downstream from the city. Following models from New York, San Francisco, Boston, Milwaukee, and Philadelphia, the legislature hoped to reduce the amount of contamination by relocating the industry to one location. Formerly independent companies would rent space there, with no privilege toward any butcher, large or small.

The Butchers' Benevolent Association sued to stop this takeover of the industry, losing in the lower courts. The association appealed to the Supreme Court, invoking the Fourteenth Amendment and arguing that the Louisiana law discriminated against the industry as a class of citizens. The butchers' attorney was John A. Campbell, who had left the Supreme Court in 1861 because of his secessionist loyalties. He returned to his home in Alabama in 1861, and Jefferson Davis named him assistant secretary of war under the Confederate government. After imprisonment and reconciliation, he moved his law practice to New Orleans. Even though he had worked on cases designed to obstruct Radical Reconstruction in the South, Campbell aimed to broaden the meaning of the Fourteenth Amendment in the *Slaughter-House Cases* to extend equal protection to any class of citizen.

Continuing the series of Supreme Court decisions that facilitated rolling back the Reconstruction amendments, 1873's *Slaughter-House Cases* separated U.S. citizenship from state citizenship. Justice Samuel Freeman Miller, a former physician with expertise on cholera, wrote a decision ruling that the Fourteenth Amendment only affected rights of U.S. citizenship, not state citizenship. With the right to charter a private monopoly that reformed an existing industry, Louisiana had not violated the butchers' rights. The decision also interpreted the Fourteenth Amendment as only specific to blacks. While this appeared to uphold the primacy of civil rights, it also gutted the universal understanding of citizenship that the amendment originally promised. States could interfere with civil rights as long as they masked their intentions under nonracial terms. State politicians could license violent intimidation by denying that vigilantes had political motivations. Later the same year, the Court's decision in *United States v. Cruikshank*, which reversed the indictment of white Louisiana militiamen who had attacked black voters, essentially exempted states from enforcing the Fourteenth Amendment, as long as states did not violate it on an official level.

In 1875, at age twenty-one, Ada wrote home expressing her uncertainty about her adoption by the Tourgées. She appreciated their love, but the memory of her early youth reminded her that she had been poor and illegitimate. She had one more year to go at Hampton, but she also wrote to announce that she was dropping out, citing her mother's declining health as the reason for this change. Most likely, Ada was homesick and yearned to be closer to friends and family. Even if Ada's mother, Louisa, was aging, the Tourgée household cared for her. Perhaps Ada was performing lower than expectations for her, leading to a feeling of inadequacy that she connected to her background. Hampton's focus on "practical education" may have been the wrong program for her, and boarding may have contributed to a sense of alienation. Given her near-white appearance, perhaps she felt out of sorts at the predominantly black institution. While many students at these schools did embrace their black identity, Ada may have questioned this path more than others did. Any combination of these feelings could have motivated her decision to move back to Greensboro. She took a teaching position nearby and married a local African American barber, Leroy William Woods, settling for the comforts of home instead of greater intellectual achievement.

The following years brought more disappointments to Tourgée and other radicals. The Compromise of 1877 gave Rutherford Hayes the presidency and removed troops from the South, ending enforcement of any Reconstruction gains. Tourgée made an unsuccessful bid for Congress in 1878 and then began writing *A Fool's Errand, by One of the Fools*, a novel based on his experiences in North Carolina. Sympathy for the cause made the book a success, selling around two hundred thousand copies and bringing monetary fortune to the Tourgée family. The following year, he followed with *Bricks without Straw*, which drew from the same experiences. However, unlike the first, this volume placed two freedmen at the center, dramatizing the conclusion of Reconstruction efforts. The Tourgées moved to Mayville, New York, to be near both family and the intellectual activity at the Chautauqua Institution.

The income from two bestsellers allowed him to live as a professional writer. For the next three years, he attempted to run a literary magazine, *Our Continent*. He had hoped it would be a weekly as expansive as the typical monthly, printed using the best quality materials. This endeavor sapped the fortunes that the two previous books brought him. While his reputation remained strong, the financial, emotional, and physical strains of this era showed in his demeanor (see figure 3.2).[20]

Another white author, George Washington Cable, had a career trajectory resembling Tourgée's. Although they were both antiracists, they had fundamental differences. Cable was born in New Orleans and served in the Confederate army. Unlike the northerner, he settled in his home state after the war. He contracted malaria working as a surveyor on the Atchafalaya River levees. After his recovery, he moved to the city and became a journalist for the *Picayune*. His collection of stories, *Old Creole Days*, portrayed antebellum life in the area. It appeared the same year as Tourgée's debut, riding the demand for regional writing. Cable became the preeminent literary writer on Louisiana, especially with northerners, but southerners resented his critiques of race relations. Just as Tourgée produced another novel a year after his first, Cable published *The Grandissimes* a year after *Old Creole Days*. This novel told the story of the Creole Grandissime family, which had both a white branch and a mixed-race branch, the product of *plaçage*. The tension of this left-handed marriage provided Cable with an opportunity to imbue mixed characters with greater depth, yet still in ways recalling the "tragic mulatto" trope. His next novel, *Madame Delphine*, continued this tendency. His expertise led to a commission from the U.S. Census Bureau to write a report on the unique racial environment of the area. The product, later published as *Creoles of Louisiana*, provided the historical background regarding the region for the 1890 census. Like Tourgée, he left the hostile South, moving to Northampton, Massachusetts, once his literary fortunes could support him. Later he became friends with Mark Twain, joining him on speaking tours and addressing racial equality.[21]

Like the progressive framers of Louisiana's 1868 state constitution, Cable believed that political/civil, personal, and social rights overlapped each other. He found distinctions of race onerous, especially when they led to segregation. Dictating who could sit where on a train led to saying who could join in politics. However, his hesitation regarding racial mixing resembled that of the more cautious of the abolitionists. His 1885 speech "The Silent South" targeted the white southerners who were sympathetic to racial equality but too timid to act. Responding to those who argued that extending wide rights to the freedpeople would cause common sociality and race mixing, he

Fig. 3.2. Photograph of Albion Tourgée sitting in his office, ca. 1890

argued, "Have we not just used their own facts to show conclusively that this is not what occurs?"[22] Cable presented the low number of interracial relationships as proof that striking down distinctions of race would not lead to more intermarriage. Fear of mixture had prevented the exercise of equality for a century. Opponents of equality had cast the slurs "Negrophiles, Negro-worshippers, and miscegenationists"[23] at their foes. However, according to Cable, racial mixture had not increased. He named three cities—Philadelphia, Boston, and Oberlin, Ohio—that had not become havens of intermarriage. Cable underestimated the prevalence of interracial intimacy, acknowledging only "three or four of such unions" in these hotbeds of radicalism.[24] He promised that "dictates of reason and the ordinary natural preferences of like for like"[25] guaranteed the minimization of interracial intimacy.

Attacks on public rights stifled interracial cooperation as well as interracial intimacy. Along with local courts and extralegal violence, the Supreme Court continued its subversion of a transformation to a broad conception of citizenship, equality, and rights. In the *Civil Rights Cases*, the justices decided a set of five complaints against racial segregation by African Americans, on the basis of the Civil Rights Act of 1875, which sought to prosecute those who would interfere with any person's access to public accommodations, including inns, transportation, theaters, and places of public amusement. The Court deemed that act unconstitutional, maintaining that the Fourteenth Amendment did not grant Congress authority to enforce such a law. The *Civil Rights Cases* followed the *Slaughter-House Cases* and *U.S. v. Cruikshank* in reversing the gains of the Reconstruction acts and amendments. By 1883, the Court had interpreted the Thirteenth Amendment as addressing blacks only; severed state citizenship from federal citizenship, leaving the punishment of mob action to local courts; and let any prejudice against African Americans short of officially reenslaving them proceed with impunity.[26]

Within the Court, the *Civil Rights Cases* decision encountered censure from John Marshall Harlan, the lone dissenter. He argued that the earlier act sought to guarantee that blacks were treated as equals, not to make them a "special favorite of the laws."[27] Beyond the Court, the decision met with protest through a rally on October 22 featuring the lawyer and orator Robert G. Ingersoll. A Civil War veteran, former Illinois attorney general, and radical, Ingersoll dissected the decision point by point in a speech that supporters later printed and distributed. He argued first that the Reconstruction amendments had made federal and state citizenship into one, which the federal government was charged with protecting. Second, he maintained that the amendments made the Constitution "color blind." In particular, the Thirteenth Amendment prohibited any kind of servitude; in other words, it made unconstitutional any distinction based on race. These notions of color-blindness and national citizenship influenced Albion Tourgée, who wielded them in his *Plessy* arguments years later.[28]

Also present at the Washington, D.C., rally was Frederick Douglass, who delivered a speech and introduced Ingersoll. Since the 1850s, he had toned down his fervent black racial identity. By this point, he warned against excessive race pride, maintaining that it would feed the divisions of the time. Now, in his sixties, he matched his belief in American interracial interaction with his personal life. His wife, Anna, had died in 1882, after a long illness. She had been illiterate throughout her life, which may have contributed to his gravitation toward radical, educated, white women. At the same time, these women found him handsome, strong, and eloquent, the representative of what the race could become. Douglass grieved his wife's death, but he was at no loss for meaningful female companionship. Ottilie Assing, the German journalist he befriended in 1855, still visited Rochester annually, and she anticipated that Frederick would propose to her, legitimizing their romance. Instead, he married his secretary, Helen Pitts (see figure 3.3). The daughter of Gideon Pitts, a longtime associate of Douglass's, she was twenty years younger than either Douglass or Assing. Their family descended from *Mayflower* passengers and was related to John Adams. When Assing heard the news, she committed suicide by drinking poison.[29]

Douglass's marriage received disapproval from both families. Although Pitts's father had worked for racial equality, he disapproved of the wedding, as did her brother. Douglass's children saw it as a form of rejection, especially since he had kept his plans secret from them. Among some of his descendants, this marriage became his mark of shame. Blacks at large took it as an insult to black womanhood, a mark against his stature as a leader, or a warning against marrying interracially themselves. Committed to living free of racial prejudice, Douglass listened to his conscience over the matter, responding, "My first wife was the color of my mother, my second is the color of my father."[30]

In reaction to the backlash, Douglass presented a more neutral stance, neither condoning nor condemning interracial intimacy. But his personal choice pointed to his true feelings. National unity had always trumped racial unity for Douglass, and his greatest hope was for a composite American nationality much like Phillips's. In an atmosphere of equality, mixture was natural, and an intermediate race, neither black not white, was constantly increasing. Later, he spoke and wrote of physical assimilation of the black race: "My strongest conviction as to the future of the negro therefore is, that he will not be expatriated nor annihilated, nor will he forever remain a separate and distinct race from the people around him, but that he will be

Fig. 3.3. Frederick Douglass; his second wife. Helen Pitts Douglass (right); and her sister Eva Douglass (center) (FRDO 3912, n.d.)

absorbed, assimilated, and will only appear finally, as the Phoenicians now appear on the shores of the Shannon, in the features of a blended race."[31] Douglass emphasized that intermarriage alone could not resolve white racism. "The pivotal issue of the Negro's relationship to America, he contended, was more moral and political than racial."[32] The mixing of races, although inevitable where there was racial equality, would not bring racial equality without a shift in politics and attitudes.

Meanwhile, shortcomings of the blood quantum system for Indian tribal membership became apparent. In 1892, Barney Traversee, of mixed Indian and European descent, pursued a land allotment from the federal government based on his Native American heritage, to no avail. The commissioner rejected his application, disliking the notion of Indians profiting from land sales. Already possessing U.S. citizenship, Traversee applied for a homestead, claiming he was actually a white man who had voted in the past, had children in white schools, and lived among whites. Traversee's willingness to test racial requirements finally paid off in 1894 when the secretary of the interior allowed him to relinquish any claim on an allotment. He could receive the homestead he wanted, but he had to cut all ties with the Sioux in exchange. He was both white and Indian, but the government would only acknowledge one or the other. From South Dakota to Montana to Hawaii to Illinois, racially mixed indigenous people tested the limits of citizenship, inclusion, and racial categorization. More often than not, the government preserved white supremacy when resolving whether mixed indigenous people (and the mixed territories they occupied) belonged in the United States. Putting episodes such as this alongside the Plessy story shows that the struggle between white supremacy and racial ambiguity involved all racial groups. Disappointments for members of one could lead to legal and legislative setbacks for any other. Conversely, for antiracists with a universal conception of American nationhood, charges against oppression of one minority group could assist the struggles of another. In this, mixed race could be an effective tool.[33]

Upon assuming leadership of the Plessy legal team, Tourgée suggested that a plaintiff be chosen who was racially mixed and light enough to appear white, to challenge racial classification in general. Tourgée and the Comité upheld the principle of national citizenship as supreme, above local mores. The expansive idea of public rights made an infraction of social rights as serious as one of voting rights or civil rights. Their target was the use of race to classify how anyone could practice one's rights. They questioned Louisiana's ability to categorize anyone, much less to assign social classes to (classify) them. Furthermore, by considering only black or white, this classification conflicted with their Creole-of-color identity, which was mixed by definition. They considered that mixed identity as their property, and they abhorred the state's disregard for it. Their mission was to remove racial categorization from the tools government had for distributing rights, in a way, recalling Phillips's prediction in his 1853 essay: "So that you will not be able to tell black from white, for any purpose that you now make the distinction."[34]

The Plessy team made a stand against the use of race to distribute rights by utilizing the complexity of mixed race. They used mixed race as a tool to dissolve categorization and held self-identification as the rule. So their mission was to preserve their particular identity, but it was also for public rights in general. While William Short had proposed acknowledging mixed offspring in private, the New England Anti-Slavery Society had been willing to defend interracial marriage in theory, and Wendell Phillips had drawn out a United States where mixture was inevitable, the Comité and its allies deployed mixed race in a high-stakes legal battle with immediate repercussions. Their success would mean success for national citizenship in general, whether Creole of color, black, American Indian, or Asian. The Multiracial Movement was to do the same, a century later.[35]

The team first used Rodolphe Desdunes's son, Daniel, to test the law. As an octoroon, the twenty-one-year-old had the physical appearance of a white person. (See figure 3.4. With no extant photos of Homer Plessy, this may be the closest approximation of the later plaintiff's looks.) They counted on an adverse ruling from the local court, which they planned to appeal to Louisiana's high court. From there, they would appeal to the U.S. Supreme Court, maintaining that racial classification was unconstitutional, whether on the state or federal level. This required the cooperation of the train company, which would instruct its conductor to arrest Daniel for not being white. The Comité found its ally in the Louisville and Nashville Railroad, which dreaded the expense of maintaining separate and equal cars. However, the company wanted to avoid negative reactions from the general (prosegregation) public for resisting the law, so it was happy to remain in the background. The younger Desdunes bought a first-class ticket on the L&N train from New Orleans to Mobile. When the conductor approached him, he acted out the script the legal team had written beforehand, stating that he was a U.S. citizen and disclosing that he was not white. The conductor did his part, executing the arrest on January 24, 1892.

The case that the Comité brought before the Orleans Parish Criminal District Court used the Fourteenth Amendment to charge that Louisiana had made and enforced a law to "abridge the privileges or immunities of citizens of the United States" on the basis of race. They had chosen an interstate trip so that they could invoke the commerce clause. Fifteen years prior, the U.S. Supreme Court had reversed a Louisiana law prohibiting racial segregation in public carriers traveling within Louisiana. One of many decisions that came with the retreat of Radical Reconstruction, this ruling favored local customs and police power. The Comité hoped to use the interstate trip as a tool to reverse that decision. Lastly, they questioned the process of determining race at all. Racial mixture made categorization a difficult business with few standards. Since Louisiana had not set up any standards, it fell on the

Fig. 3.4. Daniel Desdunes

conductor to judge, and he lacked the authority. This gained the state law another Fourteenth Amendment violation under the due process clause.

Unfortunately, the Louisiana Supreme Court reached a decision on *Abbott v. Hicks*, a similar case involving intrastate travel, before the Comité's team reached the state bench. So the new judge in the Criminal District Court, John H. Ferguson, rendered the Comité's effort moot by deciding that the Separate Car Act did not apply to interstate travel. Although Ferguson's decision limited the separation of races on interstate travel, it left intrastate travel alone. More importantly, it left alone racial classification, the Comité's real target.

Even before *State v. Desdunes* concluded, the Comité knew they would have to produce another plaintiff. Rodolphe Desdunes recruited Homer Adolph Plessy, another Creole of color who appeared to be white. They choreographed every detail of his travel, confrontation, and arrest so that they could take the case to the U.S. Supreme Court. On June 7, 1892, Plessy bought a first-class ticket on the East Louisiana Railway, going from New Orleans to Covington, a seventy-mile circuit around Lake Pontchartrain. Following the plan, he boarded at 4:15 p.m., and the conductor, who followed a lead from the Comité to the company, confronted him. They also had a New Orleans detective present to arrest Plessy, remove him, and take him to the Fifth Precinct station. The charge against him was that "unlawfully he did then and there, insisted on going into a coach to which, by race, he did not belong."[36] The punishment was either a fine of twenty-five dollars or a prison sentence of no more than twenty-five days.

Plessy's instructions stipulated that he state that he was a U.S. citizen but conceal his racial makeup. So, contrary to the popular imagination, he did not make a scene, attributing his treatment to being black. It was essential for him to withhold his identity until later and for the conductor to ascribe one to him. But it was also important for him not to claim whiteness. As prior legal cases over white identity for Creoles of color showed, that would fail. The Comité's team was going for something bigger than either securing white privilege for their light-skinned members or helping African Americans alone; they were pointing out the fallibility of racial categorization in general.

In the Orleans Parish Criminal Court, the Comité's local attorney, James C. Walker, made a plea of jurisdiction, maintaining that, since the Separate Car Act was unconstitutional, the court lacked any authority. John H. Ferguson, the same judge as in *Desdunes*, overruled this plea, commanding the defendant to plead to the facts. It was still essential for Plessy to remain silent, especially in regard to his racial makeup, so Ferguson reminded him that he would be found guilty unless his lawyers submitted a writ of prohibition against him, the judge. They had planned to produce this challenge if Ferguson overruled them, and the case went up to the Louisiana Supreme Court.

Writing for the unanimous Louisiana Supreme Court, Justice Charles Fenner dismissed Walker and Tourgée's fourteen-point petition, maintaining that the Separate Car Act was "in the interest of public order, peace, and comfort."[37] In other words, it was a reasonable use of police power. As with many courts rationalizing racial segregation, Fenner pointed to equal application of the law to blacks and whites to assert that no rights had been impaired. He indicated that he knew the importance of this case in dismantling segregation. If he let that practice weaken in Louisiana, then it could weaken in every other state with separate but equal arrangements. Admitting that these arrangements violated the Fourteenth Amendment would "necessarily entail the nullity of statutes establishing separate schools, and of others, existing in many states, prohibiting intermarriage between the races."[38] With insight into the defense team's wider goals, he knew he had to protect this use of race distinctions to defend all others. So he ruled the Separate Car Act constitutional, which put the Comité's team closer to Washington, D.C.

Tourgée delayed the argument before the Supreme Court, hoping to gain more public sympathy for the case. This would come from the National Citizens' Rights Association (N.C.R.A.), the organization he had founded in 1891 to promote color-blind national citizenship across the country and to raise awareness for the Louisiana case. For a while, he publicized the N.C.R.A. through his popular column, "A Bystander's Notes," which appeared in the *Chicago Inter-Ocean*, a Republican newspaper. Membership was free and interracial, and the executive board included figures such as George Washington Cable. Among its members were Ida B. Wells, T. Thomas Fortune, and Charles W. Chesnutt. Twenty thousand "whites and Negroes, southerners and northerners, individuals and organizations, the educated and the illiterate, the self-seeking and the selfless, the famous and the unknown" sent in registration cards by the end of the year.[39] Tourgée hoped the N.C.R.A. would reach one million members and then exert influence on the 1892 Republican convention. The organization's support for Thomas B. Reed, Speaker of the House, was in vain. Although the organization had one hundred thousand members, it was unpopular with northern blacks. Tourgée's approach differed from that of white philanthropists who excluded blacks from conversations about racial inequality. But, by this point, the problem of racial inequality had become "the Negro problem." From there, it was easy to think of racism as blacks' burden and not society's as a whole. Most whites who wanted to address inequality excluded blacks from the conversation, even though blacks wanted to participate. Some, like Tourgée, remembered the success of interracial antiracist activity from the Civil War era. Blacks started their own organizations, some of which stipulated black membership. When membership was interracial, as with the N.C.R.A., whites resisted joining because they associated the issue with blacks only, and blacks resisted joining because of distrust. Both black groups and white groups claimed interracial cooperation as an ultimate goal, but it seemed so far from attainment that they accepted separate efforts for the foreseeable future. Tourgée decided that the N.C.R.A. would not meet in person, to avoid this conundrum. Eventually, it fell short of Tourgée's expectations, becoming "little more than a list of names."[40]

In 1894, Mark Twain published a novel, *The Tragedy of Pudd'nhead Wilson*, set on the Missouri frontier before the Civil War. The story's namesake is David Wilson, a lawyer who moves to town (much like Tourgée and Cable) to establish a law firm. He gains the label "pudd'nhead" from the locals, who believe he is bookish and eccentric. Until later, when his hobby of fingerprint collecting helps solve a murder mystery, Wilson moves into the periphery, and the story centers around the slave Roxy, her son, and the son of the household she serves. Only one out of sixteen of her ancestors was black, but she has assumed a black identity because of her condition. She has a son, Chambers, with one in thirty-two black ancestors, who is born into slavery. Their genealogies take Homer Plessy's one step further, ridiculing rules of hypodescent.

Roxy's master, Percy Driscoll, has a fully white son, Tom, who is born at the same time as Chambers, and Roxy cares for both. Already, as an infant, Tom has a rotten personality. Roxy switches Chambers and Tom in the cradle, subverting her son's destiny as a slave; Chambers grows up as "Tom," a spoiled white man with refined manners, and Tom grows up as "Chambers," a kind-hearted, uneducated slave. It appears that Twain was arguing that good qualities come with whiteness and bad qualities with blackness, but he was actually magnifying the bad qualities that come with indolence and cruelty, as well as the absolutism that ascribed goodness to whiteness and badness to blackness.[41]

Percy Driscoll manumits Roxy, and she goes to work on riverboats. But her bank fails, and she loses her retirement fund. She returns to Dawson's Landing, blackmailing "Tom" into supporting her. But "Tom's" gambling habit has made him an unreliable provider. She leads him to robbing houses, selling her for profit, and (echoing the story of Thomas Jefferson's and William Short's mentor, George Wythe) murdering his uncle, Judge Driscoll. "Tom" goes to prison, and then the bank sells him to pay debts from the estate. "Chambers," who is actually Tom, becomes a white man, but he speaks and behaves as a poor black man, making him an outcast in white society—Twain's commentary on the semisuccess of Reconstruction. Wilson finally receives the respect he deserves and becomes mayor of Dawson's Landing. However, even with professional success, he is lonely. Twain set up a literary scenario that recalls the revelation of black parentage, the tragic mulatto, and the plantation myth. Just like the legal strategy of the *Plessy* team, his work drew attention to the unreliability of racial classification. *Pudd'nhead Wilson* was "a fitting gloss on the nation's rush toward racial extremism in law, in science, and in literature, and its propensity to define equal protection under the Constitution in such a way as to render the black population invisible or, what was more fantastic, to define color itself not by optical laws but by tendentious genetic theories that reached metaphysically into a lost ancestral world."[42] Similarly, the *Plessy* case was shaping up to be a capstone on legal, social, and scientific thought on race.

Tourgée's brief to the Supreme Court employed two restrictive rights arguments: First, the Separate Car Act violated the equal protection clause of the Fourteenth Amendment, giving final authority to conductors in determining a passenger's race. Furthermore, the separate accommodations often were not equal. Since racial classification, not the quality of the cars, was the team's target, they did not dwell on that. However, the Louisiana court had determined that one could sue a railway company for incorrect seat assignment, considering that an appropriate way to address such injuries.[43]

Second, the act violated the due process clause of the Fourteenth Amendment. Train conductors were ill equipped to determine race accurately. The inconsistencies between classifications showed that the meanings of race were untenable on the local, state, and national levels. Arbitrary assignments deprived passengers of property in the form of reputation. Here, Tourgée proved himself a forerunner of twentieth-century critical race thinkers, who appreciated that identity is property. Allowing a conductor to evict a passenger who was rejecting a seat assignment deprived the passenger of liberty without due process, since the passenger had the right to occupy the seat, in the form of the ticket he or she purchased. The ticket and seat were forms of property, and the law seized that "by pretended force of law."[44] However, once again, since a conductor's actions could face judicial review, it was not necessarily the last word. Other states with separate car acts worked out the details via litigation, a resolution Louisiana accepted for perfecting its law. Tourgée hoped that the Court would follow its own, national standard, rather than acquiesce to one state's.

The team employed seven affirmative rights arguments: First, the national citizenship clause of the Fourteenth Amendment conferred national citizenship to all people born or naturalized in the United States. Since federal authority bestowed state authority, this national citizenship trumped the local. Second, the federal courts had the authority to review a state's treatment of state citizenship. Third, "the free and secure enjoyment of all public privileges" was at the center of citizenship under the Fourteenth

Amendment. Even separate cars with passengers self-categorizing was unacceptable. In this case, race was the crime because it punished certain kinds of people for occupying seats and did not punish others for sitting in the same seats. Fourth, the formulation of personal rights as inalienable in the Declaration of Independence served as the foundation for interpretation of section 1. Fifth, the Supreme Court could exercise jurisdiction in regard to the right against classification, as no leading cases had negated the possibility of this right. Sixth, the Separate Car Act was not about disciplining criminality but rather about infringing on one's citizenship. Lastly, the Louisiana law also violated the Thirteenth Amendment because it put people into servitude, in particular, "the estate and condition of subjection and inferiority of personal right and privilege."[45]

This position rested on an expansive, new understanding of citizenship. Tourgée dared the justices to see the Reconstruction amendments as new founding documents with principles that could yield utopian results. "This provision of section I of the Fourteenth Amendment *creates* a new citizenship of the United States embracing *new* rights, privileges, and immunities deliverable in a *new* manner, controlled by *new* authority, having a *new* scope and extent, depending on national authority for its existence and looking to national power for its preservation."[46] He dared the justices to think in utopian terms, transforming the United States into a new, egalitarian nation that lived up to its most noble creeds. Like the more attractive parts of Jefferson's writing, Tourgée's appealed to sense rather than reason.

However strongly Tourgée argued for a broad understanding of citizenship under the Reconstruction amendments, the Court had already dismantled this construction in *Slaughter-House, Cruikshank*, and the *Civil Rights Cases*. The justices were unlikely to reverse themselves. The recent decisions' focus on blackness also hampered Tourgée. They produced a narrow understanding of who the amendments served, and he was evoking an understanding of them before that. This produced a deep contradiction: On one hand, he wanted to question categorization at all—for both state and federal government. On the other, he was asking to use judicial tools that had essentially racial meanings. He failed to show how the amendments included a right to freedom from racial categorization.

The position also rested on an expansive understanding of family and racial mixing. Tourgée's brief asked the justices to imagine interracial families, some with a white husband and some with a white wife. The Louisiana law would divide these families in ways one would find unacceptable for monoracial families. These figures demonstrated how equal protection and racial classification were incongruous. Even if the scenarios were rare, they reinforced that racial mixing did occur. They also cast interracial intimacy in a respectable way, as a producer of legitimate families. Tourgée hoped to build sympathy for the mixed figures he presented. Like the conventional tragic mulatto character, they could receive narcissist sympathy from those who saw themselves in their whiteness. Like Twain's *Pudd'nhead Wilson*, they showed that black descent did not mean inferiority of character but rather a mixed future with equality and equal protection for all.

However, if a person believed in hypodescent, then he or she would maintain that mixed people belonged on the other side of the color line; such was their tragedy. Rather than eradicate the line separating white privilege from minority blight, true believers would say that the trick is in effective detection. Mixed race could challenge racial classification, but the justices could offer more racial classification as the solution to mixed race's power. To those who were sympathetic to racial classification, more effective methods could overcome Tourgée's emphasis on physical appearance, vis-à-vis his use of a white-appearing plaintiff. You have to believe in racial equality to appreciate physical appearance and remain truly color-blind.

Tourgée had used the trope "color-blind justice" since holding the bench in North Carolina. In his Brief of Plaintiff in Error for *Plessy*, he wrote against the uses of law to make one class of people subject to another: "Justice is pictured blind and her daughter, the Law, ought at least to be color-blind."[47] Justice John Marshall Harlan adopted this saying in his sole dissent:

> The white race deems itself to be the dominant race in this country. And so it is, in prestige, in achievements, in education, in wealth, and in power. So, I doubt not, it will continue to be for all time, if it remains true to its great heritage, and holds fast to the principles of constitutional liberty. But in view of the Constitution, in the eye of the law, there is in this country no superior, dominant, ruling class of citizens. There is no caste here. Our constitution is color-blind, and neither knows nor tolerates classes among citizens.[48]

Many people associate the term *color-blind* with Harlan, praising his denunciation of his peers' decision. However, many overlook how his praise of the white race licenses white supremacy "for all time." Later, in the same opinion, Harlan also expresses his low opinion of the Chinese in the United States:

> There is a race so different from our own that we do not permit those belonging to it to become citizens of the United States. Persons belonging to it are, with few exceptions, absolutely excluded from our country.

I allude to the Chinese race. But, by the statute in question, a Chinaman
can ride in the same passenger coach with white citizens of the United
States, while citizens of the black race in Louisiana, many of whom, perhaps, risked their lives for the preservation of the Union, who are entitled,
by law, to participate in the political control of the state and nation, who
are not excluded, by law or by reason of their race, from public stations of
any kind, and who have all the legal rights that belong to white citizens, are
yet declared to be criminals, liable to imprisonment, if they ride in a public
coach occupied by citizens of the white race.[49]

Harlan maintained this antipathy for these aliens ineligible for citizenship
two years later, in another, lesser-known dissent. In *United States v. Wong
Kim Ark*, six justices agreed that a child with foreign parents born in the
United States could become a citizen at birth. This set a generous precedent
for Wong, who was born in San Francisco of Chinese, noncitizen parents and
who had tried to reenter the country after a short visit back to China. Both
Harlan and Chief Justice Melville Fuller found these "strangers in the land,
. . . apparently incapable of assimilating with our people," distasteful. Chinese
children did not deserve to become U.S. citizens "by accident of birth."[50] In
Pace v. Alabama, Harlan had sided with the majority, protecting state anti-
intermarriage laws. With these prejudices, Harlan was far from being the
avatar for color-blindness. His *Plessy* dissent, censuring racial classification,
contradicts these other positions. He copped Tourgée's catch phrase, but he
rejected broad color-blindness, equality, or racial mixture.

On the other hand, a little-known vaudeville play presented the possibilities of mixed-race Asian success at the same time that it used yellowface
minstrelsy to lampoon Chinese exclusion. Thomas Stewart Denison's 1895
comedy *Patsy O'Wang, an Irish Farce with a Chinese Mix-Up* tells the story
of Chin Sum (aka Patsy O'Wang), a half-Irish and half-Chinese man who
works as a cook in the home of Dr. Henry Fluke, a San Francisco physician,
and his wife. Denison stipulates in his director's notes, "Whiskey, the drink
of his father, transforms him into a true Irishman, while strong tea, the bev-
erage of his mother, has the power of restoring fully his Chinese character,"
providing the premise that drives the play.[51] Dr. Fluke believes that he is
privy to this information, and when Patsy becomes drunk, terrorizing one
of Fluke's patients and becoming generally unmanageable, he hatches a plan
to force-feed black tea to the cook. However, Patsy is fully cognizant of the
effects of whiskey and tea on his behavior; it is what has brought him to the
United States in the first place. He dupes the Flukes into believing that their
plan has worked, announcing in the end that he has decided to stick with

whiskey and his rowdy Irish character. In the "land of opportunity," Patsy decides to go into politics, making what the Flukes's Irish servant, Mike, calls "a shplit ticket, half Irish, half Chinay." The play closes with Patsy singing a song, to the tune of "Pat Molloy," retelling his life story and his future plans.

> A fool for luck, the proverb says, a fool O'Wang must be,
> But now I'm turned true Irishman, bad cess to all Chinee.
> And in this free Ameriky I'll have a word to say;
> I'm goin' into politics, I'll drink no more green tay.
> And for the moral of this tale, I'm sure it's very plain:
> When tipple stirs your blood too much, you'd better just abstain.[52]

On one hand, the resignation to whiskey offers a poignant twist to the story, an answer to the extreme position of the time's temperance movement, and a spoof of Robert Louis Stevenson's *The Strange Case of Dr. Jekyll and Mr. Hyde*, which was published in 1886. Much of the play involves Patsy's torment of Dr. Fluke's patient, their chasing him around, and his seeming ability to drink gallons of tea. His desire for freedom connects him to male tragic mulatto characters such as George Harris in *Uncle Tom's Cabin*. His dual nature echoes essentialist notions of racial inheritance. However, Patsy rejects the roles that people assign him. He also asserts his Irish identity even more so for others to accept him as such. Patsy would not be the last racially mixed politician to emphasize one part of his heritage to gain broader accessibility with the public.

The turn of the century was a period of increased immigration and anxiety about the eastern and southern Europeans entering the country. Some people were happy to exploit them as labor yet unconcerned with their survival, and others wished to limit their entry. The Progressives addressed the well-being of the immigrants but also wanted them to conform to their own norms. As with any period, native-born Americans became antagonistic to immigrants if they perceived a threat to their own resources. Nativism fluctuated with the fortunes of the country at large, increasing with the Depression of 1893 but contracting with the Spanish-American War. Americanization became the dominant approach for assimilating newcomers into mainstream society, emphasizing English proficiency, consumption of mass culture, and conformity to social norms. For example, Ford Motor Company's educational program held pageants that featured immigrant employees entering an eight-foot-high cauldron in their traditional garb and then exiting, well-groomed, wearing business suits, and waving American flags.

A cartoon expressed the misgivings of the time. C. J. Taylor's "The Mortar of Assimilation" shows America, personified by a woman doing laundry, stirring miniature immigrants in a cauldron-sized vessel (see figure 3.5). The ethnic stereotypes include Europeans in their Old World garb but also Asians and blacks. Rather than a pestle, she uses a spoon labeled "Equal Rights." Her weariness, along with the resistance of the newcomers, indicates that making one people out of many is a futile effort. An Irishman escaping the mortar and wielding a knife is "the one element that won't mix." However, none of them are mixing. This cartoon appeared in *Puck* magazine in 1889, appropriating symbols already associated with core, secular values. The failure of equality, of immigration, and of mixture went together in this message, just as their successes did for those who were in favor of any of the three. But there was another way. In the coming years, Frederick Jackson Turner, Theodore Roosevelt, and Israel Zangwill all praised mixture as a happy answer to some questions of inclusion, but not many. At the "nadir of race relations," minorities addressed the same issues, often corralling mixed people into their ranks.

THE MORTAR OF ASSIMILATION — AND THE ONE ELEMENT THAT WON'T MIX.

Fig. 3.5. The mortar of assimilation—and the one element that won't mix; cartoon by C. J. Taylor, 1889

4

The Color Line, the Melting Pot, and the Stomach

Like all periods of U.S. history, the end of the nineteenth and beginning of the twentieth century was a time of restriction as well as transformation. Through the publications of Herbert Spencer and others, social Darwinism influenced scholars, philanthropists, and politicians toward a view that individuals' achievement or failure depended on their physical fitness. This retooling of Charles Darwin's theory of evolution emphasized "survival of the fittest," maintaining that those who were more fit to succeed in society did, while the less fit remained at the bottom. Thus, the success of a society depended on the success of its members, who competed for survival with other individuals. Those at the bottom deserved to be there because of their inferiority. This school of thought dovetailed with the Lamarckian belief in essences, as well as practices such as craniometry, to justify the superiority of some groups (namely, northern European males) above others. At the same time, this period earned the moniker the Progressive Era, to describe the middle-class desire to eliminate the inefficiencies of society. Philanthropists such as Andrew Carnegie gave millions to establish public museums, libraries, and universities. Reformers worked for social justice, general equality, and public safety. Often, efforts such as family aid, settlement houses, and temperance involved the moral reform of the beneficiaries. At the same time that the Progressive Movement patronized its beneficiaries, expecting them to conform to middle-class norms, it encouraged civic engagement in the newly urban and industrialized era.

While social Darwinists suggested that hands-off policies would weed out the less desirable members of society, American and British eugenicists advocated antimiscegenation laws, sterilization, and immigration limitations to move nations to a higher level of development. According to Francis Galton, human civilization had thwarted the mechanisms of natural selection, allowing the less fit to survive, pulling societies toward a dysgenic state. This racialist work gained popular acceptance; for example, Lothrop Stoddard's *The Rising Tide of Color against White World-Supremacy* appeared as a conversation piece in F. Scott Fitzgerald's *The Great Gatsby* and later as a major influence on Adolf Hitler's racial thought. But this was also a period when the natural sciences began to move away from essentialist ideas of racial character, toward a Mendellian understanding of inheritance. This fitful transformation lasted through the 1920s, with racial mixing standing at the forefront of the debate. Many geneticists such as Charles B. Davenport held on to hybrid degeneracy, the belief that mixing produced weaker offspring and threatened society as a whole, while a few such as William E. Castle, who had introduced Mendel's theories to the United States, argued that racial mixing could produce superior offspring. In between were many who could apply this idea to corn, mice, and livestock but never to humans.[1]

In 1913, Davenport published *Heredity of Skin Color in Negro-White Crosses*, a privately funded project investigating complexions of racially mixed people. Because "all matings of blacks and whites [we]re illegal and the genealogies of 'colored' people [we]re usually either difficult to obtain or else unreliable" in the southern states, he chose Jamaica and Bermuda as research sites.[1] (He also included data regarding a few families in Louisiana.) Davenport had hoped to prove the theory of hybrid degeneracy through rigorous quantitative methods. Most remarkable was his methodology, which utilized a children's game of the day. In addition to recording subjects' racial makeup, his assistant compared skin color using a Milton Bradley color wheel, an educational toy that taught the basics of color theory. To do this, the research assistant asked subjects to reveal a light patch of skin on the upper arm and matched it as well as she could to the color wheel's combinations of red, blue, and yellow. The resulting report, published by the Carnegie Institution of Washington, is truly fantastic. As Werner Sollors, scholar of ethnic literature, has written, *Heredity of Skin Color in Negro-White Crosses* "looks like it was invented in a novel by Ishmael Reed or Charles Johnson."[2] Charts, genealogies, and combinations of black (N), red (R), yellow (Y), and white (W), fill the first one hundred pages. Black-and-white photos of some of the families occupy the pages after the main body of the report, with parents and children sitting together in their everyday clothes. Most are larger groups, with the largest being the "F" family of Bermuda, with seventeen members across two generations. Covering each of these pages are sheets of translucent paper that overlay outlines over the figures in the photographs. This allows coding of the individuals without cluttering the reproductions. Turning the overlays gives two versions of how Davenport saw the subjects: either impersonal data or proof of hybrid degeneracy and a threat to society. The photo of the "W" family includes a woman, her six children with a white man, and a cousin of theirs. Their lower economic status is apparent, and the mother may have been unmarried with no claim to the father's estate. However, they appear healthy and (except for the mother, who had a handful) at ease (see figure 4.1).

Fig. 4.1. Part of "W" family, pedigree 13, including a "medium-colored" mother and six of her seven children by a white man; also, a first cousin of the children

The data led to three conclusions: First, the heredity of skin color came from both parents. Second, there was no evidence that dark skin would reappear after generations of mixture. Third, mulattoes were prolific. Davenport listed these in the section "Summary of Conclusions." Having dispelled longstanding myths about racial mixing, rather than prove the threat that mixture posed, he dedicated little text to the significance of these results. As with other American eugenicists who made such discoveries, he resisted taking any position that could weaken white supremacy.

On the other hand, the turn of the century saw a change in the natural sciences, at the hands of anthropologist Franz Boas and his followers. While social Darwinists and eugenicists believed that some groups were more advanced than others along the same scale, placing industrialized Europeans at the top and indigenous groups at the bottom, Boas stuck closer to Charles Darwin's attention to adaptation as the relationship between a species and its environment, rather than the elimination of the weak from their environments. Boas's belief that any given population's development was separate from independent variables such as time altered the study of anthropology for the rest of the century, emphasizing empirical study over social and cultural hierarchies. Believing that scholarship had moral consequences, Boas greatly influenced the intellectual development of W. E. B. Du Bois, Booker T. Washington, and Robert E. Park. His leadership contributed to a major shift in the conception of race, away from a static, essentialist one and toward one that appreciated independent development and historical changes of fortune.

During the early decades of the twentieth century, the protection of white racial purity remained dominant in national conversations about racial mixture, even prevalent among minorities wishing to stabilize identities. In particular, African American leaders deemphasized the mixture among their ranks to fight racism. At the same time, praise of mixture as a means to achieve progress, equality, and utopia gained visibility in the public sphere. Because of the increased access to higher education since the Civil War, more minority voices for any of these positions joined the public record around these issues. Because of the increase in antiracist scholarship, more white voices (often associates of the black intellectuals) contributed to more liberal ways to discuss race and mixture in the United States.[3]

This chapter explores a period beginning with W. E. B. Du Bois's 1897 essay "The Conservation of Races," which succinctly expressed his project of racial stabilization, an effort to consolidate various black identities under one bloc. This would consist of four steps: first, defining what a "race" was; second, applying one label to disparate members; third, naming the duty of its members; and fourth, promoting a universal response to past collective violations. Since the whole project was to deemphasize internal differences that came about through racial mixture, this final step nurtured blacks' negative associations with whites' past sexual violations of their ancestors, giving group members a shared experience, but it also increased antipathy toward members who wore mixture in their physical features. Black nationalists since David Walker had employed some of these maneuvers, but Du Bois collected them in an intellectually rigorous format. Although Du Bois and his fellows in the American Negro Academy had just begun to vie for influence in black intellectual thought, his definition of what a race is set the basis for minority collective identities as distinctive and antagonistic to mixture throughout the twentieth century. By the 1920s, the consolidation of minority racial groups was nearly complete, with the peak of Du Bois's influence. He and other black intellectuals urged the government to quit measuring mixture in the census, further naturalizing monoracial categories for the decades that followed.

Israel Zangwill and Jean Toomer, two creative writers, praised mixture rather than sweeping it away. Zangwill's play *The Melting-Pot* provided an optimistic way to view changes in diversity by suggesting intermarriage as the happy end of immigration. Like his progressive counterparts in the social sciences, Zangwill failed when considering the role of racial minorities, producing an assimilation theory that addressed whites only. Addressing the shortcomings of Zangwill's idea, Toomer offered "the stomach" as a social metaphor that did include all racial groups. José Vasconcelos, the Mexican intellectual, also praised racial mixture during this time. Although he mainly addressed Latin America, he constantly referred to the United States, influencing the following generations of Mexican American writers on mixture, from early leaders of the League of Latin American Citizens (L.U.L.A.C.) to Gloria Anzaldúa and then to Richard Rodriguez. Toomer's statements on mixed race continued after his landmark novel, *Cane*, and his apparent disappearance from the literary scene. The chapter ends with Jean Toomer's 1936 poem "The Blue Meridian," which expressed the author's belief that all the categories of humanity would combine into one "blue" race greater than the sum of its parts, with the United States its birthplace.

Most prominent among those who were working to consolidate black identity, William Edward Burghardt Du Bois looms large over all minority racial thinking to this day. Du Bois was born in 1868, in Great Barrington, Massachusetts, a predominantly white, yet integrated, town. His mother came from a family of free blacks who had owned property for generations. She was also of Dutch descent. His father was of Haitian descent, with French and African ancestors; he left Du Bois and his mother when the boy was two years old. Later, when Du Bois's mother suffered a debilitating stroke, the family survived through support from their extended family and through young Du Bois's odd jobs around Great Barrington. He received recognition for his scholastic achievements at an early age, coming to believe that liberal education would empower himself and other African Americans. At Fisk University, the first predominantly black environment he had experienced, he adopted a black identity. Then he received a scholarship to attend Harvard University, where he graduated cum laude in 1890. Another prize allowed him to undertake graduate work at the University of Berlin. Travel throughout Europe, an introduction to worldwide colonialism, and study with prominent German social scientists greatly influenced the student, giving his intellectual work a Continental flavor. Du Bois returned, earning his Ph.D. from Harvard in 1895, the first that the university had conferred on an African American. After a short period at Wilberforce University (1894–1896), he accepted a fellowship at the University of Pennsylvania, where he worked on *The Philadelphia Negro* before beginning a thirteen-year stay at Clark University in Atlanta.[4]

In 1897, Du Bois set forth a racial theory that he retained through the following six decades of his career, in "The Conservation of Races," a lecture first given to the American Negro Academy, an elite association of black, male intellectuals who believed that those of their class could uplift the race more broadly, a group Du Bois later called the "Talented Tenth." Most notably, Du Bois's definition of race deemphasized the biological aspects, working against the idea of pure races that was still prominent in anthropology. Reliance on physical features to define what was a race had failed, producing countless standards. Instead, Du Bois focused on the less quantifiable characteristics. "But while race differences have followed mainly physical race lines, yet no mere physical distinctions would really define or explain the deeper differences—the cohesiveness and continuity of these groups. The deeper differences are spiritual, psychical, differences—undoubtedly based on the physical, but infinitely transcending them."[5] Using the Teutonic race as an example, Du Bois explained that the initial force that brought a race together was race identity and common blood. Even while Du Bois wanted to abandon all physical measures, he privileged them, producing circular reasoning: before anything else, a race existed because members of a race subscribed to the idea of that race. But whether in a distinct moment or over time, someone or a committee had to define what the race was. Du Bois was talking about group experiences; the individual must accept the group definition, even though the whole matter was subjective.[6]

To Du Bois, the other forces bringing together a race were more important, but they came behind the group identity. These were the "common history, common laws and religion, similar habits of thought and a conscious striving together for certain ideals of life."[7] This list placed the study of race with historians and sociologists. Du Bois believed in the existence of races as discernable collectives. He also believed that members of a race would collectively progress or fail together. There was a thin line between this idea of progress and hierarchies that ranked peoples. In both cases, the wish for group progress produced more demands that everyone in the group get with the program. One had to subscribe to certain criteria to be a valid member of the race. Lastly, once the definition of a particular race took hold, it rarely let go of criteria; irreverence to the tradition marked one as a traitor. Altogether, it was hard to revise the definition of a race once someone had established it.

Even though Du Bois's theory applied to all races, he was speaking for African Americans in particular, setting himself as the codifier. As the inaugural paper of the American Negro Academy, his essay also set out the goals of the organization. The academy would be "representative in character, impartial in conduct, and firm in leadership" to lead the black race toward uplift.[8] The essay ended with a proposal for the organization's creed, which also summarized the theory he presented in the essay's body. Du Bois asserted, "We believe it the duty of the Americans of Negro descent, as a body, to maintain their race identity until this mission of the Negro people is accomplished, and the ideal of human brotherhood has become a practical possibility."⁹ To reject his definition of race was to betray the race. The main concern was African Americans, but it set the model for minority antiracist thinking ever since. Asian Americans, Latinos, and Native Americans adapted his ideas, substituting their own label where Du Bois mentioned blacks. This was the foundation for minority groups' antipathy toward racial mixture in the twentieth century.

Altogether, the different races around the world created a sort of pantheon of human collectives, with each bringing its unique, intrinsic gifts. Some of the member races had more assets than others. In particular, Europeans had prospered, colonizing the rest of the world. However, that oppression stifled the gifts that people of color had to offer. Du Bois had a global concept in mind, but the experiences of different races were not interchangeable. As a diverse nation, the United States presented a microcosm of worldwide diversity. The white race had the advantage, but other minority groups had something to offer. Cooperation was possible, through political action, equal opportunity, and the coordination of elites from each group. This conception of diversity became the model for multiculturalists, but we must remember that Du Bois was an elitist who favored educated male actors and the collective uplift tradition. Adolph Reed has reminded us that "the color line," "the veil," "double consciousness," and "the talented tenth" were born of the nineteenth century. I agree and question the applicability of Du Bois's most quoted concepts in our post-civil-rights context. Just as few people question Du Bois's reliance on blood in defining races, few interrogate the use of "the color line" to discuss racial inequality.¹⁰

Why would Du Bois use such a metaphor? He surely knew of wealthy, white-appearing families who had prospered for generations. An expert on the Reconstruction and an admirer of Albion Tourgée, he was familiar with color-blind citizenship. Du Bois's reliance on physical appearance pointed out worldwide white supremacy, but it also grouped together people who had arbitrary commonalities. He did this because his project was one of racial stabilization; blacks, poor and rich, dark-skinned and light, urban and rural, belonged together. In contrast to the protection of white purity, this was an inclusive effort rather than an exclusive one. His color line had little to do with color but rather with categorization of minority groups, prioritizing unity over appreciating distinctions. Like blood, this trope relies on a metaphor (legal segregation) archaic to our times. We should substitute it with something less metaphoric for it to make sense. After all, "racial inequality" has operated through standards broader than mere color, oppressing people of all physical appearances.

I disagree with Robert Reid-Pharr's assertion that Du Bois believed that blackness was never "a final answer but always a site of contradiction, always, in a sense, a question."[11] Du Bois was constructing blackness as an answer. Knowing what a race was and what races did left one project: defining who was in the race. This cluster of ideas eschewed the biological concept of race. At the same time, it relied on the same hypodescent that dominant racial thinking in the United States enforced: one was black because one descended from at least one black person. The contexts have changed since the end of the nineteenth century, but blackness (or Asianness, or Latinidad, or Indianness) remains the answer for those who consider it a given. Du Bois's guidelines have influenced positive racial identification for all of the "dark races" ever since.

Whereas Crèvecoeur, Tourgée, and Toomer considered mixed race for its disruptive potential, Du Bois's model considered it something to stabilize. Whereas the Comité concerned themselves with public rights, this model made equality each race's project, even if members of the race had ancestors from other races. For example, Du Bois did write about the mixture in his family in his 1940 autobiography *Dusk of Dawn*; before going into his genealogy, he reflected on the lack concise racial terms available during the early part of his life:

> Just as I was born a member of a colored family, so too I was born a member of the colored race. That was obvious and no definition was needed. Later I adopted the designation "Negro" for the race to which I belong. It seemed more definite and logical. At the same time I was of course aware that all members of the Negro race were not black and that the pictures of my race which were current were not authentic nor fair portraits.[12]

Rather than meaning "of color," as in racial minorities as a whole, "colored" referred to what we call African American. Du Bois often used "colored" to refer to African Americans, as in "the colored race." When he wrote about people of color around the world, he called them "dark races." Later, Du Bois accepted "Negro," the acceptable label of the late nineteenth century. But he also knew that not all Negroes were "black," as in dark-skinned. However, by 1903, he sometimes used "black" to mean African American, the acceptable label of the late twentieth century.[13]

Still, as he wrote, "race lines were not fixed and fast."[14] As an undergraduate at Fisk, his race pride grew in leaps and bounds. He broke off courtship with a light-skinned girl because "she looked quite white" and he wanted to avoid accusations that he had married outside his race. But even with these signs of loyalty, he encountered African Americans who ridiculed these choices, making their own distinctions about race. He turned to culture, rather than science, to discuss racial belonging, regretting the divisions African Americans established within their own race: they avoided socializing with dark-skinned fellows; they pointed out Du Bois's northern (rather than southern) upbringing; and they called him a "mulatto" rather than a "Negro."[15]

The genealogy Du Bois shared in *Dusk of Dawn* included one white great-grandparent and another mixed great-grandparent. As he described, the New World, Africa, and Europe united in his family. Ultimately, though, he called his a "colored family." Considering his self-identification during his adult life, he was a black person with racial mixture in his background, rather than a racially mixed person with parents of different racial groups in his household. I am making a distinction between these two identities: mixed-race identity attempts to keep the disparate parentage in focus ("I am eggs, milk, butter, flour, sugar, and cocoa powder"), whereas monoracial identity foregrounds a recognizable result ("I am chocolate cake"). The latter has been more predominant in American racial thought, and Du Bois set a model for talking about the mixture, coming to a monoracial identity, and promoting the unity of a vast racial group. Sometimes that model leads to the "that's what they'll see you as" argument for monoracial identification. In other words, your identity is not your own, and you may not fashion it how you see fit; it belongs to the white man or to your kin.

Following the 1893 Chicago Columbian World's Exposition, which barred African Americans, blacks did participate in the 1895 Atlanta Exposition, also famous for Booker T. Washington's "Compromise" speech. Following Du Bois's and Washington's suggestions, the U.S. commission to the Paris Exposition invited Thomas J. Calloway, a black lawyer, educator, and activist, to organize an American Negro Exhibit there. Showcasing the achievements of African Americans, it displayed books, artifacts, and statistical charts to the forty-eight million visitors to Paris. Like Du Bois's book *The Philadelphia Negro*, his three albums bringing together 363 photos of contemporary African Americans aimed to show the group as realistically, but also as positively, as possible. Most of the photos were individual portraits of blacks around Atlanta, his home at the time. Some showed members of civic groups, and others captured scenes of domestic life. Altogether, they aimed to reflect the advances of a group that had been enslaved just thirty-five years before (as if all blacks were slaves). In this, Du Bois picked subjects who conformed to middle-class standards of achievement, comportment, and domesticity. He also picked subjects of all complexions. The photos had no captions, and the names of the subjects remained secret. On one hand, this characterized the group as robust, countering the idea of hybrid degeneracy by showing successful, healthy, and prodigious people with racial mixing in their backgrounds. The dark-skinned subjects were as successful as the light-skinned ones, disproving the notion that white heritage was necessary to advance.

On the other hand, the anonymity of the photos put Du Bois in the position of defining the subjects' history, racial makeup, and perspective on blackness. Who was a former slave, a child of a slave, or a descendant of a family free for generations? Light-skinned subjects may have had parents from different racial groups or mixture somewhere in their past. They may have felt deep connection to African Americans of all stations, or they may have associated only with those of similar status. Since they were silent, the context of the exhibit provided the only clues. As the mission of the exhibit was narrow, the answers it provided stabilized all the subjects to a certain kind of blackness, one that deemphasized mixture. Viewers may have accepted this purpose while viewing the subjects with apparent mixture. If sympathetic to racial progress, they may have recognized the value of the exhibit's aim, setting aside the complications. Or, unfamiliar with the U.S. context of hypodescent, they may have exclaimed, "What are these white people doing here?" This would be an appropriate reaction facing the portrait of a girl with blond hair, light skin, and narrow features (see figure 4.2). The albums featured many like her, who may have had one black ancestor in eight or even sixteen. Du Bois's project spoke for her, as Wendell Phillips did for Fannie Lawrence during the Civil War and as advocates for a "Multiracial" umbrella category did nearly a century later. In all three cases, the mixed child symbolized a future that elders had a stake in.

In 1900, Du Bois noted the inconsistencies in social sciences on African Americans in the *Southern Workman*, the magazine of the Hampton Institute, which brought scholarly writing on racial topics to the school's alumni and donors. He praised the census as "our sole source of information as to the condition of the Negro population in general." This essay was both an introduction for the magazine's readers and also a proposal to the Census Bureau in preparation for the 1910 decennial census. Along with thorough counting of the black population, Du Bois recommended that the census "class those of African descent together and not confound with them groups socially so diverse as the Japanese and Indians," two groups tangential to the topic at hand. However, he named these to discourage breaking the black race into many groups and to discourage clumping together disparate minority groups into a vague "colored" category. So that the study of African American life could employ the statistics, he argued for one racial category rather than many. He suggested, "above all, the Negro statistics should be so collected

Fig. 4.2. African American girl, full-length portrait, seated on stool, facing slightly right, 1899 or 1900 (Photograph by Thomas E. Askew)

as to be easily segregated and counted by themselves."[16] Here his scientific interests matched his ideological ones, as stated in "Conservation." African American blackness was distinctive and in need of consolidation.

While many Americans wanted to limit immigration, others believed that America could absorb all the newcomers and transform them into true Americans. Theodore Roosevelt embodied these contradictions; while he urged native Americans to have large families, restricted women's marriage choices, and excluded racial minorities, he helped develop a liberal nationalism that emphasized the values of tolerance, equality, and individual rights. He also believed that the most vigorous people (the Americans, the British, and the Australians) achieved their potency from bringing together different strains. To a degree, Roosevelt was comfortable with including southern and eastern Europeans, believing that they would assimilate and participate in national projects such as expansion.

This type of nationalism influenced many people, including Israel Zangwill, a British Jew born in 1864 who became a successful writer of fiction, poetry, and drama in England. Upon meeting Theodor Herzl in 1896, he devoted himself to the Zionist movement in 1896 and remained active in it throughout his lifetime. While his 1897 essay "The Realistic Novel" advised writers to remain true to their perspective and to keep a sense of humor, his own writing used these maxims to dramatize the social ills of his time. In 1899, an adaptation of his novel *Children of the Ghetto* was his first play to appear on a New York stage. Following the publication of his novel *Merely Mary Ann* (1903), Zangwill made the United States his home. At the same time that he defended the Uganda Plan to establish a Jewish territory in East Africa, he also praised the Pilgrims for founding "the great country in which we stand" from the modest beginnings of the Plymouth colony.[17] His position on a homeland for Jews oscillated between two options: to renationalize or denationalize; unless a state was established, he advocated that Jews integrate into the societies in which they lived. His own life reflected this position, via his success as a writer in England and America and through his marriage to Edith Ayrton, the Christian daughter of a prominent English scientist. Still, Zangwill knew America had its faults, namely, racism, xenophobia, and urban poverty.[18]

Zangwill's 1908 play *The Melting-Pot* tells the story of David Quixano, an Orthodox Jew who moves to New York after escaping from czarist Russia. David, an idealistic composer working on an "American Symphony," voices Zangwill's rejection of the xenophobia of the time. The young man ultimately falls in love with Vera Revendal, whose father led the pogrom that killed half of David's family. But the love he finds in America cures past injuries, so they can create a new, stronger America. The play is most famous for coining the term "the melting pot," a social metaphor with similarities to Hector St. John de Crèvecoeur's *Letters of an American Farmer*, Ralph Waldo Emerson's diaries, and Frederick Jackson Turner's "The Significance of the Frontier in American History." Like these predecessors, the idea that intermarriage between ethnic groups will lead to a new, superior, American type was central. Although Zangwill's position, like Wendell Phillips's and Albion Tourgée's, was iconoclastic for its time, it has become popular shorthand for the process of creating the future American.

However, the questions that *The Melting-Pot* avoided point to its faults. The primary of these was Zangwill's uncertainty regarding racial minorities, which was the case for Crèvecoeur, Emerson, and Turner, as well. Were blacks, Asians, and others participants in the melting pot and assimilation more broadly? Would they enjoy equality with whites? Was mixture acceptable in any racial and gender combination? Even a romanticized image of mixed-race comeliness would have clarified his position regarding racial minorities. Unfortunately, the curtain closed before he could answer any of these questions. Two passages in the play express Zangwill's belief that the United States would host peace between different nationalities. The first is in act 1, when David describes America as "God's Crucible, the great Melting-Pot where all the races of Europe are melting and re-forming!"[19] Like Crèvecoeur's earlier conception of the American, David has left behind the animosities of Europe, submitting to God's will to form the American from Germans and French, Irish and English, Jews and Russians. To his uncle's suggestion that there are already eighty million Americans, and David replies, "No, uncle, the real American has not yet arrived. He is only in the Crucible, I tell you—he will be the fusion of all races, perhaps the coming superman."[20] While the first portion of this speech appears relevant only to Europeans, the later portion includes racial minorities in the melting pot. The reliance on providence recalls Wendell Phillips's "United States of the United Races," which also included racial minorities.

The second speech comes at the end of the play, when David commits to his relationship with Vera. This time, he explicitly includes blacks and Asians, along with all the world's people and religions, in the melting pot: "Here shall they all unite to build the Republic of Man and the Kingdom of God. Ah, Vera, what is the glory of Rome and Jerusalem where all nations and races come to worship and look back, compared with the glory of America, where all races and nations come to labour and look forward!"[21] The play ends here, once again suggesting that the will of God will bring together all these people, making the United States an example greater than past civilizations.

Zangwill's play resisted the wish to protect purity by arguing that intermarriage was congruent with the vision of America as mixed and democratic.

At the play's October 5 debut in Washington, D.C., President Roosevelt provided an endorsement that headlined much of the play's promotion material: "That's a great play, Mr. Zangwill, that's a great play!"[22] Critical reception of the play was lukewarm, especially in Chicago and especially with most Jews, who were uncomfortable with its nonchalance regarding the disappearance of Jewish culture. Even though the *New York Times* panned the play, *The Melting-Pot* produced solid ticket sales, playing 136 times on Broadway.[23]

In the second edition of the play, Zangwill equivocated, suggesting that "only heroic souls on either side should dare the adventure of intermarriage," effectively plucking blacks and Asians out of the melting pot.[24] Instead of taking part in the "fusion of all races," he advised blacks to put their efforts into Liberia, the establishment of a black territory in the United States, or asserting their rights in the South. If the black experience was analogous to the Jewish one, then this was a recommendation for a separate homeland rather than assimilation into other nations. Zangwill considered the "spiritual miscegenation" that had produced African American cultural products as ample mixing with blacks in the United States. According to Zangwill's 1914 afterword, the same was true for the Jew as well: "The action of the crucible is thus not exclusively physical—a consideration particularly important as regards the Jew." He continued, employing scientific jargon: "The Jew may be Americanised and the American Judaised without any gamic interaction."[25] It is likely that criticism from fellow Jews led Zangwill to recant his earlier idealism. Many disapproved of his promotion of marrying out of their group, considering that trend a threat to collective preservation. His support of the Uganda Plan added to the sensitivity around his position on out-marriage. Did Zangwill have the Jews' interests in mind if he was advocating blending into America or moving to Africa? Even though he had learned of the obstacles regarding Uganda, Zangwill stood fast, preferring it to Canada or Palestine, two other possibilities for a Jewish homeland around the time of *The Melting-Pot*'s debut. When Jews opposed his hero's statements about interracial mixture, he decided to abandon universal mixture in the United States to protect his assertion that an African country was a place where Jews could preserve their cultural, religious, and biological integrity. So, in 1914, he made the melting pot a Eurocentric affair and then excused his own group from the physical mixing that the play originally defended. The new afterword effectively shut the case on whether Zangwill meant to include racial minorities in the mixing that would create the future utopian America. Then he distanced himself from this topic. In 1916, he suggested that people would naturally resist mixing and coalesce around identities such as Christian and Jew. After World War I, Zangwill turned to nonfiction to address social issues. His disillusionment grew, and he even distanced himself from the Zionist movement. Regardless, his contributions to the melting pot as a symbol grew, providing a vague, positive message about immigration, assimilation, and intermarriage throughout the twentieth century. As a 1916 theater program showed, the melting pot often aligned patriotism with these three often threatening trends, guiding readers and speakers toward thinking of them as a national boon (see figure 4.3). As with Crèvecoeur, the question of minority inclusion that Zangwill retreated from is still important to analyze because the egalitarian notions in his writings resound, even if he fumbled with the particulars.[26]

Some people opposed the idealism of the melting pot trope because it had become synonymous with the "100 percent American" campaign to transform immigrants into loyal, normative citizens. The most vocal opponents were Horace M. Kallen and Randolph S. Bourne. Kallen directly addressed Zangwill's trope in a 1915 essay, "Democracy versus the Melting Pot," which favored preserving ethnic, cultural differences, with English merely as the lingua franca of the land. He adopted Zangwill's metaphor of the symphony to describe the sound of American diversity, claiming, "So in society each ethnic group is the natural instrument, its spirit and culture are its theme and melody, and the harmony and dissonances and discords of them all make the symphony of civilization."[27] Bourne, a writer from a prestigious New Jersey family, followed Kallen's position in his "Trans-National America" (1916), which also asserted that the United States' strength came from its hyphenated citizens. Kallen later coined the term *cultural pluralism* to describe his antidote to assimilation, and it became a central tenet of the Multicultural Movement decades later. However, Kallen deemed racial mixture as one of the regrettable forces of Americanization, while Bourne overlooked it completely. Both were more interested in preserving immigrant cultures than they were in mixing bodies.[28]

Philip Gleason offered one of the most cogent (and most cited) analyses of the melting pot trope in his 1964 article "The Melting Pot: Symbol of Fusion or Confusion?" He asserted that, since 1908, its usage was more evocative as a symbol ("Millions of immigrants came fumbling into the melting pot") than as a simile ("America is like a melting pot") or a metaphor ("America is a melting pot").[29] However, as a symbol, it has been an ambiguous one with no clear theoretical framework to support it. From its earliest deployment, the melting pot's ambiguities have fostered and reflected confusion regarding its meaning. This was true for those who supported the ideas of inclusion

Fig. 4.3. Cover of theater program for Israel Zangwill's play *The Melting-Pot*, 1916

and mixing as well as for those who were opposed to them. However, the rhetorical alternatives rising in following decades lacked the adaptability of the melting pot. For example, the mosaic is an especially static symbol; once the pieces are in place, they remain there forever. The salad captures the proximity of elements, but they only produce new flavors through mastication. The quilt emphasizes a larger picture, but it puts pieces in contact only with their immediate neighbors. The stew overlooks the process of ingestion, as well as the possibility of ruining the dish. Lastly, the kaleidoscope captures the overall picture and the constant flux, but it also prohibits the individual pieces from changing. As Gleason wrote, "It is the unique merit of the melting pot that the element of ever-changing process is intrinsic to the symbol itself, and that which is symbolized, ethnic interaction, is above all an ever-changing dynamic process."[30]

At the same time that Zangwill was revising *The Melting-Pot*, Robert E. Park was shaping modern sociology, applying modern methods to social issues, including immigration and inequality. Park had been Booker T. Washington's secretary at the Tuskegee Institute before moving to the University of Chicago, where he was to have his greatest impact on future generations of sociologists. Here, he began writing about assimilation. In a liberal society, members of minority groups assimilated as individuals. Perhaps reflecting Washington's influence, he rarely addressed the relationship between exclusion and race—in other words, racism. Park trained his pupils to believe that African Americans lacked a distinctive culture; like other minorities, they would assimilate to the dominant, white culture. Even though the Chicago School wanted equality, this focus ignored racism as an obstacle. Park's definition of assimilation let whites off the hook, leaving all the work to racial minorities. What if a principal belief of the dominant group was to exclude certain minority groups?[31]

Of Park's followers, E. Franklin Frazier deviated the most, later presenting cultural and social assimilation as two processes, with racism hindering racial minorities, mixed or not. In response, racial minorities might fortify separate group identities to cope with exclusion. This separation could leave the exclusion unchallenged. They would have to choose between assimilating socially and culturally with the mainstream and becoming ethnic nationalists. The latter was the popular route, as Du Bois had chosen for himself and prescribed for others. Scholars of race from this time, regardless of their positions on culture, all consolidated racially mixed people with their minority parent group. Unsure what to do with racial minorities, members of the Chicago School followed Zangwill's unexamined praise of mixture. Just as the playwright left the question of racial minorities out of his dramatic work, the sociologists left it out of their academic work. Altogether, they naturalized the idea of hypodescent in a variety of discourses.[32]

In 1921, Robert E. Park and Ernest W. Burgess published their famous textbook *Introduction to the Science of Sociology*, providing the definition of assimilation Park had begun in 1914: the "process of interpenetration and fusion in which persons and groups acquire the memories, sentiments, and attitudes of other persons or groups, and, by sharing their experience and history, are incorporated with them in a common cultural life."[33] While inter-ethnic antagonism arose naturally, assimilation was a sign of its resolution.

Similar to the field that was to become Black Studies, the study of racial mixing had existed since first contact and then expanded during the ante-bellum period. In the early decades of the twentieth century, though, many of Park's followers, including Everett V. Stonequist, Edward B. Reuter, and E. Franklin Frazier, studied racial mixing, producing a body of work I call "Mulatto Studies." Unlike earlier American racial scientists, these scholars worked toward racial equality. They considered social forces as the primary influence on one's station, rather than intrinsic racial characteristics trans-mitted through the blood. However, even with this substitution, they char-acterized racially mixed people as intermediate between their parent groups and prone to confusion because of their mixture. Most importantly, Mulatto Studies scholars looked to mixed minorities for the progress of their minor-ity communities more so than for the progress of America as a whole. So these scholars contributed to the stabilization of racial identity into tradi-tional groups rather than exploring the unreliability of racial categories or the distinctive experience of mixed peoples.

Assimilation could occur without amalgamation, but amalgamation "naturally promotes assimilation or the cross-fertilization of social heritages. The offspring of a 'mixed' marriage not only biologically inherits physical and temperamental traits from both parents, but also acquires in the nature of family life the attitudes, sentiments, and memories of both father and mother. Thus amalgamation of races insures the conditions of primary social contacts most favorable for assimilation."[34] For the rest of the twentieth cen-tury, intermarriage became the principal indicator of assimilation, the means for minorities to enter Park's schema. With reference to Sollors's discussion of anticipation and fulfillment, mentioned in the introduction, sociologists' citation of the statistics on intermarriage repeats the prophecy of racial equal-ity to the point of overshadowing the actual promise. But it also means that the anticipation increases with repetition, becoming more consuming than achieving racial equality. Because of sociologists' reliance on signs of fulfill-ment (or imminent fulfillment) such as increasing intermarriage or mixed-race birthrates, these signs became more and more prophetic throughout the twentieth century.

As a University of Chicago doctoral student, Edward Reuter followed Park's denial of black culture in his dissertation and book *The Mulatto in the United States* (1918). Reuter assigned inferiority and superiority to racial groups, but differently than past racial scientists had; these stations came about because of oppression rather than essential capacity or worth. So his praise of mulattoes as superior was complimentary in intention. While Du Bois subordinated mixture to a stable group identity, Reuter separated mixed people into their own group. Both notions were limiting. Reuter's examples favored high-achieving figures such as Du Bois, without engaging with the scholar's ideas. The achievements of mixed people were proof of their superiority. However, Reuter characterized this set as wanting to remove themselves from blacks, ignoring that most of these achievements demonstrated deep ties to African Americans and racial justice broadly. The result, according to Reuter, was that white racism has clumped superior mulattoes with inferior blacks. At that station, the mulattoes would become their reluctant leaders. Reuter's dissertation and book was forward thinking yet echoed the tragic mulatto perfected in the 1850s. His program for racial equality was to deploy the superior mulatto on the inferior blacks to help uplift them.[35]

Everett Stonequist expanded on Park's trope of the Marginal Man, the product of bicultural or multicultural societies, in whose mind "conflicting cultures meet and fuse," embodying the processes of civilization and progress.[36] This trope readily pointed to racially mixed people, although it also applied to immigrants. The Marginal Man's "racial status is continually called in question; naturally his attention is turned upon himself to an excessive degree: thus increased sensitiveness, self-consciousness, and race-consciousness, an indefinable *malaise*, inferiority and various compensatory mechanisms, are common traits in the marginal person."[37] Unlike Reuter, Stonequist recognized that racially mixed African Americans may choose to align with African Americans. However, like Reuter, he also considered this small group—which included "the gifted mulatto, Dr. Du Bois," whose trope of "double consciousness" resembled the emotional anguish he described—the champions of the whole. If the marginal person can adjust to his or her station, then the final result may be a new social framework. Stonequist updated Josiah Nott's unstable hybrid with the possibility of racial progress, or social (rather than biological) tragedy.[38]

Others outside the social sciences answered the questions regarding how the future American would appear and what life with universal interracial intimacy would be like. One of these was Jean Toomer, author of the novel *Cane*. Born on December 26, 1894, Toomer (Nathan Eugene Pinchback) was the grandson of P. B. S. Pinchback, who had been a member of the Comité des Citoyens, lieutenant governor of Louisiana during Reconstruction, and then governor for thirty-five days after the impeachment of Henry Clay Warmoth. Toomer's family was part of the mulatto elite in Washington, D.C., and the boy grew up in a white neighborhood, apparently free of prejudice.

Later, he described his ancestry as Negro, Indian, Scotch, Welsh, German, English, French, Dutch, and Spanish. At age nineteen, Toomer first had the notion to consider himself an American, neither white nor black. He began to believe that almost all Americans possessed a number of ancestries, but few were aware of it. His conception of national identity developed in the coming years, exerting a major impact on his literary career, his personal relationships, and his spiritual quest. Toomer briefly attended the University of Wisconsin and several other colleges and universities but found it hard to settle into one field of study or line of work. A snapshot from his time in Madison features him showing off his young, muscular body, comfortable in predominantly white settings and plying his mixed, American, and national, not racial, identity (see figure 4.4). He moved to New York City, began reading broadly, and built friendships with Waldo Frank and other writers. In 1920, he returned to Washington to be with his ailing grandfather and to begin writing in earnest.[39]

In the October 10, 1920, issue of the *New York Call*, Toomer responded to an editorial by the author Mary Austin alleging that Jews had inordinate control over the critical tastes of America. While Toomer admired Austin's concern for American culture, he censured her on three points: First, the influences on American letters outside New York disproved her argument. Second, her statements resembled those of whites in the Jim Crow South who wished to keep blacks away from the polls. Third, her emphasis on ethnic origins showed no appreciation for the inequality that immigrants faced. He was certain all would join together, producing a nation of evolved spirits, "universal of sympathies and godlike of soul."[40] The race he described in the essay was yet to materialize, but its spirit was visible in some creative artists of the day.

> It is certain that it will be a composite one, including within itself, in complementing harmony, all races. It will be less conscious of its composite character than the English are of theirs, and it will be considerably more aware of the grandeur of its destiny. . . . The resultant temper will be broad, inclusive, aware of one race only, and that the American. In fine, in our future national type humanity will have again achieved the constructive association of its varied elements.[41]

He later described the race as "interracial and unique" and "structurally distinguishable from the heretofore existing types."[42] However, physical appearance was of less concern to Toomer than were the spiritual aspects of transformation.

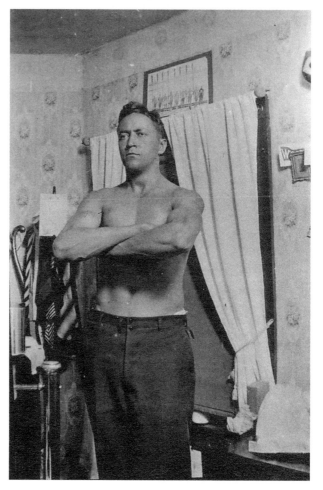

Fig. 4.4. College photo of Jean Toomer, bare chested with arms folded, 1916

Toomer directly addressed Zangwill's melting pot at two points in this article: first, referring to the distaste some Christians have for intermarriage with Jews, and vice versa; and, second, criticizing Austin's "focus on the unfused metals of the melting pot," pointing out that regardless of what some narrow-minded people think, the future American will encompass all of us, the more and the less assimilated, and the more and the less open-minded.[43] Like Phillips and Zangwill, Toomer believed it was destiny for the nation to bring forth a new, superior, moral race. Differences that some people fixated on at that point would become moot in the future.[44]

The U.S. census has employed ways of accounting mixture, on and off, since 1790, with shifts in method reflecting thinking on mixture of the times. From the census's conception through 1840, it focused on who was free and who was enslaved, to comply with the Constitution's stipulation that slaves count as "three fifths of all other persons" for purposes of taxation and congressional representation. The term "free colored persons" captured some people whom enumerators would identify as free and nonwhite, including Indians who did pay taxes, free Creoles of color in Louisiana, and people living in rural areas who were known as "triracial isolates." Reflecting a strong association of whiteness with freedom and blackness with enslavement, the language of racial categories then shifted toward color. In 1870 and 1880, the census only counted blacks and mulattoes, since the other distinction became moot after emancipation. The terms *mulatto* and *quadroon* appeared in 1890, producing such unreliable data that they disappeared in 1900. That was the same time as Du Bois labeled his photographic subjects "Negro" at the Paris Exhibition and emphasized one census category for Negroes in the *Southern Workman*. According to Kelly Miller, black sociologist and one-time dean at Howard University, Booker T. Washington advised the Census Bureau to call all people of African descent "Negro." Before disappearing for good after 1920, "Mulatto" appeared two more times. If the Supreme Court's decision in *Plessy v. Ferguson* marked the end of the retreat from radical Reconstruction, it also marked the full acceptance of the one-drop rule on a national level. Since it was legal to exclude nonwhites, it was no longer relevant to count mulattoes, and it was dangerous to acknowledge their white descent. By the 1920s, the Jim Crow version of white supremacy had become such the norm that voters, politicians, and Census Bureau officials dropped the complicated task of measuring racial mixture. So Miller also urged the bureau to quit the folly of counting mulattoes. Maintaining a third distinct racial group would further the "iniquity" that racism already exacted on African Americans.

Increased immigration from south of the border made the count of Mexicans relevant. The growth of plantations on Hawaii, which had a high degree of racial mixture, made counting its people an attainable goal. Sometimes census racial categories appeared because they seemed relevant and manageable at a particular moment, not because they figured in a grand narrative of racial identification. It is possible that the punch cards used in the bureau ran out of space with the addition of "Mexican" and "Hawaiian." Along with ideology, politics, and science, the mechanics of forms influenced these choices. Without controversy, ceremony, or press coverage, "mulatto" and "quadroon" disappeared after 1920. After seven decennials in eighty years that did categorize racially mixed people, the bureau affirmed in 1922, "A person of mixed blood is classified according to the nonwhite racial strain or, if the nonwhite blood itself is mixed, according to his racial status as adjudged by the community in which he resides," consigning mixed people to their minority parental groups.[45]

Equally as influential among blacks, but appealing directly to nationalist wishes rather than to intellectual manners, was Marcus Garvey and his Universal Negro Improvement Association (U.N.I.A.). Born in 1887, Garvey became a labor organizer in his homeland of Jamaica and studied in England, where he associated with other black anticolonialists. He had corresponded with Booker T. Washington; under Washington's influence, Garvey hoped to establish a school like Tuskegee Institute in Jamaica. He moved to the United States in 1916 and started a chapter of the U.N.I.A. in New York after a year-long speaking tour. A Pan-Africanist, Garvey hoped to improve the condition of blacks worldwide, starting businesses and advocating a return to Africa. His Black Star shipping line purchased its first craft, the *Yarmouth*, in 1919, and the U.N.I.A. grew to nearly four million members. Its *Negro World* newspaper had a circulation of two hundred thousand at its peak, becoming the most popular black paper in the United States and reaching readers around the world. Malcolm X reminisced in his autobiography about his father's activism in the U.N.I.A. as a minister in Lansing, Michigan; Omaha, Nebraska; and Milwaukee, Wisconsin. Along with a return to Africa, Garvey characterized racial purity as a primary tenet of the organization. Garvey encouraged a distinction between unmixed blacks in the African diaspora, such as himself, and those with mixture in their background, labeling those with more mixture "coloreds" rather than black. He equated the pursuit for integration with "race suicide": hatred for one's own race to compete for the hand of white women.[46] He even met with Ku Klux Klan leaders, who agreed with his ideas of racial separation.[47]

Garvey disparaged the idea of a utopia, where all would get along. Racial separation was his goal. Assimilation, whether social or physical, was unacceptable.

> Some Negro leaders have advanced the belief that in another few years the white people will make up their minds to assimilate their black populations; thereby sinking all racial prejudice in the welcoming of the black race into the social companionship of the white. Such leaders further believe that by the amalgamation of black and white, a new type will spring up, and that type will become the American and West Indian of the future. This belief is preposterous.
>
> I believe that white men should be white, yellow men should be yellow, and black men should be black in the great panorama of races, until each

and every race by its own initiative lifts itself up to the common standard of humanity, as to compel the respect and appreciation of all, and so make it possible for each one to stretch out the hand of welcome without being able to be prejudiced against the other because of any inferior and unfortunate condition.[48]

Garvey did not name the leaders, but his accusations do bring Du Bois to mind. Garvey's belief in separate development within a common humanity echoed Du Bois's. However, Garvey found the American project to create a diverse democracy distasteful. Integration was an attempt to "escape the race through an underground current of miscegenation."[49] Black intellectuals were the agents of this plan, which reflected their alleged "disloyal and selfish" agendas.[50] Although wildly popular, Garvey was making enemies, including Du Bois, who denied that the colorism Garvey cited even existed.

As editor of the *Crisis*, the N.A.A.C.P.'s official magazine, Du Bois wrote to explain the organization's defense of social equality. The organization gained a reputation for promoting miscegenation because it argued for social equality. As Du Bois clarified,

We believe that social equality, by a reasonable interpretation of the words, means moral, mental and physical fitness to associate with one's fellowmen. In this sense the crisis believes absolutely in the Social Equality of the Black and White and Yellow races and it believes too that any attempt to deny this equality by law or custom is a blow at Humanity, Religion and Democracy.[51]

Typical of the Jim Crow era, the elision of equality with miscegenation was quick, and the *Crisis* had to respond. Whether the topic was public facilities, voting, or private interaction, racists cast black men in particular as sexual predators, a fiction that antilynching activists such as Ida B. Wells worked to debunk. Even after the 1954 *Brown v. Board of Education* decision, which reversed *Plessy*, segregationists invoked the threat of interracial intimacy to bar equal access to certain resources. On the other hand, the racists had a point; with public rights could come interracial intimacy, the complication of racial categories, and the dissemination of capital across racial groups.

Speaking for the *Crisis* and the N.A.A.C.P. as a whole, Du Bois defended interracial marriage as a right. "As to the individual right of any two sane grown individuals of any race to marry there can be no denial in any civilized land. The moral results of any attempt to deny this right are too terrible and of this the southern United States is an awful and abiding example."[52]

However, similar to William Lloyd Garrison's retreat from the marriage-law campaign, Du Bois distanced himself from promoting interracial marriage. "The answer to this is perfectly clear: it is not socially expedient today for such marriages to take place; the reasons are evident: where there are great differences of ideals, culture, taste and public esteem, the intermarriage of groups is unwise because it involves too great a strain to evolve a compatible, agreeable family life and to train up proper children."[53] While intermarriage was not a crime, nor did it cause any physical harm, Du Bois issued a strong recommendation against it.

Du Bois soon found himself sparring with Warren Harding, who rebutted this stance on social equality in October 1921. In a speech to a Birmingham, Alabama, audience, the president addressed race relations as a national issue. He advocated letting "the black man vote when he is fit to vote" but also favored "recognizing a fundamental, eternal, and inescapable difference" between the races.[54] He censured lynching but also warned against social equality. Blacks should develop "a heredity, a set of traditions, an array of aspirations all its own," along with "leaders who will inspire the race with proper ideals of race pride, of national pride, of an honorable destiny, an important participation in the universal effort for advancement of humanity as a whole."[55] Harding's suggestions to African Americans resembled Du Bois's and Garvey's programs of separate development, but with the assumption of inferiority. Lastly, even though interracial intimacy was not the topic at hand, he condemned racial amalgamation. "Racial amalgamation there cannot be."[56]

Du Bois responded to Harding in December. First, he gave the president "every ounce of credit he deserves" for defending voting rights, education, and economic justice. Second, he delineated the two possible meanings of "social justice," pointing out Harding's elision. The president had confused the question of equality with compulsory intimacy, a tactic that forced blacks to concede that any interracial interaction—for example, Booker T. Washington's dinner at the White House—was a "disgrace."[57]

But amalgamation had happened, was happening, and likely would continue. If Harding meant that it should not happen, then the majority of blacks would agree with him. As Du Bois responded,

> We have not asked amalgamation; we have resisted it. It has been forced on us by brute strength, ignorance, poverty, degradation and fraud. It is the white race, roaming the world, that has left its trail of bastards and outraged women and then raised holy hands to heaven and deplored "race mixture." No, we are not demanding and do not amalgamation, but the reasons are ours and not yours.[58]

This fulfilled the fourth step in the project of racial stabilization: promoting a universal response to past collective violations. Slave narratives of the antebellum period by Harriet Jacobs, William Wells Brown, and Lewis Clarke had introduced the notion of house slaves and field slaves to the general public, suggesting that the house was the site of sexual violence while the field was the site of brute violence.[59] This provided a two-prong rebuttal against the notion that slave owners were kindly providers, but it also homogenized slave experiences along two poles. But Du Bois added two judgments to the account: first, the interracial intimacy had always been forced; and second, all offspring were bastards. The sexual exploitation of black, Indian, Asian, and Hispanic white women did occur, but Du Bois's analysis populates all mixture in the past with lecherous white men. In response to this violence, shame, and silencing, all interracial intimacy takes on the specter of rape. All mixed offspring, who you can spot by their physical appearance, are products of shame. Any perceived advantages they may or may not have also recall the rape. In reality, interracial relationships have been more varied than this. Du Bois, Garvey, and their peers had not invented this rhetoric, but they did rearticulate minority antipathy toward racial mixing during the twentieth century into a sort of reverse colorism that held light-skinned kin as privileged, suspect, and poisoned by whiteness.

Meanwhile, Jean Toomer provided an example debunking the idea that racially mixed people had to identify with their minority parent group because society was so restrictive in past eras. In 1922, at the invitation of the head of a black school in Sparta, Georgia, he went south to be its temporary principal and to immerse himself in what he considered to be a dying black culture. This experience was the impetus for *Cane*, the manuscript that literary figure Waldo Frank helped him find a home for. In a 1922 letter that Toomer wrote to Frank, he used language prescient of late-twentieth-century racial theory, explaining that he only used the term *Negro* when he wanted to evoke an emotion associated with the black experience and that he no longer thought of people according to their "color and contour." Instead, he saw "differences of life and experience," which often directed him to racial experiences.[60] At times, he described races as knowable and distinct, but rarely ever cultural. While he never went as far as to suggest that race was a social construction, he often equated it as a lived experience that individuals may encounter differently. However, his attempt to jettison physical appearance in favor of social descriptors was incomplete, as he still referred to racial groups as discrete bloods and races. When Boni & Liveright published *Cane* in 1923, Toomer accepted that the firm might market his book as Negro literature. But he directed them to avoid calling him a Negro in advertisements or materials going out with review copies, even though black life was at the center of the book. When they disappointed him, he wrote Horace Liveright, "My racial composition and my position in the world are realities which I alone may determine. . . . As a unit in the social milieu, I expect and demand acceptance of myself on their basis. I do not expect to be told what I should consider myself to be."[61] He directed the publisher to refrain from insinuating that he was "dodging," or racially passing for white. Echoing his grandfather's peers in Reconstruction Louisiana, he maintained that his identity was his own private property, knowable to himself but elusive to others. Predicting the mixed-race identity theory emerging in the 1990s, he maintained his right not to justify his ethnic legitimacy. While few examples of this individualism reveal themselves in the public record, Toomer's position proves that racially mixed Americans surely could identify in unconventional ways.

At the time, *Cane* was like no other piece of fiction by an African American author. Its modernist sensibility brought new forms to an exploration of traditional black culture. Toomer's belief in an emergent Negro found favor with Alain Locke, who published excerpts of *Cane* in *The New Negro* (1925), his landmark collection that announced a change in consciousness and a cohort of African American writers, artists, and musicians, often synonymous with the Harlem Renaissance. Some of these figures, including Locke and Langston Hughes, acknowledged racial mixture in their backgrounds but also subordinated it to the goal of promoting a vibrant, unified black race. Critics anointed Toomer the stylistic vanguard of that literary movement, even though he primarily wanted to be known as an American writer. Later, Toomer claimed that Locke had included the excerpts without his permission, and he avoided being in any future collection that revolved around the racial identity of the authors. The experience of pigeonholing increased Toomer's distaste for conventional thinking, and even before *The New Negro* appeared, he had attended the Institute for the Harmonious Development of Man, south of Paris, France. Founded by Greek-Armenian mystic Georges I. Gurdjieff, the institute taught his philosophy of Unitism, which maintained that the remedy for the ills of war, materialism, crime, and the Great Depression lie in "transcending the multiplicity of particularities and individualities."[62] Many scholars have considered Toomer's involvement with Gurdjieff as the end of his literary career, overlooking his continued (yet unpublished) productivity through the decades after *Cane*, when he incorporated the mystic's formulation into his writing.

In 1930, James Weldon Johnson, author of *The Autobiography of an Ex-Colored Man*, which told the story of a man who racially passed for most of his life and came to regret abandoning his race, invited Toomer to contribute to the second edition of his *Book of American Negro Poetry*. Toomer responded,

I aim to stress the fact that we all are Americans. I do not see things in terms of Negro, Anglo-Saxon, Jewish, and so on. As for me personally, I see myself an American, simply an American.

As regards art I particularly hold this view. I see our art and literature as primarily American art and literature. I do not see it as Negro, Anglo-Saxon, and so on.

Accordingly, I must withdraw from all things which emphasize or tend to emphasize racial or cultural divisions. I must align myself with things which stress the experiences, forms, and spirit we have in common.[63]

Toomer associated the idea of race with experience and affiliation. He also rejected the notion that he must pledge allegiance to the collective black experience that Du Bois had articulated. Johnson replied, respecting his wishes, but asserted that the time was too soon to emphasize the fundamental unity of all Americans. However, Toomer maintained that the time was right and set his efforts toward describing a country that reflected his mystical vision. As a utopian, he lived in the world he wanted now, rather than later.

At the same time that Toomer was attending the Institute for the Harmonious Development of Man, Mexican educator and politician José Vasconcelos was writing his own version of the melting pot. His essay "La Raza Cósmica: Misión de la Raza Iberoamericana" was at the center of this project, but he spoke on mixture throughout his career. While focusing on Latin America, Vasconcelos's statements are relevant to racial mixture in the United States for two reasons: First, he constantly addressed race relations in Mexico's northern neighbor, even as a counterpoint. Second, his ideas have exerted a great influence on later Mexican American thinkers, including the Chicano movement, Gloria Anzaldúa, and Richard Rodriguez.

Born in 1882 in the Oaxaca region of Mexico, Vasconcelos was the son of a government official and a pious matron. He described himself as being of mostly Spanish descent, with a drop of Indian blood and a grain of African culture, which supposedly gave him more emotionality than most whites. Because of his father's customs post, his family often moved between border towns and seaports. Part of his elementary school education was in Eagle Pass, Texas, an experience that broadened his perspective. Vasconcelos came of age during the rule of Porfirio Diaz, dictator from 1876 to 1880 and 1884 to 1911. Positivism, the school of thought hailing from French philosopher August Comte, influenced Gabino Barreda, who had studied in France and shaped Mexican education during Diaz's rule. Barreda introduced positivism to the National Preparatory School. Diaz, to bolster his own authority among the elites, sponsored the theory, shaping Mexicans of Vasconcelos's generation. Vasconcelos came to believe that societies progressed from a theological to a metaphysical to a positive phase in a sequential and quantifiable manner. As with social Darwinism, positivism allowed the conclusion that dominant societies had reached that point because of their inherent superiority.[64]

In 1909, Vasconcelos joined the Ateneo de La Juventud, a group of fifty young intellectuals who aimed to remove Diaz from office, mainly because the leader had allowed so much foreign capital to affect the nation's economy and to diminish traditional Mexican culture. This group disavowed positivism, aiming to formulate new paradigms for the era after the dictator. Trained as a lawyer and dedicated to politics, Vasconcelos was already a prolific writer when he left for Washington, D.C., to represent the Anti-Reelection Club supporting Francisco Madera in the Mexican Revolution. At this time, Vasconcelos criticized Comte for his disregard for art and metaphysics and placed these at the center of his philosophic thought from then on. But his linear, progressive tendencies swayed his thought for decades, whether he addressed art, education, or racial mixing.

In 1913, Victoriano Huerta, one of Diaz's generals, assassinated Madero and took office. Vasconcelos supported Venustiano Carranza, a former revolutionary and usurper of Huerta, until Carranza sent him north of the border again to gain business interest from the United States and Canada, an endeavor that reminded Vasconcelos of Diaz's open policy toward foreign investors (see Fig. 4.5). Splitting ranks with the new leader cost Vasconcelos the directorship of the National Preparatory School. Upon Vasconcelos's return to Mexico, Carranza arrested him, but he escaped, lived in New York City, and then moved to Peru. Álvaro Obregón's 1920 victory over Carranza allowed the educator to return, and the new president named him rector of Universidad Nacional Autónoma de México, which led to his becoming minister of education. During the early 1920s, Vasconcelos built his greatest legacy as the father of modern Mexican education. He opened over one thousand rural schools that also served as community centers. Promoting literacy, he distributed copies of world classics throughout the country. In the public arts, he sponsored the muralist movement, which decorated public buildings in a traditional Mexican style. This initiative also advanced the careers of Diego Rivera and José Clemente Orozco, who became internationally recognized artists. This arts program reflected his perspective since finishing his training that Mexico had great potential. Achieving it involved resisting foreign influence, whether financial or cultural, and drawing from the country's own traditions.

Fig. 4.5. José Vasconcelos in Washington, D.C., 1914 (Photograph by Harris & Ewing; courtesy of Harris & Ewing Collection, Library of Congress)

Vasconcelos began lecturing on racial mixture as early as 1921, four years before the publication of "La Raza Cósmica: Misión de la Raza Iberoameri-cana," the essay that predicted a new race combining the better features of "*el negro, el indio, el mongol y el blanco*," the four groups populating the earth. While he had abandoned Comte and positivism, he retained that way of thought in predicting that the union would be the result of three stages of development. The first was "material," which focused solely on obtaining the necessities of life. Mixture happened only by force, and war was the only means of conflict resolution. The second, "intellectual," stage used strategy, calculation, and scholarship to improve on past errors. This is where Vasconcelos placed most modern nations. Unfortunately, the intellectual stage also led to rationalizations against racial mixing. The final stage, which was beginning to take hold and would result in a mixed population, was "esthetic." People would rule themselves and abandon the ways of the previous two. Passion, beauty, and happiness would be the inspiration for peoples' lives, which would be full of creativity and spirituality. Vasconcelos opposed the protection of racial purity, speaking out against movements such as Nazism and the Ku Klux Klan. But he did believe that Europeans had brought advancements to the other less developed people of the world during the current, "material," phase. He acknowledged that the white race was in a position of power and pointed out that it brought technology, religion, and education to the others, readying them for the next stage. His theory abhorred the elimination of any group, aiming to fuse them all together into one. This would begin in Latin America, which already has begun mixing all the races. Displaying his own contradictions, Vasconcelos critiqued the Anglo tendency toward pure races but wished to include the United States in his vision. He disavowed his northern neighbor's white supremacy but excused Europeans for colonialism.

The people in the esthetic stage would let love and beauty direct the interracial unions producing the cosmic race, rather than the greed, power, or desperation that led to mixing during European colonialism. However, Vasconcelos framed this in eugenic terms, claiming that only people of comparable beauty, intelligence, and health would be attracted to one another, so that they could produce beautiful, intelligent, and healthy—yet mixed—offspring. The less beautiful, poor, and unhappy would no longer mate, causing their ills to disappear from the population. Ultimately, the qualities spread among all races would rejoin in the new race. The next year, in his book *Indología*, Vasconcelos wrote on the encounter between Spanish and indigenous in particular. He pointed to the creation of a large mestizo group throughout Latin America as proof of how quickly the development of the cosmic race could happen, challenging the racial scientists who believed that mixed groups were less prolific. *Indología* expanded on his prior warning that the isolation of pure races would lead to their demise. He praised the Spanish for bringing their best qualities to the New World and for creating the mestizos, the mixed group spanning the Americas that would be the start of the cosmic race.

Vasconcelos developed his own version of Bolivarist thought in 1921, promoting the idea of a unified Latin America. Even though his pride in Mexico was most immediate, he professed that this should be within the context of bringing together the republics of Central and South America. Their division into twenty-plus countries allowed for Anglo-American preeminence, so he opposed the idea of a Pan-American union—or *Monroismo*, after the United States' Monroe Doctrine. His ultimate goal was to join people on this side of the Atlantic with Spain, which he considered to be the motherland. He longed for a coalition that would bolster the cultural, financial, and anti-imperialist interests of its Spanish-speaking constituents. He later described it as pan-Iberian, including Brazil and Portugal, linguistic cousins.

During the early 1920s, Vasconcelos envisioned Spanish America as a peer with North America, coexisting in peace and enriching the hemisphere with their many traditions. At the same time, he thought that the two cultures were incompatible, and he resented the United States' meddling in Mexican affairs, whether investing, helping Huerta overthrow Madero, or landing troops at Vera Cruz. He was fond of his schooling experience in Texas and thought Americans were generous on the personal level, but he also found American mass culture generic. As he later described,

> All the cities, built according to the pattern of New York, have their Broadway, with bright signs announcing the same plays, films, and merchandise. In addition to Broadway, there is always the commercial street, the Main Street made famous by Sinclair Lewis in his novel. And it has been repeated to the point of satiety that customs, foods, ideas are also all the same, cut according to the pattern.[65]

Even with the incompatibilities between North America and Latin America, Vasconcelos believed that their passage through the three stages was inevitable. The prospect of universal transformation allowed him to set aside the differences between the two.

The 1920s continued, with Vasconcelos experiencing a level of influence, productivity, and stability higher than in previous periods of his life. When it became clear that Mexican president Plutarco Calles was arranging a puppet ruler to take over when his presidential term ended in 1928, Vasconcelos decided to run for president himself. His campaign had strong support, especially among the youth, but he experienced a resounding defeat, gaining just 111,000 votes against Ortiz Rubio's two million. Vasconcelos's supporters and journalists suspected it was a fraudulent election, and the educator hoped for an uprising like the one that removed Diaz; but without help from the Mexican military, that remained a dream. He fled Mexico and moved from Texas to California and then throughout Latin America and Europe as an exile for the next eleven years.[66]

Meanwhile, Jean Toomer made some of his most explicit statements on mixture following his 1931 marriage to Margery Latimer, a white author he had met in a Gurdjieff group he led in Portage, Wisconsin, the previous summer. In a statement he wrote shortly before his wedding, he explained his faith in a new race in America, which he considered himself a member of. This new race

> is neither white nor black nor in-between. It is the American race, differing as much from white and black as white and black differ from each other. . . . But the old divisions into white, black, brown, red, are outworn in this country. They have had their day. Now is the time of the birth of a new order, a new vision, a new ideal of man. I proclaim this new order. My marriage to Margery Latimer is the marriage of two Americans.[67]

Similar to Vasconcelos, Toomer believed in a societal transformation toward unity and peace. However, unlike the Mexican thinker, he saw himself as a participant in the process, a member of the new, mixed, heroic race. He maintained that it was common for Americans to bring together the bloods of many ethnic groups and that this combination was bringing forth the true Americans, the one label he approved. Later, he wrote, "here in America we are in the process of forming a new race, and . . . I was one of the first conscious members of this race."[68]

Word of the nuptials came out a few months later, nationwide. As *Time* wrote, describing a party with the couple's friends in Carmel, California, "No Negro can legally marry a white woman in any Southern State. But Wisconsin does not mind, nor California."[69] The article described a Gurdjieff exercise that Toomer, "who has a small mustache and few Negroid characteristics," led guests through and then quoted his assertion that "Americans probably do not realize it, but there are no racial barriers anymore, because there are so many Americans with strains of Negro, Indian and Oriental blood."[70] Cognizant of periodicals that would like to sensationalize their marriage, Toomer made sure to include racial minorities in his public statements about the process of mixing that had already begun.

Then Toomer went even further in distinguishing himself from Zangwill, coining his own symbol: "As I see America, it is like a great stomach into which are thrown the elements which make up the life blood. From this source is coming a distinct race of people. They will achieve tremendous works of art, literature and music. They will not be white, black or yellow— just Americans."[71] The metaphor had faults, switching from the body's digestive system to the circulatory system (thus eliding the obvious outcome of digestion), but it was evocative, suggesting a transformation from solid food into life-sustaining liquid. Zangwill's and Toomer's symbols were scientific, but while the melting pot worked within the realm of industry, the stomach was part of a human body. The former was part of the real world, while the latter imagined a body capable of anything. In this regard, Toomer suggested that creativity will be the activity of the new Americans, reflecting a high esteem for artists.

In the introduction to a would-be book on the matter of the Americans, Toomer expanded on the idea of the stomach, asserting that a country's strength depended on its capacity to "digest, assimilate, and transform all the diverse materials present in it," turning all of its food into a distinctive blood, as well as the "people, bodies and souls, and customs and culture special to it."[72] He continued, directly addressing Zangwill: "It has been said that America is a melting-pot. Rather I would view it as a stomach. Rather I would view it as the place where mankind, long dismembered into separate usually repellant groupings, long scattered over the face of the earth, is being re-assembled into one whole and undivided human race. America will include the earth."[73] Just as food dies when one eats it, racial groups would die as the country transforms them. Suggesting that this activity was important to undertake on a personal level, he added, "This is true of the individual members of a nation."[74] Toomer believed in just one pure race, the human race, and he echoed the notion that this land will be the site of Acts 17:26's "one blood." While he believed that there already were many who fit this description through their mixed backgrounds and that this transformation involves the whole earth, those who shared these values with him were the ones he called the Americans. Just as oxygen and hydrogen lose their form when they make water, humans become indivisible beings when their diverse parents create them.[75]

In a 1935 essay from Toomer's unpublished papers, he recounted many of his life's experiences—moving between various groups and being the target of a variety of racial slurs and accusations of racially passing. Whereas most Americans lived their whole lives with people similar to themselves, maintaining "queer unreal views of the people of other groups," Toomer viewed his own life as "not typically American."[76] He had moved through many circles, making each his own in a Whitmanesque sense. He hoped this would characterize American life in the future and suggested that it would take more than three hundred years to "consolidate and blend the mixtures existing here into an American people."[77] Toomer described his utopia as dependent on racial mixing. It would be the site of civic values, most notably, humanism. However, he also feared that his vision may fall the way of Whitman's, with a hundred years passing without any development.[78]

The poem that began as "The First American" in 1921 and appeared as "Brown River, Smile" in 1932 was published in the *New Caravan* in 1936 as "The Blue Meridian." It was an homage to the American people reflecting Gurdjieff's philosophy of Unitism. "The Blue Meridian" suggested how the pursuit for wholeness was a means for the country to reconcile its differences. Three meridians divided the poem's 843 lines into three stages in the transformation. The black meridian, which was first, stood for longing before the second, white, meridian, which referred to awakening or rebirth. The final meridian was blue, representing the final transcendent union.

> Blue Meridian, banded-light,
> Dynamic atom-aggregate,
> Awakes upon the earth;
> In his left hand he holds elevated rock,
> In his right hand he holds lifted branches,
> He dances the dance of the Blue Meridian
> And dervishes with the seven regions
>   of America, and all the world.[79]

In this last stage, old races and old religions were the fodder for the creation of "the man of purple or blue," who possessed a higher consciousness, able to create new morals, much like the Nietzschean superman that Zangwill mentioned. Frederik Rusch called this figure "The Blue Man." These are not literal skin pigments but rather spiritual states. The use of such hues deemphasized recognizable, racialized, physical descriptions.[80] Even though the poem appeared in limited circulation, with little critical response, later scholars considered it Toomer's second-greatest achievement behind *Cane*. While that novel focused mostly on the past in order to preserve it, "The Blue Meridian" considered the past as a stage in progressing toward a utopian future. His approach relied on the humanities rather than the sciences. He emphasized the equality among peoples rather than ranking them, as the racial scientists did. Still, he predicted linear stages for humanity, dabbling in positivists frameworks, just as his Mexican counterpart did. When Toomer and Vasconcelos employed scientific and humanistic discourses, their arguments suffered, just as Thomas Jefferson's did when he switched from political theory to natural sciences in *Notes on the State of Virginia*.[81]

The similarities between Toomer's and Vasconcelos's visions are remarkable, but it is unlikely that they knew each other. The latter was an exile from Mexico for eleven years. During that time, he alternated between esteem and bitterness toward the United States. He suspected that Washington had interfered with his election bid, but he also praised the administrations that dealt fairly with Latin America. In the prologue to the 1948 edition of "La Raza Cósmica," he commended U.N.E.S.C.O. for its "Statements on Race," but he also adopted hierarchies from past racial scientists. By this point, he held Spanish culture as highest and reinvigorated the Catholicism of his youth. He credited Christianity with correcting even the bad mixes between advanced and inferior peoples. He directly addressed Zangwill's 1914 afterword, agreeing that blacks had been excluded from mixture in the United States, except for their "spiritual penetration" in the realm of popular culture. He also pointed out that "the powerful North American nation has been nothing but a melting pot of European race."[82] It took another fifteen years for mainstream American sociologists to admit this fact. As Nathan Glazer and Patrick Moynihan wrote in 1963, "Yet looking back, it is possible to speculate that the response to The Melting Pot was as much one of relief as of affirmation: more a matter of reassurance that what had already taken place would turn out all right, rather than encouragement to carry on in the same direction."[83] They pointed out an important fact: Zangwill's intervention was really an anesthetic for anxiety over changes in diversity. Its entry into our national, civic vernacular provided a positive way to speak about ongoing changes, whether one is for, against, or indifferent to intermarriage.

5

Say It Loud, I'm One Drop and I'm Proud

Following Zangwill's removal of blacks and Asians from the melting pot, it became a symbol of white consolidation, rather than the mixture of all people in the United States. Similarly, sociologists' uncertainty about the role of racial minorities in American life led to the persistence of assimilation as a whites-only affair. Hector St. John de Crèvecoeur had focused on Europeans because they were the only people eligible for American citizenship at the end of the eighteenth century. Assimilation theorists of the twentieth century did so because they mistook whites as the only shapers of American society. Beyond intellectual realms, white privilege remained the norm in matters of property, policy, and politics, as well as culture. Regardless of one's position on race relations, whites benefited from the "possessive investment in whiteness" that protected their interests. During this time, society bestowed whiteness as a privilege on more ethnic types. Later in the century, their descendants would enjoy whiteness as normal, and still privileged.[1]

At the same time, minority groups developed group identities that made social movements for racial equality possible. These relied on rank-and-file members working toward clear goals, coalescing around common values, and making visible expressions of racial pride. The consolidation of blackness by way of W. E. B. Du Bois became the model for Hispanics, Asians, and Native Americans, allowing them to confront white supremacy in unprecedented ways. But the tenets common to these movements often led to antipathy toward their mixed brethren. The mass media broadcast images of African Americans facing fire hoses, Mexican Americans calling for a boycott of grapes, American Indians occupying Alcatraz, and Asian American student sit-ins, entering the national consciousness and leading to local and federal attention to civil rights.

It became natural to think of the story of social movements as representing distinct "food groups," one for each racial constituency. African Americans had the most prominent civil rights movement, supposedly beginning with Rosa Parks's arrest in 1955 and ending with Martin Luther King, Jr.'s assassination in 1968. In reality, mass action campaigns for racial justice had taken off with A. Philip Randolph's planned march on Washington in

1941 and the notion of "Double Victory" with the United States' entry into World War II. Minorities hoped that victory abroad against fascism would accompany victory at home against racism. Hispanics, Asians, and Indians followed, after the black movement had peaked. The principal mixed-race social movement, which aimed to include a Multiracial identifier on the census, seemed to sprout in the 1990s, its tardiness a result of the sudden appearance of racially mixed people after the 1960s. Around the same time, leading titles in critical whiteness studies appeared, equipping readers with the analytic tools to examine the ways of white folks, which many people had taken for granted.[2]

Maintaining these separate but equal narratives produces a handful of results limiting the use of race as an analytic tool: It provides dogmatic founding myths for each racial group. It suggests that social movements have finite beginnings and ends. Social justice efforts become mutually exclusive, with little cooperation between them. It enshrines the stable, collective identities each group devised, fostering nostalgia for some past period's thinking and hampering innovation. Lastly, and most importantly for this project, maintaining six narratives gives the impression of a hush around mixed race from the 1930s to the 1990s. Persons, events, and images of black unity, Hispanic unity, Asian unity, and Indian unity are recognizable, but mixed-race people are negligible, seeming to disappear into their parent minority racial groups' struggles, only to reappear with *Loving v. Virginia* and again with the activism around the 2000 census. Minorities promoting racial unity as well as whites protecting racial purity have denied or demonized interracial intimacy, marriage, and mixed-race people. Working for racial equality and stabilizing racial identities have gone hand in hand. This has been the norm even before the signature social movements of the twentieth century.

But a closer look reveals that mixed race was at the center of twentieth-century U.S. history, even though traditional collective identities stigmatized mixture. Foreign wars extended our spheres of influence but also compelled the country to include those whom we were liberating in the body politic. Similarly, changes in immigration led to more interracial families. The progressive mass media helped naturalize the acceptability of interracial relationships through message movies. Even the mainstream civil rights narrative had integration at its core. Disaggregation into six narratives became the norm, with mixed race one of the newest. I bring all of these into one, showing how mixture has been at the center of issues about race throughout the twentieth century. I tie it together at the opening of the 1990s, when scholars noticed that whiteness had consolidated as well. While this chapter offers a sketch, it presents a new, inclusive approach to the period. I argue that this approach brings together more themes than food-groupism does, by definition. This chapter draws together episodes across U.S. history illustrating the centrality of racial mixture, meanwhile acknowledging that the terms have shifted and changed across time and place. Mixed race has been a site where multiple historical themes intersect, even when participants have tried to minimize it. Thus, thoughtful conversations about mixed race can produce narratives about familiar historical periods that keep more themes in view.[3]

Stabilization facilitated many of the twentieth century's social movements, but it also led to the disappearance of interracial intimacy from the historical record. Likewise, beyond the Mulatto Studies of Reuter, Stonequist, and later Chicago School pupils, which went hand in hand with consolidating blacks, works about mixed-race identity seemed to disappear as well. Demographically, the numbers of mixed people may have been low, regardless of which racial groups were interacting. But the urge toward stabilization obscured their numbers and silenced their voices. I offer as an example the Manasseh Club, an organization supporting interracial couples in the Midwest from the 1890s to the 1920s. The most prominent chapter was in Chicago, but the organization possibly started in Milwaukee and resettled in the larger city. While interracial marriage was legal in Illinois and Wisconsin, it still met with hostility from blacks and whites, as did common law interracial relationships. Similar dynamics silenced these relationships in other cities and in many racial configurations. The Manasseh Club countered the social ostracization that these couples faced, providing a social base, mutual aid, and connections to other organizations open to interracial marriage, for example, the Baha'i faith and the Communist Party. The Manasseh Club's membership was selective, seeking gainfully employed married couples and excluding more informal relationships. Its annual fundraising ball attracted fifteen hundred people in 1908, advertising in the *Chicago Defender*. Both the city council and the state of Illinois recorded its existence as a nonprofit organization, and its numbers grew after World War I.[4]

By 1932, the society faded away, occasionally appearing in historians' accounts of the region. No academic journal has printed an article about the Manasseh Club, no peer-review press has published a monograph focusing on its career, and no descendants have revived its mission. The Manasseh Club's members were regular people, and no record of violent or scandalous events preserve its name. The dissolution of the Manasseh Club may have occurred because of the increased acceptance of mixed people in Chicago. Or maybe the members sought solidarity through other organizations. Most likely, pressures to raise their children to identify as black led to their dispersal. The second generation probably let the memory of the organization fade,

and now the Manasseh Club exists mostly in the footnotes. In turn, this contributed to the perception that interracial intimacy and racially mixed people
were a new phenomenon that came about after 1967, the year the Supreme
Court ruled state laws against interracial marriage unconstitutional.

The work of Caroline Bond Day, an African American anthropologist,
resisted the trend of the mixed-race issue fading away. In her 1932 Harvard
University thesis, Day addressed kinship with African Americans while
keeping racial mixture in sight. The title of her project, "A Study of Some
Negro-White Families in the United States," spoke to these concurrent
themes. Day gathered biographies and photos of 346 mixed families. Like
C. B. Davenport, she included body measurements, placed subjects' skin
colors on a scale, and delineated genealogies into quarters, eighths, and six-
teenths. Instead of using a research assistant, she interviewed the subjects
herself or sent questionnaires by mail. Many of the subjects were prominent
racially mixed African Americans of the time, including W. E. B. Du Bois.
She also included her own family. (See Fig. 5.1.) However, rather than use
fractions to measure degeneracy or ignore fractions to consolidate blackness,
Day used them in a more descriptive way, prefiguring a celebration of mixture by mixed-race activists later in the century.

Day was aware of how some newcomer white ethnicities were assimilating into full citizenship, and she protested the second-class status that successful African Americans endured. As she wrote in a draft version, "Here is
a group who buy homes, send their children to school, patronize whatever in
civic life they are allowed to, and on the whole are law-abiding citizens. Yet
apparently generosity, humility, forbearance, adaptability, a sense of humor,
and a high standard of living are not qualities which make most for citizenship today?"[5] This passage did not appear in the final manuscript, but it did
express her political intentions for her project. It also showed the limitations
of her understanding of the immigrant experience, as well as her chauvinism
in favor of those from her social set. While collecting data, she encountered
some resistance, but the middle-class, educated subjects she solicited generally appreciated the value of her work and cooperated with her requests.
Ultimately, hers was an antiracist work, even if she employed methods similar to those of mainstream physical anthropologists. The resulting thesis contained over four hundred photographs, mostly from the albums of the families themselves. Some of these appeared as group photos, but many more of
them were headshots (cropped from larger prints) arranged into family trees.
Like the *casta* paintings and Davenport's work before it, captions divulged
the subjects' racial makeup. Her use of their real names resisted the norm in
anthropology, giving the people identities. It also diverged from Du Bois's

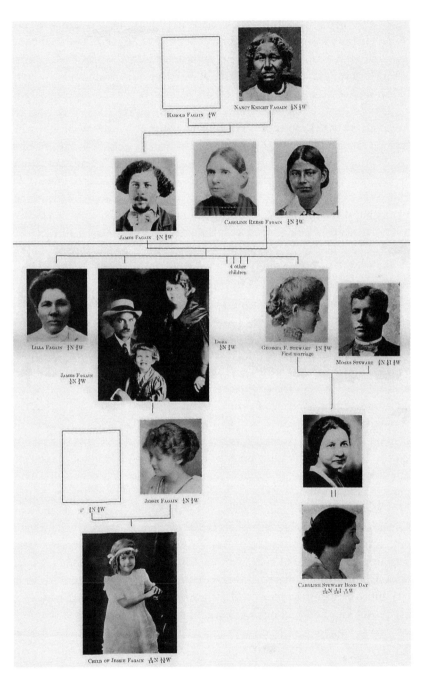

Fig. 5.1. Caroline Bond Day, "A Study of Some Negro-White Families in the United States" (Peabody Museum, Cambridge, Massachusetts, Chart 13: Fagain, Plate 34)

Negro Exhibition, which minimized individual personalities for the sake of the project as a whole.[6]

A shift occurred during the mid-twentieth century, as demonstrated by writers such as Richard Wright, Ralph Ellison, and James Baldwin, who acknowledged that both the collective innocence of blacks and the unified understanding of blackness had already ended. Their writings expressed the notion that black identity was created from inside the race as well as from outside. Regardless, scholars, creative artists, and regular folk continued to defend the idea of black particularity, even though the complicity of blacks in foreign wars, the worldwide consumption of American culture, and the spread in proficiency in black idioms made innocence untenable. As Robert Reid-Pharr has written, "We are, so the discourse of American racialism would have it, the blameless race. The black has been and is the victim of slavery, the casualty of segregation, the sacrifice at the altar of white supremacy."[7] This is not to deny that these things have occurred but rather to interrogate the innocence blacks confer on themselves. While the forms of oppression differ among minority groups, it is possible to substitute their signature experiences in Reid-Pharr's passage. None of us is as innocent as we would like to believe. We all benefit from American imperialism, show our faces in the global media, and cop each other's cultural forms.

All of this work to stabilize racial identity reflected the four steps of W. E. B. Du Bois's project of racial stabilization: defining what a "race" was; applying one label to disparate members; naming the duty its members must undertake; and promoting a universal response to past collective violations. The end result was to associate with mixture the loss of cultural and human resources, making it a threat to the collective progress of that race. These tenets appeared in later scholarly work, regular discussions, and other minority social movements. They have influenced our understanding of the middle decades of the twentieth century as several narratives. The black movement's influence on other groups' movements led to dissemination of that antipathy toward mixture. Du Bois's influence on these other groups may be partial, but through his broad influence on racial thinking, the antipathy bears his mark. Unfortunately, I have to do exactly what I decry, examining one group at a time, to illustrate these connections with Mexican Americans, then Native Americans, then Asian Americans.

Because of the acknowledged *mestizaje* in Mexican Americans' experience, their perspective on mixture was often more accepting. Still, twentieth-century Mexican American racial justice hails directly from Du Bois, as the premier Mexican American organization, the League of United Latin American Citizens (L.U.L.A.C.), modeled itself after his notion of the

Talented Tenth. During the 1930s and 1940s, its goals resembled those of the N.A.A.C.P.: school desegregation, voter registration, and Mexican American access to public facilities and juries. A generation later, young Chicanos modeled their activism after the Black Power movement. The Brown Berets imitated the paramilitary attire, confrontational tactics, and autonomous organization of the Black Panther Party, growing to twenty-eight cities by 1969. During the same period, pride in Chicano identity developed a cultural nationalism based on a return to Aztlán, the legendary home of pre-Columbian Mexicans. Again, Chicano activists paralleled simultaneous developments in the Black Power movement: more emphasis on style, more exclusion of women, less critique of social class.[8]

On one hand, Chicano activists adapted praise for their mixed past from José Vasconcelos. On the other, they adapted his message to their own context. Rather than praise their Spanish forebears for bringing civilization to the New World, they hailed Aztlán. In December 1969, the first National Chicano Youth Liberation Conference composed "El Plan Espiritual de Aztlán," a document recognizing the "proud historical heritage," the "brutal 'gringo' invasion of our territories," and the powerful "call of our sangre."[9] Its prelude concluded, "With our heart in our hands and our hands in the soil, we declare the independence of our mestizo nation. We are a bronze people with a bronze culture. Before the world, before all of North America, before all our brothers in the bronze continent, we are a nation, we are a union of free pueblos, we are Aztlán. For La Raza todo. Fuera de La Raza nada."[10] This explicitly called for racial unity and loyalty. Like black nationalism of the time, this turn in the Chicano movement led to an indictment of interracial relationships: those who partook of them were traitors to cultural pride and unity. Some studies showed that rates of intermarriage between Mexican Americans and non-Hispanic whites stabilized during the 1960s and early 1970s. Velia García Hancock, a pioneer in Chicano Studies, wrote, "intermarriage results in a weakening of ties and declining sense of responsibility and commitment to La Raza."[11] These indictments often targeted women, whose exogamy evoked *La Malinche*, the Nahua woman who aided Hernán Cortés during his conquest of Mexico. Since 1519, her reputation has blended with other legendary figures, often casting her as traitorous. Along the way, she has picked up the nickname *La Chingada* (the fucked one), which adds layers of victimization and mishap to her reputation. The Chicano movement continued this usage, evoking the destruction of the Aztecs that followed her relationship. Opponents to interracial relationships deployed these meanings on Mexican American women in particular.

Vine Deloria, author of *Custer Died for Your Sins*, the 1969 manifesto for American Indian activism that inspired the founders of the American Indian Movement (A.I.M.), compared various minority experiences with American racism. As he explained, whites left Asians alone once they minimized them as a threat to white social mores. Similarly, whites left Mexicans alone once they realized they would stick to themselves. While the white man had different methods of oppression for different racial groups, many whites considered race relations as a one-size-fits-all matter, suggesting that if you addressed the concerns of those protesting blacks, then you must be addressing the concerns of every other group. (In general, the term *race relations* hesitates, making cooperation the prime goal rather than exposing and indicting racism.) In addition to more activism, Deloria called for more appreciation for the distinctions between blacks and Indians, in particular. Blacks were an indelible problem that required active exclusion from all aspects of society. Indians presented the opposite challenge, forcing incorporation of the people, or at least their land. "Laws passed by Congress had but one goal—the Anglo-Saxonization of the Indian. The antelope had to become a white man."[12] Beginning with the Pickering Treaty, which promised peace and mutual respect with the Six Iroquois Nations in 1794, the federal government had broken every agreement it ever made with American Indians and then had taken their land and expected them to assimilate into the United States. "In looking back at the centuries of broken treaties, it is clear that the United States never intended to keep any of its promises. Like other areas of life, the federal government adapted its policies to the expediency of the moment. When the crisis had passed, it promptly proceeded on its way without a backward glance at its treachery."[13] Rather than sexual exploitation, Deloria characterized this treachery as the prime offense against his people. He had not invented this collective response to past violations, but he did articulate Indians' collective wariness of any new commitments the U.S. government vowed to uphold. In a way, the relationship between the two parties was like a marriage gone bad, and Native Americans' indictment of the white man's treachery resembled complaints by a married person to an unfaithful spouse. This trope played on past encounters with white patriarchy, for example, Oglala Sioux Chief Red Cloud calling U.S. presidents, the makers and breakers of treaties, "Great Father."

Custer Died for Your Sins did not address racial mixture as it related to Indians, but Deloria did address the figurative power of mixture with Indians in the past. Reflecting on his three years as executive director of the National Congress of American Indians (N.C.A.I.), which promoted coordination between tribal governments to address treaty rights, Deloria had the near-daily experience of whites coming by his office to proclaim that they had Native American ancestors. Usually, this was in the distant past, removing any possibility of familial relations with Indians. Often it was a female ancestor, a tribal princess evoking the feminine, loving, and loyal qualities of Pocahontas. Deloria mused, "I once did a projection backward and discovered that evidently most tribes were entirely female for the first three hundred years of white occupation. No one, it seemed, wanted to claim a male Indian as a forebear."[14]

Deloria credited black youth with participating in the civil rights movement, articulating the wrongs of racial oppression, and creating a sort of racial nationalism. His impression was that Indian students were far more complacent, a result of society's efforts to absorb them rather than exclude them. A.I.M.'s founding national director, Russell Means, cited the agitation by Students for a Democratic Society (S.D.S.), the Weather Underground, and the Black Panthers as models for his organization's movement. As Leonard Peltier, imprisoned participant in the 1975 Pine Ridge Reservation shootout, wrote, "Instead of disappearing, dissolving as a people, as we were expected to do, we found a new social consciousness and a new sense of ourselves in the human cauldron of the cities."[15] He considered A.I.M. one of the movements of the time, along with antiwar, the New Left, and Black Power. The occupation of Alcatraz in 1969, the takeover of the Bureau of Indian Affairs in 1972, and the siege at Wounded Knee in 1973 all bore the militant spectacle of the black and brown movements.[16]

With regard to racial mixture, the system of blood quantum established by the Dawes Act raised the stakes for all Native Americans, not just the activists. Offspring with too much mixture could not claim allotments, and too much out-marriage could diminish a tribe's numbers. These incentives created a paradox: measuring mixture was instrumental, but monoracial identity was imperative. The Indian Reorganization Act of 1934 claimed to return self-government to tribes, but it also compelled some tribes to rely on blood quantum more than they had previously.

W. E. B. Du Bois's sympathies with Japan during its war with Russia led him to announce, "The awakening of the yellow races is certain," after Japan's 1904 victory.[17] A consummate postcolonialist, Du Bois drew parallels between Asians and Africans through most of his career. Later, visiting China as an exile in 1959, he met with Chairman Mao and maintained that Asia would be the first to rebuff European capitalism. As World War II drew to a close, he predicted that racial prejudice would cause the Allies to fail in bringing equality to the world. The tradition of exploitation along racial lines undermined other forces for social change, even formal equality. More importantly for this project, though, Asian American activists of the 1960s counted W. E. B. Du Bois, the Black Panthers, and Malcolm X as direct influences, along with revolutionaries from Asia, Latin America, and Africa. They combined these, producing an outlook that asserted, "The people, and the people alone, are the motive force in the making of world history."[18] In turn, this slogan inspired Asian American activists to think of themselves as agents of change for their communities. Often, this was through grassroots organizing connecting domestic and international policies, communities in America and in the countries of their descent, and commonalities between various Asian ethnicities in the United States. The Black Panther Party's creed of community service, self-defense, and antiwar protest attracted many allies with Asian American youth. Similarly, Chicano and Latino groups such as the Brown Berets and the Young Lords influenced Yellow Power, showing how connected all these groups were in the 1960s. Treating them as separate movements perpetuates the notion of races as separate, working for their own ends, and progressing or failing independently.[19]

Pressures to choose racially similar partners persist, especially outside of those who subscribe to the panethnic "Asian American" ideal. As legal scholar and commentator Frank Wu reflected on his youth, "When I was a boy, I once asked my mother if she would love me if I married an American girl. She answered that she would love me if I married a foreigner. But she added that she would love me more if I married a Chinese girl."[20] With only one Asian American girl in his class, Wu had no idea how to accomplish this task. Over the years, he found that his parents' ethnocentrism existed in families of various Asian origins. Acceptance of children's interracial dating choices generally reflects acculturation; the longer a family has been in the United States, the more open they may be. Still, decades after Wu's conundrum, 69% of Chinese American parents strongly agreed or agreed with the sentiment "I prefer that my children marry someone in the same ethnic group," showing how conditioning toward endogamy continues.[21] Members of younger generations are more accepting of intermarriage; still, half of the children agreed with the statement.

However, antipathy toward interracial intimacy seems less prevalent among Asian American cultural nationalists than among analogous groups for other racial groups, perhaps because their lower numbers made prohibitions of interracial relationships unrealistic. The umbrella ethnicity, Asian American, brought together people of various ethnic origins, emphasizing their similar experiences of exclusion. Writing about the benefits of Asian American panethnicity, Yen Le Espiritu argues that "Asian America, by definition, is multiracial and that this multiraciality provides us the critical space to explore the strategic importance of cross-group affiliation—not only among Asians but also with other kin groups."[22] For Asian Americans, distaste for mixture seems to come more from the rank and file than from the intelligentsia constructing the consolidated group identity.

Once each group established this stabilized racial identity, it could progress in its own way. This resulted in many narratives about race in the United States—one African American, one Hispanic/Latino, one Native American, one white, and so on. In researching, writing, and teaching U.S. history, it requires revisiting any historical period over and over to get a fuller picture. In contrast to the separate-but-equal narratives of the 1940s–1960s, I present a list of events from those decades that had interracial intimacy at their core. They were all part of a post–World War II wave of liberalism that compelled the United States to live up to its credo against fascism. This continued during the Cold War, as the government cast the nation as the leader and champion of freedom, in opposition to the Soviet Union. Domestic racism persisted, often as a stumbling block for foreign policy. So, through several administrations, the State Department, the president, and the nation's image makers worked to remove the stumbling block.[23]

America's entry into World War II in 1941 precipitated reform of immigration laws, a legacy often excluded from the domestic civil rights movement. Since Japan was our enemy, China became our friend, which called for a change in the Chinese Exclusion Act. The War Brides Act of 1945 made it possible for some Asian spouses and adopted children of military personnel to enter the country. While the McCarran-Walter Act let racial quotas stay, it did end the racial exclusion of Asians that had stood for seventy years.[24]

With the 1948 decision in *Perez v. Sharp*, the California Supreme Court overturned that state's anti-intermarriage law. The same year, the first official transracial adoption of a black child into a white family took place in Minnesota. Adoption continued as a site of making the American family interracial with adoptions from Korea that began in 1953. Activists such as Bertha and Harry Holt, who adopted eight war orphans, believed in bringing children from the Third World into the American way of life.

Popular culture of the middle decades of the twentieth century also naturalized racial tolerance. In particular, Hollywood joined forces with the State Department in countering the damage that news about racial strife exacted on the nation's global public image. During World War II, N.A.A.C.P. executive secretary Walter White worked with movie makers and the Office of War Information to create propaganda emphasizing tolerance and racial equality. This continued after the war, resulting in increased visibility for African

Americans in films. Message movies cast blacks and whites together, treating integration favorably.[25]

Hollywood movies such as *Sayonara* (1957) and *South Pacific* (1958) portrayed interracial relationships and racially mixed people in more positive ways, sometimes allowing mixed couples to live happily ever after. Some, such as *The World of Suzie Wong* (1960), made self-conscious statements about racism, hinting that interracial romances may succeed. At the same time, others, including *Show Boat* (1951), *Pinky* (1949), *Love Is a Many-Splendored Thing* (1955), and *Imitation of Life* (1959), continued the Tragic Mulatto trope, with the mixed character failing at love. These also cast white women as the mixed female characters. When minority men courted white women characters, they either turned down the possibility of romance in favor of helping their people, as in *Island in the Sun* (1957), or suffered a broken heart before consummation, as in *The King and I* (1956).[26]

Civil rights campaigns working toward integration were inherently interracial. They aimed to provide access to minorities, but they also aimed to transform the social realm, giving equal access to all. Like the New England Anti-Slavery Society, they undertook an interracial endeavor that often put them in danger. The long campaign that started in the 1930s and resulted in *Brown v. Board of Education* worked against the Jim Crow fear of social and sexual equality. The Montgomery bus boycott aimed to transform transportation into an integrated place accessible to all, evoking Louisiana radicals' conception of public rights. The Student Nonviolent Coordinating Committee (S.N.C.C.) was founded as an interracial organization in 1960, and its daring placed a diverse set of college-age youth together for voter registration. The photography of Herbert Randall, who documented 1964's Freedom Summer in Hattiesburg, Mississippi, captured how the workers' interracial composition challenged the mores in the South and the North. For example, one snapshot showed a young, interracial pair enjoying some down time (see figure 5.2). While innocuous to our post-civil-rights perspectives, this scene violated longstanding social boundaries. The couple's relationship may have been platonic, but it still proved all those who had fought political equality correct: it would lead to social equality and then intimacy. Segregationists throughout American history were right, and those who defended integration often pointed out that interracial intimacy was a minor threat in comparison to preserving inequality. During the civil rights movement of the 1950s and '60s, attacks by southerners on white activists gained sympathy from the nation at large. In turn, S.N.C.C. produced many leaders of the New Left. Later reflections by activists and their mixed "movement children" attested to the values that brought them together.[27]

Fig. 5.2. Volunteers relaxing, June 1964 (Photograph by Herbert Randall)

Since the 1940s, the dismantling of state anti-intermarriage laws had picked up pace, but in 1957, half of the states still had them in place. Consensual interracial intimacy on the local level often challenged state laws, making their enforcement nearly impossible. Some interracial couples in such communities brought cases that would invalidate the state laws across the country. Mildred Jeter and Richard Loving grew up in Central Point, Virginia, a town that, like rural triracial isolates, had featured interracial interaction and mixing between blacks, whites, and Indians for generations. This part of Caroline County practiced different standards of segregation than other parts of the South, so Richard, who was "white," and Mildred, who was "Negro," attended separate churches and schools but started dating after meeting at a local dance that welcomed blacks and whites. Richard also worked as a hand on Mildred's father's farm, further confounding the hierarchy that usually existed between black women and white men. To avoid Virginia's Racial Integrity Act, the couple married in Washington, D.C., in 1958, and returned to live with her parents. Though few in Central Point cared, word got to the county sheriff, who arrested the newlyweds. They received a suspended sentence, banishing them from the state for twenty-five years.[28]

The early 1960s featured a string of signature events that the Lovings witnessed from Washington, D.C., including sit-ins in Greensboro, North Carolina, federal troops escorting James Meredith as he registered at the University of Mississippi, attacks on the Freedom Riders, and Birmingham's attack on nonviolent protesters. Often a moderate on matters of race, John F. Kennedy addressed the nation on June 11, 1963, to encourage the creation of sweeping civil rights legislation. Mildred Loving, sensing the relevance of their case to the news, wrote Attorney General Robert F. Kennedy about their case, curious whether this act would address interracial marriage. In turn, the American Civil Liberties Union and the N.A.A.C.P. assisted the Lovings in bringing their case to the Supreme Court. Although the Court had decided in favor of school desegregation, it was hesitant to address inter-racial marriage. The Lovings' team built its arguments around a precedent that the 1964 *McLaughlin v. Florida* Supreme Court case set by prohibiting the punishing people of different races who lived together because it made them a special target and violated their equal protection. In a unanimous decision, the Court ruled in favor of the Lovings, making anti-intermarriage laws in seventeen states unconstitutional.

Even though Chief Justice Earl Warren recognized marriage as "one of the 'basic civil rights of man,' fundamental to our very existence and survival," the effort to remove anti-intermarriage laws seems tangential to the popular civil rights narrative. Even though the Lovings' marriage coincides with the events in Birmingham, Selma, and Washington, D.C., few scholars include it with voting rights and desegregation. Ten of the most popular recent books about civil rights have no mention of *Loving v. Virginia* in their pages. While scholarship about the topic has grown since the 1990s, most of these titles fill the holes historians of the civil rights movement have left open because of antipathy toward the topic. Until integrated into the broader narrative, monographs about intermarriage merely cover a niche topic. Three beliefs underlying this marginalization come to mind: Many people consider the right to marry interracially less important than voting or desegregation, as if the pursuit of happiness were less important than life or liberty. Fewer people have voiced the desire to marry freely; it seems to be a subject less worthy of our attention, with that choice being treated like a deviant behavior. Lastly, interracial intimacy is perceived to be a betrayal to one's minority-parent racial group. Considering the underlying antipathy toward mixed race that I have mapped in this chapter, this is likely the root of its exclusion from the master narrative on civil rights.[29]

By the early 1990s, scholarship on assimilation had come to realize that the "new man" of Zangwill's melting pot was white, and assimilation had become synonymous with the consolidation of white ethnics. Sociologist Mary C. Waters's *Ethnic Options: Choosing Identities in America* begins by surveying the literature on assimilation, with the contention that it was always about ethnic whites. Her interviews with sixty adults and analysis of census data show that many people see race and ethnicity as biologically rooted and discernable by physical appearance. At the same time, non-Hispanic whites (those who racially identify as white and who do not check "Hispanic or Latino," which has referred to an ethnic group consisting of members across the major racial groups since 1970) have been able to practice symbolic ethnicity, "choosing among elements in one's ancestry and choosing when and if voluntarily to enjoy the traditions of that ancestry."[30]

Sociologist Richard D. Alba's *Ethnic Identity: The Transformation of White America*, the product of extensive surveying in New York State, adds to Waters's arguments that ethnicity among non-Hispanic whites is undergoing a major shift: "Ethnic distinctions based on European ancestry, once quite prominent in the social landscape, are fading into the background; other ethnic distinctions appear more highlighted as a result. In a sense, a new ethnic group is forming—one based on ancestry from *anywhere* on the European continent."[31] Overall, he argues that ethnic identity among whites of European origin is more and more a personal and voluntary matter. While past decades may have placed more importance on ethnic identity, currently, white ethnic identities are more nominal. However, in a society with racial and ethnic divisions, those who are unable to practice the symbolic ethnicity that Waters and Alba write about find themselves at a disadvantage because of their physical appearance, even if they have reached the same cultural and socioeconomic level as whites. More importantly, these results show that the melting pot has been a success in producing what Zangwill's 1914 afterword would allow—a seemingly ambiguous, conglomerate, and European "real American."[32]

With intermarriage as a central feature in assimilation theory, minorities who intermarry receive more praise than those who do not. However, this habit is a smokescreen for the third trend: even with the mid-twentieth-century civil rights movement, changes in immigration, and the abolition of anti-intermarriage laws, preserving white racial purity is still a priority for non-Hispanic whites, the nation's historically predominant group. At 69.1% of the population in 2000, they still are predominant. The percentage may have dropped from 75.6% in 1990, but the feared majority-minority moment is still well into in the future. In regard to interracial marriage, Waters shows that middle-class, non-Hispanic whites see racial difference as a higher barrier to intermarriage than religion or social class. Prior to the publication of *Ethnic Options*, Waters's 1988 longitudinal study with Stanley Lieberson showed that endogamy between non-Hispanic whites was higher than one would expect, given the number of generations their subjects had been in the country. Even those who were from mixed non-Hispanic backgrounds showed a preference for some portion of common ancestry.

Census data from 2000 show that 96.3% of all married, non-Hispanic whites across all age groups are married to other non-Hispanic whites, a rate higher than that of any other non-Hispanic racial group. Blacks and Asians follow with 90.7% and 90.6% endogamy rates, respectively. The rate for Native Hawaiian/Pacific Islanders is 54.5%, and the rate for American Indians is 45.1%. Across racial groups but especially among non-Hispanic whites, individuals have devised ways to avoid sounding racist when talking about why they have never considered interracial marriage, often beginning with the disclaimer "I'm not prejudiced, but . . ." and continuing with rationalizations that deflect attention away from how they feel about the matter, for example, to consideration of whether mixed children "will be accepted or not accepted." Similarly, non-Hispanic whites are likely to maintain that romantic accidents bring them together with their mates, rather than the remnants of historical inequality, the conditioning they receive from their families, or limited access to opportunities. Explanations for why they have so few minority friends follow the same rationales. However valid the sentiments are, the separation among the races remains. Few dare to make their personal lives interracial, and even fewer commit themselves to making opportunities available to minorities, which can lead to more interracial interaction. So, instead of measuring minorities' uphill battles in gaining acceptance, we should look at non-Hispanic white resistance to intermarriage as the true indicator of assimilation. Until the rate of endogamy among non-Hispanic whites drops, there should be a moratorium on celebrating the curative power of racial mixing.[33]

As a counterpoint to the separate-but-equal thinking of cultural nationalists, Albert Murray, critic, novelist, and peer of Ralph Ellison, provided a statement on the mixed nature of American culture in his essay "The Omni-Americans." Like Ellison, he believed that both black and white influences ran deeply within all of American life. Writing in 1970, Murray deplored constricting preconceptions of American life, whether from social scientists labeling black people's urban problems or cultural nationalists rejecting the United States as their homeland or writers perpetuating clichés about black despair. He maintained that understanding culture is key in understanding

identity, but it also reveals how people relate to power. So Murray's attention to music and literature served a greater purpose than mere popular culture analysis; we can find this approach in later historians who take leisure
seriously. Because the African American experience was the one with which
Murray was most conversant, it was his focus. However, he disliked the tendency to think of the United States as a nation of only two races, black and
white. Instead, everyone developed basic American characteristics, becoming "omni-American," black, white, and Indian. As Murray asserted,

> American culture, even in its most rigidly segregated precincts, is patently
> and irrevocably composite. It is, regardless of all the hysterical protesta-
> tions of those who would have it otherwise, incontestably mulatto. Indeed,
> for all their traditional antagonisms and obvious differences, the so-called
> black and so-called white people of the United States resemble nobody in
> the world so much as they resemble each other.[34]

Murray emphasized the American tradition we all share, considering
the differences reflections of a vital pluralist society. At the same time, he
acknowledged racial inequality and urged his readers to see beyond the roles
that narrow-minded intellectuals would conscribe Americans to. Murray
addressed the issues of cultural mixture and equality but left racial mixture
alone. This omission protected him from announcing that racially mixed
people symbolized those two themes. As the post-civil-rights era continued,
more people would confuse the three. The tendency to believe that progress
is a linear function of time joined the belief that the successes of the 1960s
were complete. Conservatives emphasized a sort of color-blindness that disavowed race as an analytic tool, discouraging liberals from ever evoking it.
A generation later, censure for racially insensitive statements created a new
racial etiquette. At the same time, most Americans lacked the ability to discuss race. When images, arguments, and sentiments praising racial mixture
emerged, many mistook them for brand-new ideas. Ambiguous bodies, mere
cultural mixture, and token successes became signs that the United States
had reached an age when race no longer mattered.

6

The End of Race as We Know It

After the civil rights legislation of the 1960s, census data became a tool to enforce fair voting, housing, and employment. However, the 1970 decennial missed 2.5% of the population, approximately 5.3 million people. The percentage undercount for African Americans was 7.7%, while the rate for whites was 1.9%. Only ten thousand of the questionnaires had any question asking about Hispanic or Latino descent, as the decision to count them arose very late in the planning. These were the long versions of the form that the bureau decided to use as a sample to estimate the percentage of the population originating from Latin America. The undercount of racial minorities showed that the census was failing at one of its central uses, making the work before the 1980 decennial more crucial than ever.[1]

In the face of lawsuits from city governments and civil rights organizations, the bureau dedicated more resources toward reaching hard-to-count populations in 1980. As before, the media joined in, publicizing the increase in field workers, offices, and paperwork but also covering the bureau's misfortunes. The data from 1980 showed that the population was larger than the bureau expected by four million people. Once again, there was an undercount, but the difference between black undercount and white undercount was 5% rather than 5.8%, as it had been in 1970. Rather than appearing on a sample of forms going in the mail, the Hispanic-descent question was on every form. Also known as the Hispanic ethnicity question, it attempted to capture a group of people who could be from any of the standard racial groups, as there are whites, blacks, Indians, and Asians from Latin America. The survey's design placed the question four spaces below the race question, with the hope that Hispanics would pick a standard racial group and then say where they were from. Results showed that 7.5 million Hispanics (40% of them) picked "Other" as their racial group, producing data that was less effective for civil rights enforcement. However, reflecting the tenor of the Reagan administration, the bureau's director, Vincent Carraba, announced that the bureau would not adjust the undercount. He cited the increase in the population as one reason, asserting that it corrected the matter. His other reason was the difficulty in chasing down illegal aliens, a large group unworthy of the effort. The Census Bureau was successful in most of the fifty-five lawsuits against it, but it still had challenges heading toward the next decennial.

The 1990 data showed a 2.1% undercount, with rates for blacks, Hispanics, and Native Americans at least twice the average. (It was slightly lower for Asians, at 3.1%.) The number of Hispanics picking "Other" on the race question increased to over 10%, making it the fastest growing racial group in the United States. Those who were looking to limit immigration from Mexico and other countries were concerned with the trend, as were those who were aiming to fortify civil rights. The increasing number of Hispanics made the "Other" problem one of the most crucial between the 1980s and 1990s. The immediate hypothesis for its popularity was that respondents misunderstood the question, with an implication that poor language skills impaired their comprehension. In reality, many people of Hispanic descent think about racial identity differently, prioritizing national origin before the four racial groups of the post-civil-rights U.S. milieu. For example, one might look for, say, *la raza dominicana* before looking for the white race. Also, Hispanics more readily acknowledge the racial mixture in their heritage than Americans do. To be Dominican or Mexican or Puerto Rican is to have white, Indian, and black ancestors. Hispanics' immediate parents may not be of different racial groups, but they do have mixture in their national histories. In 1990, many who acknowledged this *mestizaje* picked "Other," and the Census Bureau looked to minimize these responses. Mixed-race identity—that of Americans with parents from different racial groups—was secondary, but altogether Hispanics and the racially mixed contributed to the crumbling reliability of monoracial categorization.

This is where the dominant story regarding multiple checking picks up, with the Association of MultiEthnic Americans (A.M.E.A.) and Project R.A.C.E. (Reclassify All Children Equally), the two leading organizations in the Multiracial Movement of the 1990s, which aimed to include some form of multiracial identifier on the census.[2] However, their campaign was just one of the forces that resulted in multiple checking in 2000. I argue that the unitary understanding of race was already under attack. While I appreciate the work of the Multiracial Movement, I recast this story, highlighting the behind-the-scenes decisions in the federal government about which identities to address and which to suppress. Equally as important was the public testing to make enumeration more effective. Rather than privilege what racially mixed people said about their own identities, I also include discourses on mixed race from those who were not mixed themselves. Including all these voices emphasizes how positive ideas about racial mixing have remained in circulation. They may lack a traceable genealogy from one creator to another, but they have reemerged nonetheless.

One of the most visible artifacts of this period was *Time* magazine's "New Face of America," which used a computer-generated face to symbolize the mixed and diverse future of the nation in 1993. Beginning in 1985, though, a wave of philosophers had called for the abolition of all racial categories. While they worked independently of the Multiracial Movement, they shared the activists' hope to dismantle race as we knew it, with an appreciation of mixed-race identity as the first step. No matter how idealistic their prescriptions were, these writers, activists, and politicians believed that mixed-race Americans could contribute to an improved America with racial equality and new human types. Public acceptance of interracial marriage and mixed people seemed to be higher than ever. The voices of these subjects had more access to media than in past eras. And media outlets were producing more and more content reflecting the United States as harmonious. All these forces led to the employment of racially mixed people as a sign of post-civil-rights-era success. By examining the moment more broadly, I show that the issue at hand was not just mixed-race identity, which put Multiracialists on a pedestal, but a changing understanding of race altogether.

The early 1990s were the coda on what Michael Omi and Howard Winant have called "anything but a slow, steady evolution to a 'color-blind' society."[3] Both neoconservatives and neoliberals abandoned racial politics, even as the Rodney King beating and Los Angeles riots amplified the idea that we live in, as Andrew Hacker called it, "two nations, black and white, separate, hostile, unequal."[4] On all levels of society, whether politics, popular culture, or day-to-day interactions, Americans quit acknowledging race, even as racial inequality persisted. Various discourses asserted that this state of affairs was the result of anything but race, usually culture (i.e., "culture of poverty"), which often stands in for race. This denial served those who were antagonistic to racial justice, those who thought racism was a thing of the past, and those who rarely stopped to think about it. As Eduardo Bonilla-Silva wrote in 2001, "In contrast to race relations in the Jim Crow period, however, racial practices that reproduce racial inequality in contemporary America are (1) increasingly covert, (2) embedded in normal operations of institutions, (3) void of direct racial terminology, and (4) invisible to most whites."[5] The racialized social system that oppressed minorities for much of U.S. history persisted, in different forms, and despite the social movements of the mid-twentieth century. Even though it appeared that our society was becoming more equitable during these years, an ideology of "color-blind racism," which attached nonracial causes to apparent racial inequality, had arisen, exonerating whites of any responsibility for minorities' trials.[6]

As champions of color-blind policies, the Republican Party opposed affirmative action and other race-based programs of the previous era. Gaining majorities in the House of Representatives and the Senate in 1994, they pressured President Bill Clinton into ratifying massive welfare reform. The resulting Personal Responsibility and Work Opportunity Act fulfilled Clinton's promise to "end welfare as we know it." Even with these changes, the fragile job market, lack of health care, and expensive child care persisted, meaning few real gains for the poor. This chapter's title echoes the president's sound bite because of the similar problem with the new view of mixed race in the United States: in the 1990s, even with increased visibility of mixed people, public acceptance of racial mixing, and the success of some figures, race did not end, nor did everyone understand its complexities.[7]

This aggressive conservatism persisted in regard to other issues as well. Even before the Republican Party's Contract with America, the early 1990s featured a backlash against multiculturalism, as well as political correctness. Some scholars claimed that multiculturalism threatened to balkanize the country; one of these was Arthur Schlesinger, Jr., who authored *The Disuniting of America: Reflections on a Multicultural Society*. The former liberal's essay accused those who wanted a more pluralistic education system of being a threat to the unifying American identity that has brought together many ethnicities for over two centuries. He asserted that the new emphasis on difference replaces assimilation with fragmentation, integration with separatism. "It belittles *unum* and glorifies *pluribus*."[8] He sketched a contest between the one nation and the many people, a position that other opponents of multiculturalism expressed at this time.

Twentieth-century social groups supporting interracial couples and mixed-race people began with Manasseh Clubs in Chicago and Milwaukee between the 1890s and 1920s and continued with the Penguin Club and others in major cities through the 1940s and then with groups such as Interracial/Intercultural Pride, the Biracial Family Network (B.F.N.), and the Interracial Family Circle (I.F.C.) through the late 1970s and early 1980s. A.M.E.A. was founded on November 12, 1988, in Berkeley, California, by representatives of fourteen charter organizations from across the country, becoming the first national federation of its kind and defining itself as an educational organization that "promoted a positive awareness of interracial families and multiethnic people and families."[9] Among the officers, Carlos A. Fernández, a Bay Area attorney, was elected as president, Ramona Douglass as vice president, and G. Reginald Daniel, a scholar on mixed-race identity, as secretary.

In order to transform a dominant ideology of mixed-race people and inter-racial couples as dysfunctional or pathological, A.M.E.A. chose political advocacy work as its central function. In its early years, the organization thought of itself as a budding business venture; reflecting the professionalism of its executive committee, A.M.E.A. quickly drafted two-year and five-year plans. In order to have an effect on the national level, it published a quarterly newsletter and drew on the commitment of its member organizations, which included existent chapters of I-Pride, B.F.N., and I.F.C. Within five years, A.M.E.A. hoped to launch an educational and legal defense fund, to establish a multicultural resource center, and to staff a political action committee that would lobby for a Multiracial category on federal forms, with the ability to check all races that applied. Limited resources and staff made some of these goals unattainable, but A.M.E.A. did gain 501c3 (nonprofit) status within a few years and began using a national 1-800 number. In future years, like other Multiracial groups, it used the Internet to publish its newsletter and to communicate with its members. Through its alliances with other groups, A.M.E.A. also tracked state and federal decisions affecting its constituents.[10]

Susan R. Graham, a white mother of two mixed children in Roswell, Georgia, founded Project R.A.C.E. after her experience of having to pick just one box on school forms for her son, whose father was black. The main goal of the organization was to achieve "a multiracial classification on school, employment, state, federal, census, and medical forms requiring racial data."[11] Graham cited the mental health of the children as the main motiva-tor for her activism. "It's for the self-esteem of multiracial people. They have every right to call themselves biracial and for other people to recognize them as biracial, because that's what they are."[12] She believed that children should not have to pick one aspect of their heritage or the other, to reject one parent or the other, or to be placed with a race they may not want to identify with. Multiracialists often wanted to distance themselves from African Ameri-can identity by emphasizing their white identity. On one hand, embracing whiteness happens within the context of structural benefits, rather than in a vacuum. On the other hand, claiming Multiracial identity does not necessar-ily corrode the racial order, lead to a whitening process, or diminish efforts for civil rights. This embrace of whiteness received censure, as it was callous to black inequality, and it skirted the issue of economic, social, and political gains that come with white identity.[13]

In arguing for a Multiracial category, Graham applied the term *biracial* to her children as if it had always existed, rather than making sense in a specific historical moment. Labels for racially mixed people have always reflected the times and ideologies from which they sprouted. *Biracial, multiracial,* and *interracial* began as terms to describe the presence of two or more racial groups, like a biracial committee. Appropriating them to describe the experience of having parents from two or more racial groups staked a claim for personal identity, but it overlooked how the understanding of race has changed through time, location, or mere inclination. Parents such as Graham wanted to free children from narrow choices, but they ultimately restricted their choices to two terms of their picking—biracial or multiracial.

Regardless of these critiques, the Multiracial groups recognized that the census is a race-making tool as well as a numeric account of race. In other words, we think of races falling into certain categories because we see these categories on certain forms; changing the forms can have an effect on changing the vernacular on race. While A.M.E.A. and Project R.A.C.E. may have had different approaches, their efforts reflected optimism that they could change the discourse on race in America. Their activism provided a moment when mixed-race people themselves were voices in this conversation, accepting the role of hero.

The desire among mixed-race people to claim a label of their own was a byproduct of the Multicultural Movement, which aimed to bring a "greater degree of attention to minorities and women and their role in American history and social studies and literature classes."[14] They followed the pattern that other underrepresented groups set, each vying for recognition. Voicing group identities promised recognition for each member's personal identity, and this constituted the appeal of multiculturalism. However, in working to raise awareness for specific minority experiences, advocates often lost sight of the broader structures of inequality. Even with the best of intentions, some within the Multiracial Movement exhibited such short-sightedness. In fact, sociologist Rebecca Chiyoko King framed the Multiracial Movement as a conflict between individual and group rights, arguing "that it is because the Census attempts to recognize both *individual* racial/ethnic identities and *collective* racial identities *simultaneously* that the change in the Census has been so controversial."[15]

Meanwhile, studies by psychologists reached opposing conclusions regarding a Multiracial category. Some maintained that mixed-race youth develop healthy self-esteem without a custom racial label to pick; that there is no significant difference between the social adjustment of mixed children and that of other children of color; and that factors such as single-parent homes, less contact with noncustodial parents, and narrow discussions of matters of race affect positive psychosocial adjustment for mixed teens more than self-naming does. Others emphasized themes of belonging, alienation, and prejudice in regard to mixed-race children. Theirs were particular experiences that society had little sensitivity toward.[16]

In the early 1990s, the media grasped onto the movement as a viable topic, and publishers produced academic titles, making innovative writing around the subject of identity bounteous. The foremost of these scholars, including Maria P. P. Root and G. Reginald Daniel, saw themselves as part of the movement, counseling the organizations and providing research that bolstered their aims. In 1992, psychologist Root published *Racially Mixed People in America*, the first collection to bring together scholarly pieces on a variety of topics around mixed-race identity. *Racially Mixed People in America* asserted, "The emergence of a racially mixed population is transforming the 'face' of the United States. The increasing presence of multiracial people necessitates that we as a nation ask ourselves questions about our identity: Who are we? How do we see ourselves? Who are we in relation to one another?"[17] According to Root, these questions became more relevant because of the "biracial baby boom" that started with the 1967 *Loving v. Virginia* decision. She predicted a "full-scale 'identity crisis' that this country is ill equipped to resolve."[18] As she claimed,

> The presence of racially mixed persons defies the social order predicated upon race, blurs racial and ethnic group boundaries, and challenges generally accepted proscriptions and prescriptions regarding inter-group relations. Furthermore, and perhaps most threatening, the existence of racially mixed persons challenges long-held notions about the biological, moral, and social meaning of race.[19]

Root suggested that the mere presence of racially mixed people acted as a catalyst for change. As she later wrote, "Everyone who enters into an interracial relationship or is born of racially different heritages is conscripted into a quiet revolution."[20] In reality, it required more than that, whether in the post-civil-rights era or prior. Mixed race as an antiracist force is most effective in conjunction with more comprehensive efforts.

Besides the challenges of quantifying a "biracial baby boom" at the core of the Multiracial Movement's impetus, this position suggested that racially mixed people were new and that nothing short of mutual romance, legal marriage, and long-term dedication to multiracial identity counted as interracial intimacy. This disqualified relationships between people we see as too similar, extramarital relationships, and mixed people who decided to live monoracially. In reality, definitions of who is mixed and what is mixture have changed. A supposed explosion in interracial relationships implied that race always has been taboo in the United States, in all pockets of the continent, throughout our history, when there have been many cases of mutual acceptance. Lastly, celebrating the trends of recent decades casted a triumphal regard on the civil rights movement of the mid-twentieth century, as if the 1960s civil rights, immigration, and intermarriage legislation marked the end of inequality, and the world started anew in 1967.

During the same period, some thinkers on race, including philosophers Naomi Zack, Kwame Anthony Appiah, and Paul Gilroy, went even further than proposing a new Multiracial identity, arguing that racial categories themselves were invalid. Of these, Zack focused the most on mixed race, maintaining that, since "all racial identities rest on ideologies that require energies of determination and control—of will—to maintain," the idea of mixed race is contradictory, and racial purity is untenable.[21] For Zack, nothing good could come from the idea of race, which had faulty science as its basis. Central in her work was "a strong repudiation of all racial identity—black, white, and even mixed race."[22] As she claimed, "The illusion of mixed race needs to be written and talked out before the illusion of race itself can be dispelled."[23] A racial nominalist, she believed that race exists in name only, ignoring the fact that race is a lived experience. Ironically, though, she privileged mixed race as the last type of racial identity to discuss before abolishing racial categories altogether.

In the end, Zack avoided praising mixed-race Americans as a sign of an improved America. Even her concept of microdiversity, which recognized the "racial difference within individuals," was something she wanted to discard along with the other schools of racialist thought. Her prescription went even further: "The next step after microdiversity is racelessness. . . . I propose that we write ourselves out of race as a means of constructing racelessness or removing the constructions of race. And our language itself, or at least English, underscores such a move."[24] Unlike Root, Zack worked outside the Multiracial Movement, and she only saw value in discussing mixed-race identity as a means to dismantle it in the end. This was similar to some other Multiracialists' optimism, but instead, Zack wanted to abolish racial names rather than to invent a new one. However, avoiding the labels would not change the lived experience of racialized peoples, nor does the coinage of a new label. As Michael Omi and Howard Winant suggest, rather than an illusion, race becomes real through historically situated processes of racialization or, as they call them, racial projects. Philosopher Ronald R. Sundstrom agreed with this intervention, arguing that mixed race does exist as a social reality, one different from traditional racial identities (even with dual membership in both), and one that can contribute to the liberatory concerns of the traditional racial groups. On the other hand, abandoning race would "gravely hamper" those struggles.[25]

Second among these race abolitionist was Kwame Anthony Appiah, professor of philosophy at Princeton University and author of *In My Father's House: Africa in the Philosophy of Culture*. Racially mixed himself, he was a collaborator with Henry Louis Gates Jr. (a former colleague at Harvard University) on *Transition* magazine, the *Africana* encyclopedia, and *The Dictionary of Global Culture*. In both Appiah's 1985 essay "The Uncompleted Argument" and its expansion in *My Father's House*, he complimented Du Bois for moving away from biology but critiqued the reliance on a common history, because identifying with historical events of a people produces circular reasoning; you have to pick the people you want to identify with to pick the events you want to identify with. Appiah advocated, "If we let go of racial essence, logically, we'd have to let go of racial hierarchy."[26] He continued, "The truth is that there are no races: there is nothing in the world we can ask race to do for us. As we have seen, even the biologist's notion has only limited uses, and the notion that Du Bois required, and that underlies the more hateful racisms of the modern era, refers to nothing in the world at all."[27] Appiah argued that race has no scientific basis, and membership is arbitrary. While this position was first stated in the earlier essay, it gained attention when the book was named the *New York Times* Notable Book of the Year and was the recipient of the African Studies Association's Herskovits Award. In the end, Appiah acknowledged that people will cling to racial essence, often as a "badge of insult," for past experiences of oppression, but he warned that this can lead to cultural nationalism.

This cultural nationalism was exactly what Paul Gilroy, author of *The Black Atlantic: Modernity and Double-Consciousness*, opposed. His book aimed first to "repudiate the dangerous obsessions with 'racial' purity which are circulating inside and outside black politics," claiming that *The Black Atlantic* was "an essay about the inescapable hybridity and intermixture of ideas." Secondly, it pled against "the closure of the categories with which we conduct our political lives."[28] Gilroy defended an instability and mutability of black identities, whether in the United States, the Caribbean, Africa, or the United Kingdom. Rather than race, he offered diaspora as an analytic tool, using the ship as a symbol of trans-Atlantic crossings, the disruption of nationality, and a place where identity was born or reborn. The book repeatedly endorsed hybridity and mixture, but his choices of which cultural products to praise (soul music and hip-hop) and which to dismiss (black rockers Jimi Hendrix and Bad Brains) revealed a deep conservatism regarding what blackness was. At this work's foundation was the belief in a black race with a distinct set of cultural forms, even if he called people of African descent a diaspora. *The Black Atlantic* practiced the same circular reasoning Appiah criticized, and he ended up practicing the nationalism he abhorred by making it transnational.

Through the early 1990s, A.M.E.A. made great strides in lobbying for recognition. As news media attention to the Multiracial issue increased through the early 1990s, Fernández often appeared in print, saying, for example, "It's offensive for young people to confront this—a white parent and a nonwhite parent and to have to choose between them. It's also an intrusion into the family that is unjustified."[29] Like Albion Tourgée did in his brief before the Supreme Court, this lawyer presented interracial families to decry the state's faulty classification. However, this was a matter broader than mere identity; he and others on A.M.E.A.'s executive committee also cared about how a Multiracial identifier would affect race-based government initiatives, making a point of expressing solidarity with traditional minority groups. "It's wrong, destructive and very negative to think that those of mixed race are setting themselves apart from any of their ancestral groups, particularly blacks," Fernández stated in the *New York Times*, well before opposition to the category arose from established civil rights organizations and the ethnic press, which proposed variations of multiple checking in which respondents would indicate that they were Multiracial and then specify all the races or ethnicities that applied.[30]

On the other hand, Project R.A.C.E. cared more about getting a Multiracial category. As Graham testified before Congress in 1993,

> I care about accurate data, too. But I'm not a scholar, statistician, attorney, or lawmaker. I'm just a mother. A mother who cares about children, and whether I like it or not, I realize that self-esteem is directly tied to accurate racial identity. More and more parents all over our country are instilling new pride in our multiracial children. Can we say we have succeeded if our children leave home only to be denied an equal place in our society?[31]

The organization successfully promoted legislation to include the category on the local level in Illinois, Ohio, Georgia, and Michigan, with Florida, Indiana, and North Carolina following close behind. States such as Maryland, Texas, and Minnesota were much slower to introduce the new category.

Even though every census since the civil rights era had produced undercounts with racial disparities, the Reagan and Bush administrations maintained that the standards for counting race were sufficient. Similarly, even though the Other group was growing more quickly than any other, the dozen years of Republican preeminence resisted any considerable change in the terminology around race. Finally, in 1993, Congressman Tom Sawyer, a Democrat from Ohio and chair of the Congressional Subcommittee on Census, Statistics, and Postal Personnel encouraged Katherine Wallman, the statistical policy chief at the Office of Management and Budget (the agency whose Directive 15 had guided the standards and terminology around race on federal forms since 1977), to call for congressional hearings on the matter. The committee rejected two of the four proposals it received: one to make Middle Easterners/Arabs a racial group and another to move Native Hawaiians from Asian and Pacific Islander to Native American Indian. The third was to make Hispanic a racial group rather than an ethnic designation; even though this one received minimal support from its constituents, it persisted through the three hearings that year because it could alleviate the trouble that Other presented for demographers.

Visibility for the Multiracial Movement increased in June, when Fernández and Graham testified before the Congressional Subcommittee on Census, Statistics, and Postal Personnel concerning the need for some type of Multiracial identifier on all federal forms that collected racial data. Congressman Sawyer said that the Multiracial category was "an issue coming to a ripeness that makes it difficult to ignore." He claimed that, as a nation, "We are really at the threshold of another major adjustment in the way we think of ourselves as a people."[32] However, appealing to the technocrats, he also repeated three truths about racial statistics: "First, many people agree on the need to continue collecting ethnic and racial data. Second, the data must be uniform across the government. Third, racial categories must be relevant to the public, or the public won't cooperate."[33] While the decision process promised to be a long one, this was a period of great optimism for A.M.E.A. and Project R.A.C.E. The subcommittee's decisions could lead to changes in the federal O.M.B. Directive 15. But the first step was to initiate research on the proposals, which various federal agencies solicited in 1993.

The two organizations differed on the structure of the race question that should appear on the 2000 census. A.M.E.A. wanted a two-part reporting standard that would ask if someone was Multiracial and then ask for the respondent's parents' races. They also wanted to discern whether one's parents were mixed race. Project R.A.C.E. was in on these discussions but abandoned the two-part question because "it took up too much space."[34] Fernández and A.M.E.A. declared that they wanted to create statistics that were accurate, continuous, and relevant, displaying concerns with semantics, data collection, and enumeration. But Graham and Project R.A.C.E. consistently addressed the more emotional aspects of adding a Multiracial category.[35] A.M.E.A. and Project R.A.C.E. both considered themselves extensions of the civil rights movement, but their differences in style and strategy strained the relationship between them. As Reginald Daniel has written, A.M.E.A. was more conciliatory, while Project R.A.C.E. was more confrontational. Regardless, they both highlighted mixed race as a positive force in race relations.[36]

The fall 1993 cover of *Time* magazine's special issue on immigration presented the portrait of a young adult woman with brown eyes and hair, who smiled out to the reader. The text said, "Take a good look at this woman. She was created by a computer from a mix of several races. What you see is a remarkable preview of . . . The New Face of America: How Immigrants Are Shaping the World's First Multicultural Society."[37] Inside, *Time*'s managing editor revealed the tool that made the woman on the cover possible: Morph 2.0 image manipulation software. He called her "a symbol of the future, multiethnic face of America,"[38] then divulged her genealogy:

> A combination of the racial and ethnic features of the women used to produce the chart [at the center of the magazine, which places seven men and seven women of distinct ethnic backgrounds at each axis], she is: 15% Anglo-Saxon, 17.5% Middle Eastern, 17.5% African, 7.5% Asian, 35% Southern European and 7.5% Hispanic. As onlookers watched the image of our new Eve begin to appear on the computer screen, several staff members promptly fell in love. Said one: "It really breaks my heart that she doesn't exist." We sympathize with our lovelorn colleagues, but even technology has its limits. This is a love that must forever remain unrequited."[39]

This write-up, along with the cover image, another computer-generated tour de force at the center of the magazine, and the context of the magazine's articles made the special issue the example par excellence of the imagined mixed-race American (see figure 6.1). The magazine issue was in production at the same time that Congress held its 1993 hearings on race and the census, but there was no mention of those developments. *Time*'s product showed that mixed race had joined the set of viable topics for a news weekly independent of the Multiracial Movement. However, this does not mean that mixed race was particularly special to the editors but rather that it was something that could sell some magazines. After all, the preceding issue profiled evangelist Billy Graham, and the following featured corporate downsizing.

The *Time* special issue bound intermarriage together with immigration as two forces transforming the United States, rather than presenting either topic on its own. Gallup polls showed that 48% of adults approved of marriage between blacks and whites in 1991, 6% more than those who disapproved. This reflected a shift from the 1983 iteration of this question, which resulted in 43% approval and 50% disapproval. On the other hand, in July 1993, 65% of

Fig. 6.1. "The New Face of America," *Time*, November 18, 1993

adults believed that immigration should be decreased, and between 44% and 62% believed too many immigrants were entering from Africa, Latin America, Asia, and the Middle East, the most popular opinion for each region. Europe was the one exception, with 52% believing the number of immigrants was "about right." The Gallup numbers indicated more antagonism toward immigration than toward intermarriage. *Time* had to deploy one as a mechanism to deal with the other. If immigration was inevitable, at least there was the hope that immigrants would be productive, buy goods, and marry native-born Americans. Rather than arguing for a limit to mixing, the special issue presents it as a cure. This strategy may have failed for more conservative readers, but it was effective for others.[40]

When *Time* presented immigration on its own, it communicated trepidation more often than hopefulness, resulting in an ambiguous message. After all, the undocumented worker or illegal alien represented the ills begotten of the 1965 Immigration Act, which did away with the national quotas system set up in the 1920s, whether it was immigrants sneaking across the United States–Mexico border or stowing away on freighters from China. By 1993, the shortcomings of the 1986 Immigration Reform and Control Act, which granted amnesty to some seasonal laborers and undocumented residents, had become clear, and the state of California was just one year from Proposition 187, which hoped to deny social services, health care, and public education to undocumented immigrants. In the 1990s, the new color-blind racism combined with traditional forms of nativism, producing a new racial nativism on both ends of the political spectrum. Analysis of the magazine as a whole shows the trepidation that *Time* communicated along with the optimism, resulting in tension between these two tendencies.[41]

The optimistic authors in the magazine included Pico Iyer, who epitomized the United States through cheerful consumerism of fast food, nighttime dramas, and hip-hop. Thomas McCarroll reported on the increase in corporations' spending on ethnic marketing once they realized that African Americans, Asian Americans, and Latinos spent $600 billion on consumer goods and could make up 30% of the economy by the end of the decade. This trend continued with "Art of Diversity," which praised Gloria Estefan's appearance on MTV Latino, the dramatization of *The Joy Luck Club*, and the latest title by Nobel-winning poet Derek Walcott as indicators that newcomers have changed the Eurocentric nature of American culture. This simplified the matter of assimilation by suggesting that recent immigrants introduce more change than previous immigrants had. This also naturalized some items as being mainstream, rather than coming from older immigrant groups at other points in U.S. history. Examples of these include spaghetti,

St. Patrick's Day, and Santa Claus, which have become so ordinary that few people think of them as coming from anywhere in particular. Celebrating the products of Asian, Latino, and Caribbean immigrants as special suggests that those of past European immigrant groups are the norm.[42]

Other authors regretted the hyphen in ethnic American identities, but Christopher John Farley celebrated it as a connection to another place, connecting his piece to Horace M. Kallen and Randolph S. Bourne, who had done so before: "To be an immigrant artist is to be a hyphen away from one's roots, and still a thousand miles away. But it is often that link to a foreign land—another way of seeing things—that allows such artists to contribute ideas to American culture that are fresh and new. That slim hyphen, that thin line that joins individual Americans to their past, is also what connects all America to its future."[43] Farley suggested that the immigrant revitalizes the United States and allows for the country to enjoy a new future. In this, the immigrant's connection to the past was an asset, rather than something to forget through Americanization. Farley also offered the street fair "with various booths, foods and peoples, all mixing on common sidewalks" as a replacement for Anglo-conformity theories of assimilation.[44] This is useful in its focus on urbanity and free movement, but it forefronts commodification rather than interaction. Passersby get to consume cultural products but never learn anything about the vendors (assuming that the wares and their handlers hail from the same place). If you do not like the looks of a thing, there is no reason to go near it. You can go home, whistling the tune from the indigenous flute music you heard during your outing.

On the grim side was a series of articles that cast immigration as a threat, even though they did address issues of equality, inclusion, and access. John Elson presented a history of legislation that seemed more permissive over time, but he then cast aspersions on the 1980 Refugee Act, which was too lenient and vulnerable. In reality, newer legislation permitted a few entries but also redefined foreignness in timely but still restrictive ways. Elson shifted from the progressive narrative to cast aspersions on the agendas of Jimmy Carter and Ted Kennedy, Democrats. Bruce Nelan's "Not Quite So Welcome Anymore" explained the difference between legal immigrants, illegal immigrants, and asylum seekers, but it ultimately pointed out that many Americans believed that there should be restrictions for all three groups. Senior editor at the *National Review* Richard Brookhiser praised white, Anglo-Saxon Protestants as the founders of the country, as well as the industrious, utilitarian, conscientious, and civic-minded source of the American character. His "Three Cheers for the WASPs" blamed the decline in these values on wanton nonconformity.[45]

However, the most evocative of the negative articles was "America's Immigrant Challenge," in which Steve Liss named the core preoccupation of the whole publication: "Even more startling, sometime during the second half of the 21st century the descendants of white Europeans, the arbiters of the core national culture for most of its existence, are likely to slip into minority status," a prospect that "hardly pleases everyone."[46] In reality, with Hispanic whites joining the ranks of non-Hispanic whites, whites constitute the largest and fastest growing racial group in the United States. With the past transformations of Irish, Italians, Jews, and others into mainstream whiteness, this group always has increased. However, the article's plea depended on ignorance of these trends, letting the fear of white demographic diminution stand. While few people may have spoken openly about it, this fear of racial extinction surely resonated with readers, just as the fear of racial impurity had for much of U.S. history. By voicing this fear, these negative articles spoke more truth about how Americans thought, voted, and acted on immigration than did the other articles, which explored what they bought, the movies they saw, and how advertisers communicated to them.

Time's principal article on interracial marriage, "Intermarried . . . with Children," profiled five couples. Reuben and Marna Cahn received the blessings of only three parents, until the birth of their baby son won over the last, who had refused to attend the wedding. The same was true for Kyoung-Hi Song and Robert Dickson, demonstrating how the birth of a child validated socially questionable marriages. Two others (Tony Jeffreys and Alice Sakuda Flores, and Candy Mills and Gabe Grosz) spoke of the prejudices their friends expressed, even in mixed company. Kathleen Hobson and Atul Gawande designed a wedding ceremony with readings in both Hindu and Christian texts to prevent scaring relatives who did not want to expose their children to other beliefs. They also described the common ground between them: "an upper-middle-class upbringing in tight-knit families, a Stanford education and a love of intellectual pursuits."[47] This list contained the set of values the magazine was promoting: the pursuit of prosperity, commitment to family, liberal arts education, and self-improvement—some of the same Puritan characteristics Brookhiser applauded. Like the other articles, this one called for the preservation of these values in the arena of heteronormative families.

The article's author, Jill Smolowe, quoted anthropologist Karen Stephenson, who said, "Marriage is the main assimilator. If you really want to effect change, it's through marriage and child rearing."[48] Smolowe denied that this was assimilation in the Eurocentric way, but her descriptions suggested that it was—with some cultural accommodation. The end result was a promotion of the traditional sense of assimilation. Still ambivalent about the challenges of interracial marriage, the piece offered, "Such pain is evidence that America has yet to harvest the full rewards of its founding principles. The land of immigrants may be giving way to a land of hyphenations, but the hyphen still divides even as it compounds. Those who intermarry have perhaps the strongest sense of what it will take to return America to an unhyphenated whole."[49] Like Farley and others, Smolowe regretted the hyphen, but she saw intermarriage as key in dissolving it. Since there never was an unhyphenated whole, it is impossible to say what that was like, but there are two principal ways to read this closing wish: that Americans will become one tawny race snacking on chips and salsa or that the mere appearance of mixed-race children will inspire the elders to trade in their racial and ethnic differences (and practices) and behave—like W.A.S.P.'s. The article suggested that traditional, heteronormative values were necessary to initiate this change, but children could guarantee it. As she wrote, "Perhaps [Candy Mills's] two Native American-black-white-Hungarian-French-Catholic-Jewish-American children will lead the way," conferring on them the responsibility of being racial heroes.[50]

At the center of the magazine's special issue was a chart with seven women from various ethnic groups across the top and seven men from the same groups along the side—what I call "The Miscegenation Matrix." It allowed readers to pick racial types they identified with and then imagine producing children with a man or woman of some other type. Alternatively, exploring the spread was like visualizing the copulation of another pair of adults racially different from oneself. The choice of racial types subscribed to typological categories of past racial science, limiting many people to their physical features. In other words, the labels asserted that *this* was what Middle Easterners, Italians, Africans, Vietnamese, Anglo-Saxons, Chinese, and Hispanics looked like. The seven men and seven women all had the same facial expression, unremarkable hairstyles, and a lack of facial hair, making those physical features uniform. Nor were any of them short, fat, or middle-aged.

The article accompanying the chart, "Rebirth of a Nation, Computer Style," explained how the staff created these faces, using Morph 2.0 to find a medium between points on each source face. Of physical features, eyes, skin color, and neck shape were the most crucial in producing a successful blend. Most of the "morphies" were fifty-fifty combinations between their two progenitors, but in some cases the designers used more of one feature than another to create a face that complied with notions of masculinity and femininity. The author joked, "One of our tentative unions produced a distinctly feminine face—sitting atop a muscular neck and hairy chest. Back to the mouse on that one."[51] This was an admission that their process involved making conscious decisions and exclusions. Like many media producers, they described their work in naive terms that emphasized aesthetics, but these choices were never neutral, no matter how inchoate they were. They produced faces with no personalities, experiences, or histories that real people share with their ancestors. These were free of any struggles to come to the country, the day-to-day difficulties as minorities in the United States, or the challenges that arose when two disparate people entered into a relationship. Lastly, the layout proposed that this is the first generation of mixing, as if it were a new phenomenon.

Time's centerfold evoked *casta* paintings of colonial Mexico, which William Short had likely seen while a treaty negotiator in Spain. Time's grid replaced that display of wealth with one of hygienic fitness. Otherwise, the concerns were the same in eighteenth-century *casta* paintings and 1993's "Rebirth of a Nation, Computer Style": quantification of heritage, prurient voyeurism, and making sense of changes in diversity. The Miscegenation Matrix lacked the racial names for each of the forty-nine combinations, as well as the background, clothing, or occupations. But the homogeneity of their look made the labels unnecessary. Instead, these naked, young, fit bodies symbolized the perpetuation of centrist values. Rather than appear in the field, villa, or wilderness, they appeared before an empty background, doing nothing. Perhaps the blankness was a conception of the blank palette of imagination. More likely, it suggested that they were *tabula rasa*, blameless, disinterested in historical inequality, silent regarding prejudice, offspring of one man and one woman, healthy newborns of the future United States. These were also characteristics readers could wish for themselves.[52]

Like the figures from the centerfold, The New Face was fresh, clean, and symmetrical, reflecting the appealing, feminine set of features her designers assembled. Following John Berger's maxim "Men act, women appear," The New Face did nothing but smile out to the viewer, enigmatically.[53] If we accept Laura Mulvey's assertion regarding the predominance of the male gaze in narrative film and popular culture more broadly, then we can say that The New Face was available for men to ogle.[54] Her appearance also brought the narrative to a halt. This happened, physically, as the passerby in B. Dalton Books stopped to see what this pretty face was doing on *Time*. The pause also happened in thinking about her as a symbol of a multicultural United States. In the narrative about racial mixing, her smile symbolized a pause before widespread mongrelization, the end of white demographic predominance, or the filling of neonatal wards with mixed-race heroes, here to end racial strife.

However, the presentation of the woman on the cover differed from that of the people in the centerfold grid, offering another aspect to interpret.

While the forty-nine others appeared on a white background, she appeared with a washed-out representation of the Miscegenation Matrix behind her. Rather than "SimEve," mother of them all, as Donna Haraway described her, she was the daughter of them all, racial mixing carried to its logical end. Rather than cultural annihilation, white demographic minoritization, or strife, *Time* predicted a cheerful end result for current trends. Mixture, as symbolized by The New Face, our future daughter, would produce beauty, equality, and peace, benefits to society as a whole. These joined the narcissistic *tabula rasa* that the forty-nine morphies reflected. Rather than dissolving race altogether, The New Face suggested that an abundance of race and interracial intimacy was the way of the future. As with other superficial praise of mixture, from the Tragic Mulatto to *The Melting-Pot*, *Time*'s special issue excused readers from engaging with racism at all.[55]

The first popular reuse of The New Face appeared in the *National Review*, the unabashedly conservative biweekly, in 1994. The front of its February 21 issue placed *Time*'s cover on an imaginary wall, with an African American youth leaving the scene, having marked The New Face in black ink with a beard, mustache, and the words "Demystifying Multiculturalism," the title of the publication's own special issue on diversity. Inside, John O'Sullivan praised *Time* for moments of good journalism (including his colleague Richard Brookhiser's elegy for the W.A.S.P.), but he took the other magazine to task for "exiling America's central tradition, based upon Anglo-American institutions and the English language, to a nativist limbo."[56] Regarding The New Face, the editor claimed, "Problem is, she doesn't look very multicultural. She is a perky all-American girl from deepest suburbia."[57] If "multicultural" meant minority and "deepest suburbia" meant privileged, then O'Sullivan was calling her a racially white girl whom others had mistaken as mixed. Instead, he was referring to the minorities who had achieved enough success to move into predominantly white areas. That narrative buttressed neoconservative, color-blind, meritocratic notions that needed just one token minority to confirm them, dismissing all those who failed to do so.

In September 1994, the cover of *Mirabella* imitated The New Face by presenting the image of a tanned model glistening in the southwestern sun. A caption asked, "Who is the face of America?" and a write-up inside told the story of how this model was chosen. By hinting, "Maybe her identity has something to do with the microchip floating through space, next to that gorgeous face," the editors revealed that she was computer-generated.[58] They continued, "America is a melting pot. And true American beauty is a combination of elements from all over the world. Is our cover model representative of the melting pot? All we're sure of is that her looks could melt just about anything."⁵⁹ In a cheeky tone similar to *Time*'s, *Mirabella*'s editors described her as an object of desire. Also a composite of several women, the cover model on *Mirabella* was similar to The New Face before her.

In Carla K. Bradshaw's exploration of the role physical appearance plays in mixed-race people's lives, she explained how many people treat them as the Beauty and the Beast, especially when their racial makeup is unknown. "This increased attention to physical appearance is expressed in such labels as *exotic, beautiful* or *fascinating* (the Beauty)," referring to the popular notion regarding mixed people's good looks. She continued, "Obstacles to claiming racial belonging unambiguously leave the individual constantly vulnerable to rejection and identification as 'the Other' (the Beast)."⁶⁰ But *Time*'s and *Mirabella*'s staffs made a mystery of each of their cover stars' origin and put her good looks at the center of her identity, making her the Beauty. Then, by revealing that she is not real, they make her into the Beast, unnatural and without humanity.

As the decade proceeded, even more thinkers outside of the Multira-cial Movement praised racial mixing, most notably David Hollinger, Stanley Crouch, and Arthur Schlesinger, Jr. Hollinger, historian and author of *Postethnic America: Beyond Multiculturalism* (1995), suggested that inter-racial marriage, double-minority mixed-race people, and the Multiracial Movement threatened predominant racial thinking, which he described as a pentagon with a racial group at each point. Each point was far from any other, making mobility between them nearly impossible. He offered Alex Haley's choice to neglect his Irish heritage in *Roots* as a case of conformity to the pentagon. Those who made similar choices subscribed to terms of white supremacy rather than exploring more inclusive identities. Concerning mixed race, he wrote, "While the demand to add mixed race to the federal census can be construed as merely an effort to turn the pentagon into a hexagon, the logic of mixed race actually threatens to destroy the whole structure," joining Maria P. P. Root's suggestion that those who assert a mixed identity intrinsically dismantle racial categories.⁶¹ This assumed that mixed and traditional identities were mutually exclusive. From that point, it was easy to reject African American, Asian American, and the like as labels of oppression, embracing Multiracial as a curative that dismantles racial categories. While it is possible to adopt a primarily Multiracial identity rather than traditional racial labels, mixed-race people often construct racial identities that can be any combination thereof—for example, both Asian and mixed. Merely being mixed race does not disrupt the racial order. Antiracist activism, concern for universal equality, and political action might. But praise of mixed race alone is barely a starting point.

Later in *Postethnic America*, Hollinger asserted, "Mixed race people are performing a historic role at the present moment: they are reanimating a traditional American emphasis on the freedom of individual affiliation, and they are confronting the American nation with its own continued reluctance to apply this principle to ethno-racial affiliations."[62] Mixed-race Americans who moved between racial, ethnic, and social groups did challenge observers' conceptions of affiliation. However, did being mixed automatically do this? Was it not possible to be mixed and uphold racial, gender, and class hierarchies? Could others with less racial mixture practice diverse affiliations? Hollinger praised voluntary affiliation but then conscripted racially mixed people to the role of hero responsible for us all. Besides, exercising options requires a high degree of privilege; poor people, regardless of heritage, have a harder time choosing where to live, whom to socialize with, and how to shape familial relationships. So dispersing opportunities, not genetic material, would reshape affiliations, and that is not a task that racially mixed people can achieve alone.

In a 1996 *New York Times Magazine* essay, cultural critic and novelist Stanley Crouch predicted, "One hundred years from today, Americans are likely to look back on the ethnic difficulties of our time as quizzically as we look at earlier periods of human history, when misapprehension defined the reality."[63] Rather than bland uniformity, Crouch expected the rise of a vibrant culture of cross-assimilation. Accompanying the text were photos of mixed-race youth between five and fourteen years of age, along with captions providing their parent racial or ethnic groups (e.g., "Saira Asim, 10, Pakistani/African-American," "Daniel Cohen-Cruz, 11, Russian-Polish Jewish/Puerto Rican," and "Paloma Hagedorn-Woo, 12, Chinese/American Indian/Filipino/Scottish"). These were The New Faces who would precipitate the demise of racial and ethnic discord. By 2096, they would be great-grandparents, the last generation to remember ethnic difficulties, just as our own great-grandparents were the last to remember ice boxes—except that the past use of racism reverberates more powerfully in life outcomes than does the past use of food-preservation appliances.

Historian Arthur Schlesinger, Jr.'s *The Disuniting of America: Reflections on a Multicultural Society* (1992) had joined in the claim that multiculturalism threatened to balkanize the country. Six years later, the 1998 expanded edition argued that racial mixing would defeat the multiculturalists who overemphasized difference. Emphasizing the institutions that join the nation's diverse population, the first chapter presented a roll call of American figures who have placed mixture at the center of American identity, including Hector St. John de Crèvecoeur, George Washington, Herman Melville, Ralph

Waldo Emerson, and Israel Zangwill. In defense of "the original theory of America as 'one people,' a common culture, a single nation,"[64] Schlesinger claimed that the nation was becoming more racially mixed. "Tiger Woods— one-fourth Thai, one-fourth Chinese, one-fourth black, one-eighth white, and one-eighth American Indian—foreshadows the future. We can, I am sure, count on the power of sex—and of love—to defeat those who would seek to divide the country into separate ethnic communities," as if statements of ethnic belonging were the same as prejudice and as if American segregation happened because of mean people's irrational needs, not the corralling of resources toward those who have historically possessed them—in other words, white supremacy.[65]

Woods had come to national fame between the publication of the first and second editions of Schlesinger's book, and he served as the ideal example for the author to invoke—mixed race, comfortable with all his backgrounds, successful in predominantly white arenas, and more interested in unifying people than in pointing out their differences. Heroization of the athlete had started in 1996, after he left Stanford University to become a professional golfer. In Gary Smith's 1996 *Sports Illustrated* Sportsman of the Year write-up, "The Chosen One," he wrote of Woods fulfilling his father's prophecy to have more impact than Nelson Mandela, Mahatma Gandhi, or the Buddha. His mother echoed, "He can hold everyone together. He is the Universal Child."[66] Participating in a popular debate about whether fame, riches, and commercialism would defeat Woods, Smith asked, "Who will win? The machine . . . or the youth who has just entered its maw?"[67] In the end, he sided with the young athlete, suggesting that in consuming him, we "swallow hope in the American experiment, in the pell-mell jumbling of genes. We swallow the belief that the face of the future is not necessarily a bitter or bewildered face; that it might even, one day, be something like Tiger Woods' face: handsome and smiling and ready to kick all comers' asses."[68] This language may have been an appropriate match for Woods's talent; however, it also reflected the flattering stereotypes—for example, that mixed-race people are "the race of the future," "the best of both worlds," and "bridges between parents' races"— that many people ascribe to racially mixed people.

When Woods appeared on *The Oprah Winfrey Show* on April 24, 1997, to discuss winning the Masters golf tournament for the first time, the following exchange concerning his racial identity brought him even more attention than his record-breaking achievements at Augusta had:

OPRAH: Does it bother you to be called African American?

TIGER WOODS: It does. Growing up, I came up with this name: I'm a "Cablinasian," *Ca*, Caucasian; *bl*, Black; *in*, Indian; Asian. I'm just who I am, whoever you see in front of you.

He explained that he did not want to deny any part of his heritage, and when presented with forms asking to check a box for racial background, he could not settle for just one. "I checked off 'African American' and 'Asian.' Those are the two I was raised under, and the only two I know." This became a defining moment for Woods, giving a conclusive answer about his racial makeup, as well as a moniker for what to call it. His statement "I'm just who I am, whoever you see in front of you," left space for people to identify him by his appearance, and his dark complexion, broad features, and wooly hair led to the label black for many.

Journalist Jack E. White used reactions to Woods's "Cablinasian" statement as an entry into examining the "melding [*sic*] pot" and "America's failure to come to grips with the perplexing and rapidly evolving significance of racial identity in what is fast becoming the most polyglot society in history."[69] This language conveyed the anxiety over growing diversity, along with the belief in linear progress and American exceptionalism. *Newsweek* voiced the opinion that "'alternative,' ethnic ambiguity confers both individuality and a sense of shared values. Tiger Woods . . . represents the most exciting facet of this matrix."[70] In regard to the growing number of mixed-race Americans, the article's authors wrote, "They can throw light on the nation's racial irrationality, even pressure it. But this alone does not ease it, any more than Tiger Woods is the happy ending to our unhappy racial saga. He is merely the next chapter, and they, along with him, 2 million strong, and counting."[71]

Conservatives presented Woods as proof that merit trumped race in America. *Washington Post* columnist James K. Glassman asserted, "In fact, Woods is making $60 million in large part *because* he is black. . . . Tiger Woods may be just the guy to change things—not by being portrayed as a phony victim but by being celebrated as a master of a very difficult, very beautiful game."[72] The *Economist* praised Woods for claiming "no special privilege" for his race, abstaining from playing the race card, and getting over whatever racial obstacles there may have been. A 2001 feature from this magazine named Woods as proof that "the idea that there is a specific racial barrier in modern American sport, as opposed to barriers of poverty and background that apply to all races, looks increasingly hard to sustain."[73] Woods has been a convenient rebuttal against those who emphasize the few opportunities for racial minorities.

The first verbal attack on Woods's racial identity came from Fuzzy Zoeller, a fellow pro golfer who, upon finishing thirty-fourth when Woods won the 1997 Masters nineteen under par, commented, "That little boy is driving well and he's putting well. He's doing everything it takes to win. So, you know what you guys do when he gets in here? You pat him on the back and say congratulations and enjoy it and tell him not to serve fried chicken next year. Got it?"[74] Assuming Woods would conform to stereotypes of food popular with blacks when choosing the menu for next year's Masters dinner menu, Zoeller continued, "Or collard greens or whatever the hell they serve."[75] The press was quick to censure the elder athlete, and K-Mart, his major sponsor, dismissed him. In the end, Woods accepted an apology from Zoeller, but the lesson was clear: even with Wood's explicit statements about his racial identity, many considered him black, based on his physical appearance, the predominance of the "one-drop rule" in U.S. racial history, and the press's moniker "the black golfer."

The second rejection of Woods's self-naming came from a bloc of African Americans leaders whom *Ebony* magazine surveyed in July 1997. On one hand, Hugh B. Price, president of the National Urban League, credited Woods with not denying any part of his heritage, and Douglas Wilder preferred to be called "American" above any classification that confused skin color with background. The former governor of Virginia stated, "We shouldn't tell him how to classify himself. As long as he is forthright about who he is, and he has been forthright about it, then Black America should rejoice in his historic achievement."[76] However, others, such as Kweisi Mfume, president and C.E.O. of the N.A.A.C.P.; Jesse Jackson; and Sharon Robinson, daughter of baseball legend Jackie Robinson, described race in America as either black or white and urged Woods to choose accordingly. As Leonard G. Dunston, president of the National Association of Black Social Workers, claimed, "I respect his right to make his own personal choices, but it's very, very clear that in this country, race is a political category defined by those who are numerically in power. By definition, then, Tiger Woods is viewed as an African-American, whether he chooses to accept this or not."[77] Repeatedly, these figures urged Woods to adopt a more traditional way of identifying that emphasized his black heritage. A later statement by Colin Powell echoed the sentiment that one is black if one looks black. Lisa Jones, daughter of Amiri Baraka, censured Woods for neglecting a variety of issues facing blacks, whether A.I.D.S., the prison-industrial complex, or black-on-black violence. Woods claimed one kind of clear racial identification, but this set of black voices wanted a different one. He claimed his identity as his own, but they claimed it for the race. Was it possible for a public figure to retain private control over the matter—especially after he had made his identity a public matter? His divergent sense of public and private revealed itself again in 2009, with the exposure of his marital problems.[78]

Woods has not appeared in *Ebony* since that 1997 article, but *A. Magazine*, a similar monthly geared toward Asian Americans, has written about him over a dozen times, often placing him in its annual "aList" of most noteworthy Asians in America or its late-1999 list of "100 Most Influential Asian Americans of the Decade." After Woods described himself as "Cablinasian," writers at *A. Magazine* asserted that they, and Asian Americans at large, wanted "a piece of him" too and that his insistent recognition of his Asian ancestry "won him the hearts of Asian American sports fans."[79] On the other hand, in regard to the Asian reception of Tiger Woods, a sketch on *The Chris Rock Show* featured the comedian's survey of opinions on the golf star, including a group of Asian shop owners in Harlem who said they did not consider Woods as Asian. "Not even this much," one said, pinching a speck between his fingers. Their answers suggested that they considered him the same as, say, James Brown. In Thailand, Woods's fame overshadowed his mother's nonelite status, his father's participation in the U.S. military presence in Asia, and his black ancestry, making him more acceptable than he would have been as a native *luk kreung* (half child).[80]

Following the controversy of Woods's *Oprah* interview, he released a "Media Statement" to explain his racial heritage and to provide "the final and only comment" he would make on the subject. It read,

> My parents have taught me to always be proud of my ethnic background. Please rest assured that is, and always will be, the case—past, present, and future.
>
> The media has portrayed me as African-American; sometimes, Asian. In fact, I am both. Yes, I am the product of two great cultures, one African-American and the other Asian. On my father's side, I am African-American. On my mother's side, I am Thai. Truthfully, I feel very fortunate, and equally proud, to be both African-American and Asian!
>
> The critical and fundamental point is that ethnic background and/or composition should not make a difference. It does not make a difference to me. The bottom line is that I am an American . . . and proud of it! That is who I am and what I am. Now, with your cooperation, I hope I can just be a golfer and a human being.[81]

In no uncertain terms, Woods (and his handlers at I.M.G., the sports, fashion, and media-management company) spelled out his sentiments about his mixed background. He made no apology for past statements that seemed to privilege one heritage over another and dismissed any expectation that he make any more statements on his racial identity.[82]

Woods became internationally recognizable, making headline news when arriving to play in international tournaments. His philanthropic ventures aided disadvantaged children by giving them outlets to practice the sport of golf. Between his endorsements for American Express, Nike, and others, and his victories, Woods has topped *Forbes*'s list of highest-paid athletes and top celebrities. However, he has abstained from making statements on race (and definitely not on racism) since this early instance, making him a poster boy for color-blind meritocracy as well as racial progress. Even with his reticence on racial topics, Woods became "perhaps the busiest symbolic tool in the history of fictional or nonfictional mixed race characters."[83]

Even though Woods, the most prominent mixed-race figure to date, brought more attention to the topic, increased visibility for the Multiracial Movement brought increased opposition, mainly from more traditional civil rights organizations but also from scholars concerned with demographics. From 1993 to the congressional subcommittee's final decision in 1997, civil rights leaders, journalists, and scholars opposed the Multiracial category through the same activities as those who promoted it—lobbying, advising federal agencies, and stating their positions in the media. During these years, representatives from the N.A.A.C.P., the National Council of La Raza (N.C.L.R.), the National Congress of American Indians (N.C.A.I.), and others voiced their arguments in the same news pieces that noted the advances of A.M.E.A. and Project R.A.C.E. They raised any of these four points: First, beyond civil rights issues and racial identity, the Multiracial category was also relevant to fields such as health, education, and immigration research. Many of these academics emphasized the challenge in constructing continuity with past census data. Others pointed out the limitations of practicing statistical projections, even with one variable, intermarriage, in mind.

Second, the new category resembled other middling mixed-race statuses around the world, most notably Apartheid-era South Africa, where "Coloured" was an official classification for mixed, East Indian, and light-skinned peoples. In exchange for support for the Apartheid system, people with this designation enjoyed greater privileges than the indigenous black majority did, but they still held a secondary status behind whites. Michigan state representative Ed Vaughn, who opposed Project R.A.C.E.'s efforts there, often repeated this argument, naming places such as Haiti, New Orleans, and much of Latin America, where the intermediary mixed classes put greater distance between the white rulers and the darker oppressed.

Third, the category would negatively affect race-based government initiatives, such as voting rights, fair employment, and equal housing. Even though mixed-race people made up a small percentage of the population, opponents envisioned a flight to that category that would harm the larger racial groups. Billy Tidwell, research director for the National Urban League, in the press and in his own testimony before Congress, went as far as to predict that 10% of the black population would desert that classification. While African American groups were the most vocal about this threat, Latino, American Indian, and Asian groups voiced the same opinions. Between the 1993 congressional hearings and O.M.B.'s final decision, many of these groups issued statements against adding a new category, sponsored research into its effects, and lobbied against it.

The irony was that the Multiracial Movement, which claimed it was relevant to civil rights, gained the ire of premier organizations. People in the movement saw themselves as visionary, but others saw them as misguided, repeating that, considering the persistence of racial oppression, it was too soon to add the new category. As opposed to the promises of a new multiracial identity, they imagined a dystopia if the Multiracial identifier came into being. Warning that it would come at the expense of blacks, journalist Itabari Njeri asserted, "If African Americans are not included in the designation— and in a way that ensures our hard-won constitutional protections—there should be no such designation."[84] Lisa Jones even accused Multiracialists of trying to steal mixed African American figures such as Langston Hughes, an act insensitive to a history "where black people have had their every gift confiscated and attributed to others."[85] Jon Michael Spencer made explicit the opposition between black consolidation and the possibility of a Multiracial category:

> It has been by our numbers and unity, both a result of the one-drop rule, that we have made strides in attaining civil rights in this country. In fact, from the days of slavery we were Colored, Negro, Black, Afro-American, and African American together, and together we have come this far "by faith." By that faith and determination black leadership and grassroots activism have pushed the needs of the black community and the ideals of the country to the forefront of the national consciousness and of political agendas.[86]

With this perspective, it was clear to Spencer that "we need to count every black or part-black as black."[87] Like the others, he evoked a very traditional and popular way of thinking about the black experience, one that apotheosized the civil rights movement to the point of resistance to unfamiliar means to make gains for racial equality. By railing against new modes of identification, these opponents defended older modes resembling hypodescent.[88]

Few critics voiced the fourth objection, but it drove at the fundamental presumptions of the Multiracial category: it often perpetuated the idea that racially mixed people were a new phenomenon in the United States, an untenable position, since there has been racial mixing since first contact. A "biracial baby boom" beginning only after *Loving v. Virginia* is questionable because it relied on parsing out interracial marriages from past iterations of census data, which allowed for only one race. This gave the impression that racially mixed people spawned within the past decade or so. Secondly, the number of mixed births appeared to skyrocket because determining who had racially mixed parents became more difficult as one looked back further in time. But ignoring those generations results in their erasure. Lastly, asserting a "biracial baby boom" relies on voluntary self-identification with two or more races, when that data simply did not exist before 2000. While immigration reform, the end of anti-intermarriage laws, and social integration have changed society immensely, accounting for past mixed births is a complex matter that existing statistics may or may not corroborate.[89]

The three principal tests that the Census Bureau ran between 1995 and 1996 were the Current Population Survey (C.P.S.), the National Content Survey (N.C.S.), and the Race and Ethnic Targeted Test (R.A.E.T.T). The first gathered data on how people answered the Hispanic-descent question, revealing that people with some national origins were more likely to answer it than others. The second used different formats of the question to see what might reduce the Other respondents. Among other things, the third included a Multiracial category in hopes of decreasing use of the Other category, but the results showed that Hispanics were still likely to pick more than one group, even when the instructions prohibited it. In hopes of respecting Hispanics' modes of identification and avoiding the need for more tabulation, the Census Hispanic Advisory Committee and most Hispanic organizations decided against the proposal to make Hispanic a racial group.

These tests, conducted by phone, mail, and door-to-door enumerators, also assessed the efficacy of a Multiracial category, leading to a conclusion that 1.6% of all Americans would choose it. At the same time that O.M.B. stated, "We would not make a change unless we were convinced it would increase the accuracy and the value of the data collected," Graham expressed her dedication to the cause, leading up to the final congressional hearings before O.M.B. would make its decision. "So even if the O.M.B. doesn't do the right thing, we're not going away."[90] If there had been any question about

Susan Graham's political leanings, they found resounding answers in June 1997. A resident of Speaker of the House Newt Gingrich's congressional district, Graham had been trying to get an appointment on his calendar for two years. When she finally got a ten-minute slot, she presented the case to the congressman, and he quickly agreed, "This is the right thing to do for the children."[91] Over the coming weeks, Gingrich issued a number of statements supporting the category. As he wrote to O.M.B. director Franklin Raines, "I believe that we can begin to address the country's racial divide by adding a multiracial category to federal forms and the United States Census while simultaneously phasing out the outdated, divisive and rigid classification of Americans."[92] He also made it clear that this endorsement was part of his broader conservative agenda that coupled the new category with dismantling affirmative action programs. As Kim M. Williams, author of *Mark One or More: Civil Rights in Multiracial America*, summarized, "Democrats wanted multiracial recognition *without* adverse civil rights consequences; Republicans wanted multiracial recognition *with* adverse civil rights legislation."[93]

At the same time, Representative Tom Petri (R-Wisconsin) pushed legislation called the "Tiger Woods Bill" that would establish a national Multiracial category. This was independent of any endorsement from the golfer or the Multiracial groups. By this point, Woods no longer addressed the matter, but Project R.A.C.E. was happy to receive the support. Success by Petri, who also had a dismal civil rights voting record, would supersede any O.M.B. decision. The weeks leading to the federal agency's recommendation were hopeful for A.M.E.A.'s and Project R.A.C.E.'s goal, even though opponents continued their arguments against it.[94]

The Tiger Woods Bill never went to a vote, and civil rights organizations that had not participated in the 1993 hearings made statements at the 1997 hearings. Having learned that the low percentage of people who might choose Multiracial would affect African Americans nominally, the N.A.A.C.P.'s representative supported multiple checking. On the contrary, the National Asian Pacific American Legal Consortium and the National Congress of American Indians, learning that their constituents' higher rates of out-marriage could mean changes in their representation, called for further testing or no change at all. Finally, on October 30, 1997, the Congressional Subcommittee on Census, Statistics, and Postal Personnel and O.M.B. announced that they would allow Americans to check off as many race categories as they want. This followed an earlier O.M.B. recommendation that the Multiracial category

provided no useful information and the research showed that there is no general understanding of what the term means. Further, having a separate category would, in effect, create another population group, and no doubt add to racial tension and further fragmentation of our population. To provide information about their mixed racial heritage, individuals should be able to check one or more of the historical categories that have been used for the past twenty years.[95]

Federal agencies found "Multiracial" too ambiguous, and they decided to go with a method that would protect the civil rights interests of more traditional racial groups. Lessons from C.P.S., N.C.S., and R.A.E.T.T guided them to place the Hispanic-ethnicity question before the race question, in order to decrease the number of responses of "Other."

At the same time, the decision enacted a simple idea that A.M.E.A. had introduced four years earlier with its proposed reporting standards: allowing respondents to pick more than one race. As O.M.B. director Raines further explained, "We're allowing people to express that multiracial heritage in whatever way they view themselves."[96] While this statement may come across as terse and patronizing, it does point out the flexibility of multiple checking. For years leading up to this moment, Graham and others in the Multiracial Movement wanted to call mixed-race people "exactly what they are" but took for granted that all agreed with the Multiracial label, which was a gross simplification of most people's heritage. O.M.B.'s solution made it clear that the government was enumerating membership in (and across) racial groups, leaving the matter of fine-tuning for individuals to sort out some other time with lower stakes. Multiple checking allowed for a variety of self-identification that reflects a group of people who may be any combination of white, black, Asian, Indian, or otherwise. O.M.B. promoted a conception of mixed race as consisting of the legacies of standing racial groups that still depend on racial enumeration. Rather than adopt a new vocabulary to describe the mixed-race experience, it opted for a new method of employing the standing vocabulary, taking the wind out of the racial heroes' cape.

Fernández, who had concluded his term as A.M.E.A. president by this point, responded that although he preferred the Multiracial category, the decision was "the best compromise possible at this time."[97] Also disappointed, Graham said that the recommendations "fall short of what is needed for accuracy and clarity on the United States Census and on federal forms. Multiracial children deserve the dignity and inclusion of having a racial term that describes exactly who they are."[98] She lamented, "We do not want to be the check-all-that-applies community. We want to be the multiracial community."[99] While these two indicated that they would continue to advocate for the Multiracial category and hoped that the census would enumerate those who checked two or more racial groups separately, Ramona Douglass, the new president of A.M.E.A., called the decision a "victory for the whole country in the sense that Americans will no longer be cubby-holed into rigid categories. This decision really puts it to all of us to look at each other and how we identify in a different way. The country is no longer one or two races, and that's been obvious for a long time."[100] Representative Petri said he was satisfied with the decision, marking the end of the Tiger Woods Bill, and Candy Mills, editor of the newsletter *Interrace*, responded, "Let's not argue about semantics. After all, our children defy racial categories—even the multiracial one."[101]

In the end, 2.4% of the U.S. population checked two or more races on the 2000 census, or approximately 7 million out of 281 million people. In total, there were sixty-three possible combinations, with the four most common combinations being white and black, white and Asian, white and American Indian/Alaska native, and white and Other; 5% of blacks, 6% of Hispanics, 14% of Asians and 2.5% of whites identified with two or more races. The number of people checking two or more races also varied by state, with Mississippi at the low end with less than 1%, and California at top with 4.5%.

However, in addition to those who picked two or more races were those who picked Other as their one race, 5.5% of the population. Once again, many of these were Hispanics. This was more than double the two-or-more respondents, producing a total of nearly 8% challenging the singular understanding of race. Mixed-race identity is just part of this shift. The efforts of the Multiracial Movement did raise consciousness of the issue, but many other trends made the changes of the 2000 census possible. These include the visibility of positive symbols of mixing such as *Time*'s New Face of America and pro golfer Tiger Woods. Only two positive symbols by 2000. But they also include the crumbling reliability of monoracial identification in the U.S. Census Bureau. Looking further, the agents for change also resonate with past figures such as Wendell Phillips, Albion Tourgée, and Jean Toomer. Altogether, these voices help us see that the events of the 1990s are part of a tradition of progressive thought on mixed race.[102]

7

Praising Ambiguity, Preferring Certainty

At the beginning of the 2000s, Gallup polls indicated a higher acceptance of interracial marriage than in past decades. Public conversations about the Multiracial category made front-page news. The success of mixed celebrities seemed to prove that racial prejudice had crumbled. However, three centuries of racial thinking that relied on firm categories conditioned Americans into needing to know each other's racial identity in order to process him or her. Since racialization by origin, appearance, and custom has exerted such a force on life in the United States, knowing a person's race is a prominent way to understand his or her background, tastes, and priorities. More often than not, though, it requires making generalizations. What one understands as white, black, Hispanic/Latino, Indian, or Asian is the product of one's own perspective, which has limitations. Members of any of these groups can recount exchanges in which someone has made presumptions about them because of their physical appearance. In the current, post-civil-rights moment, each of these groups has signature encounters that have risen to cliché. In addition to revealing that many people are ill equipped to understand the lives of others, these microlevel experiences reveal how deeply racialization influences us.

Racially mixed people also have signature experiences, the most prevalent being the "What are you?" moment, in which a new acquaintance asks for one's racial background immediately upon meeting. It is reductive, assuming that one's makeup is the whole of one's identity. It is also dehumanizing, requiring that a mixed person justify his or her existence as an object. Often, the question comes out of context, with a jarring effect. Sometimes it comes right after learning one's name (or even before), revealing that the inquisitor cannot proceed without knowing the answer to the question. Since physical appearance persists as the primary way Americans discern racial identity, the ambiguity of a racially mixed person can produce a mystery for many. In turn, this produces the wish to solve the mystery. The most eager of these new acquaintances holds racial identity as the primary way to understand another person; and the question becomes a mystery to solve, and receiving an answer is very satisfying. On an interpersonal scale, this is the way

Americans praise ambiguity but prefer certainty. The mystery is exciting, but the solution is what they really want.

More often than not, the "What are you?" moment comes from a benign wish to get to know an ambiguous-looking person better. The speaker may consider blended features to be exotic and stories of mixed backgrounds especially interesting. Since the development of the Tragic Mulatto, who was exceptionally beautiful if female or exceptionally dashing if male, positive notions around comeliness have surrounded racially mixed people in the United States along with the more prominent negative notions. In the current moment, it appears that positive notions match the negative.

Some mixed people, such as Vin Diesel, star of *Pitch Black*, *XXX*, and *The Fast and the Furious*, have made a point of concealing their racial makeup. Whether the moviegoing public knew he was mixed or not, it delighted in the urbane, confident, muscular values he embodied. As Rob Cohen, his director in *The Fast and the Furious* and the *XXX* franchise, said, "He's a new American. You don't know what he is, and it doesn't even matter, because he's everybody. Everybody looks at Vin and goes, 'I see myself.'"[1] However, the public withheld higher adoration from Diesel, in part, because it could not categorize him. This is because, while Americans praise ambiguity, they prefer certainty. In general, they have settled on monoracial ways of understanding racially mixed people, rather than adopt more complex paradigms that appreciate the ambiguities they initially praise. Even though laws against interracial intimacy are a memory, acceptance has surpassed past levels, and mixed figures are more visible than ever, the tensions between stabilization of racial identity and defense of racial mixing have remained relevant.

Since April 2001, when the Census Bureau released basic data on race from the previous decennial, several areas of discourse made titillation over blended physical appearances even more explicit. More so, they helped Americans process physical appearances, backgrounds, and public figures that many had never encountered before. In turn, they helped Americans express their thoughts in a liberal way. The first decade of the twenty-first century has been a short period of time, recent enough that one might miss the connections. But placing recent discourse on ambiguity on a continuum reveals the historical roots that connect it to past and future episodes.

The use of racially mixed people as symbols of progress has been most prominent in visual representations of mixed faces and bodies. Some were models showcasing goods in print ads. Some were actors, whether box-office draws (such as Vin Diesel, Halle Berry, and Keanu Reeves), smiling faces populating commercials, or extras diversifying a mise-en-scène. Others were regular subjects in photographs illuminating some point about American demographics. Regardless of which type, their presentation divulged the subjects' racial backgrounds. For example, photos accompanying Stanley Crouch's *New York Times Magazine* article "Race Is Over" featured several mixed-race children whose future would be free of racial discord. The captions provided each of their racial makeups. Articles in cognitive psychology did the same, creating more computer-generated mixed faces to quantify people's attraction to racially mixed faces. Art photography such as Kip Fulbeck's "Hapa Project" collected headshots with each subject's self-description, plus the ethnicities in their backgrounds below. Along with illustrating the ambiguity-certainty paradox, this subset illustrates the American propensity for scientization—in other words, labels, quantifiable measurements, and the authority of those who work with these methods. These representations were the newest in a long tradition: *Casta* paintings from eighteenth-century Mexico did the same thing, giving names to the array of racial combinations in the Spanish colony. Eugenicist Charles B. Davenport charted mixed people's complexions using the spectrum from the Milton Bradley Color Wheel toy. Caroline Bond Day also measured complexions and offered fractions of racial makeup in her book *A Study of Some Negro-White Families in the United States*, which praised the achievements of mixed African Americans. The New Face used Morph 2.0 software to create specific combinations of features from supposedly representative ethnic appearances.[2]

On one hand, marketing and advertising executives claimed that their usages reflected the changing face of race, that the United States was becoming more diverse and mixed. But they were also very frank about their true motivation: to appeal to more kinds of consumers. When using the appeal of mixed race to sell movie tickets, the values the actors embodied were part of the commodity. In cover articles, learning a mixed star's racial makeup was an added value to the purchase, as the pieces usually explored their background. This subset of trends guided the mostly nonmixed public in how to discuss racial makeup, ambiguous appearance, and celebrity. They reflected ongoing discourses on mixture in the United States, guiding reactions to the cases that followed.

Consumer D.N.A. tests illustrated the ambiguity-certainty paradox as they recast the tensions in ways both new and old. At a fee, the curious sent a swab of cell tissues to companies such as DNAPrint and received results saying where their genetic material came from. The points of origin coincided with the earth's continents, reinforcing the notion harking back to proslavery racial scientists: that different races had fixed origins. At the same time, results from the Human Genome Project reemphasized that the differences between what we call races is nominal, following Ashley Montagu and the other scientists of the twentieth century who worked to put an end to racial science. While multiple checking was an issue that racially mixed people saw as their own, D.N.A. tests appealed mostly to people without racial mixture in their immediate background. Like the box checking of the 2000 census, the molecules achieved a figurative power, helping the public grasp racial mixture. Counting them helped Americans manage the mysteries of genetic makeup. Even more, it helped them interpret the racial mixture of the people they encountered. Consumer D.N.A. tests relied on recent breakthroughs as well as age-old notions. With the expansion of common knowledge about scientific advances, these contradictory ideas circulated simultaneously, and Americans cobbled together meanings that included them all.[3]

The third of these phenomena of the early 2000s was the emergence of Barack Obama on the national scene. His white grandparents moved from Kansas to Hawaii, where their daughter met his father, an international student from Kenya. Obama was born in 1961, but his father soon left to seek a Ph.D. at Harvard and then move back to Kenya. The boy's mother remarried a few years later, to an Indonesian businessman, and the family moved to Djakarta. She sent Barack back to Hawaii to attend a prestigious prep school and live with his grandparents. He attended Occidental College in Los Angeles and then transferred to Columbia University. In March 2004, journalist and novelist Scott Turow wrote, "No other figure on the American political scene can claim such broad roots within the human community. Obama is the very face of American diversity."[4] In July, Obama spoke at the Democratic National Convention supporting John Kerry's candidacy for president and offering his racial makeup as a case of the universal relevance of the American dream.[5]

Like the mixed girl whom Wendell Phillips presented to the Sixteenth Ward Republican Association, *Time* magazine's New Face of America, and Tiger Woods, Obama was a symbol of equality, progress, and utopia. As usual, Americans needed to hear his racial makeup to know how to process him and then to confer universal praise on him. The tension between complex ambiguity and easy-to-comprehend certainty continued when he announced his candidacy for the president of the United States in February 2007. Although debates shifted over the coming months, they lingered throughout his campaign. The question whether he was black enough, measuring his mixed experience against arbitrary criteria of authenticity, was simultaneous with reminders that he was mixed. By his Election Day victory, three forces fixed Obama as black: First was the label *black president*, a moniker that made his interracial family apocryphal. Second was the link many observers made between slavery and that event. Many newscasters drew a straight line from slavery to the civil rights movement to November 4, 2008, as the resolution of those difficulties. Third, and closely related, was the connection the media made between Obama and African Americans more broadly, making it their victory, more than one that any American could appreciate. Others declared his victory the arrival of postraciality, a condition where racial difference no longer mattered and racial identity was merely descriptive. It was easier to understand Obama as either of those certain categories, even if the latter was an antilabel, than to understand him as mixed. A smaller set of writers reminded us of his mixed background, praising him as a bridge between all races, noting a boost in mixed-race self-esteem, and anticipating a further breakdown of predominant racial thought. But their explications lost out to the black and postracial labels. More broadly, these shifts show that many people settle on a monoracial (or raceless) understanding of racially mixed Americans, rather than behold the ambiguity that is so attractive to them. The conflict between demonizing and heroizing racial mixture persists. Because the desire for racial certainty remains, even with monumental social change, putting these cases in conversation produces a warning against taking contemporary praise of racial mixing and racially mixed people at face value.

The use of racially mixed models to cast social change in a positive light continued from the 1990s. Even without verbal cues, their appearances in print ads, commercials, and film scenarios evoked favorable associations with youth, diversity, and style. Their unconventional physical features brought an enigma to the products they represented. Racially ambiguous bodies serve as a riddle to solve or an exercise of reverse engineering when the answer is present. Sometimes the cipher remains, but most often discovering the makeup is the ends. As Caroline Streeter suggested in her essay "The Hazards of Visibility" regarding mixed-race females appearing as symbols of racial harmony, "Yet when we look closely, it is clear that a deep ambivalence about miscegenation undergirds these images, whether they are designed to seduce the viewer with a mixed race woman's sexual availability or to convince us that buying jeans somehow constitutes antiracist activity."[6] While Streeter described how the desire for mixed bodies and the desire for racial equality were independent of each other, her analysis applies to the conflict between fascination with ambiguity and the need for certainty.

For decades, modeling and casting had reinforced white normative standards of beauty, best shown by the lack of minority supermodels until the 1970s and later. Like many fields, these industries like to congratulate themselves for integrating since then, but selling products has been their ultimate concern, not social change in itself. Consideration of racial minorities in marketing strategies rose with appreciation of them as consumers. By the 1990s, the abundance of products and the variety of people to sell them to around the world made a change in media representations common sense. But marketers often depicted their reactions as timely rather than late. In these self-congratulatory spells, executives were explicit about the bottom line, revealing that profits, in dollars and cents, were the certainty that they were seeking. For example, a *Newsweek* piece appearing after Tiger Woods's ascent covered how corporations began using ambiguous ethnicity to sell their wares. Through the words of a Calvin Klein spokesperson, author John Leland revealed that corporations were using mixed celebrities, the Internet, and MTV to reach more and more young consumers. "Companies like Nike, Calvin Klein and Benetton are working ethnicity as an idiom of commerce; it adds value to a pair of sneakers or a cotton T shirt. At a time when young people are buying corporate conceptions of 'alternative,' ethnic ambiguity confers both individuality and a sense of shared values."[7] The article claimed that mixed celebrities were "altering the lines of racial phenotype," as if white norms of beauty were oppressing people, rather than racism, the hierarchical social structure based on perceived physical differences.[8]

However, the executives have not invented this strategy by themselves. They purveyed the images and values that the public desired. Consumers, both as a whole and in particular markets, wanted to see more minorities in the media, so executives created representations that affirmed an integrated, diverse United States. They realized that more audiences would respond to ambiguous bodies, not out of their own ingenuity but because they paid attention to how consumers thought. As Gia Madeiros of K. K. Branding explained, "Basically, people want to see a little bit of themselves in the images they see, even if it's just part of what they see, and this is what we give them."[9] Along with this minute narcissism was the cipher that many people see in racially mixed figures; they enjoy seeing the ambiguity, but they want to solve (or dissolve) it.

By 2001, many advertisers, marketers, and casting directors demanded a multiracial look, often in the same breath as reflections on the latest decennial census data. Paula Sidlinger, a casting executive citing scores of requests for the mixed look, said that a mix of Asian facial features and kinky hair, for example, conjured up an immediate sense of both globalization and technology. "The blended look says 'we're all in this together' and that the 'world's getting smaller.'"[10] However, just as readily as these executives put mixed youth on a pedestal, they admitted that tapping into markets was their objective. As one director of multicultural insights and strategy suggested, "Multiracial consumers are giving us a jump start on how America is going to look in the future," reflecting a belief that "the multiracial market today provides the best glimpse at the future of the U.S. consumer marketplace."[11] Those 2.4% who chose two or more races on the 2000 census supposedly proved that it is a small world after all. Emphasizing mixed Americans under eighteen, these movie makers, advertisers, and casting directors would have us believe that three million youths are the future for everyone.

In December 2003, the *New York Times* published an article by Ruth La Ferla, "Generation E.A.: Ethnically Ambiguous," that profiled more executives who made the motivations explicit. *Teen People's* managing editor, Amy Barnett, reflected on the use of racially mixed models in its pages: "We're seeing more of a desire for the exotic, left-of-center beauty that transcends race or class. [It] represents the new reality of America, which includes considerable mixing. It is changing the face of American beauty."[12] Ron Berger, C.E.O. of Euro R.S.C.G. M.V.B.M.S. Partners, stated that the company was seeking out these models to appeal to young consumers: "Today what's ethnically neutral, diverse or ambiguous has tremendous appeal. Both in the mainstream and at the high end of the marketplace, what is perceived as good, desirable, successful is often a face whose heritage is hard to pin down."[13] This article, like many of its type, asserted that Beyoncé's blond hair, Jennifer López's masquerade as an Asian princess in Louis Vuitton ads, and Christina Aguilera's East Indian costumes in *Allure* magazine reflected "a current fascination with the racial hybrid," confusing the combination of cultural fetishes with the relationships and offspring of real people. These images appealed to Americans' notions, but they also appealed to consumers of American products worldwide. American producers were selling the idea of cultural and physical mixing to global markets. Models with features evoking places around the world possessed what Peter Lichtenthal, senior vice president of global marketing at Estée Lauder called "broad, universal appeal."[14]

Ironically, one of the most resonant examples of praising ambiguity but preferring certainty came from a mixed-race creator, Kip Fulbeck, whose "Hapa Project" utilized a once-derogatory term meaning "half" in native Hawaiian to describe a diverse group of mixed Asian Americans. The term has become very popular as a descriptor among this group. Its usage by student organizations such as Hapa Issues Forum, various mixed-race discussion boards on Yahoo! Groups, and even a chain of sushi restaurants in Colorado divorced it from issues of native Hawaiian sovereignty, blood quantum, or colonial appropriation. In regard to racial mixture, Hawaii has become "an idealized and even exoticized history of multiracial unity and acceptance" for mainland mixed Asian Americans.[15] Fulbeck, a visual artist and professor at the University of California–Santa Barbara, photographed over a thousand subjects from the shoulders up, without clothes, accessories, or makeup. Within the traveling exhibition, a color photo of each model appeared with two answers to the question "What are you?" beneath. The first was the subject's own answer, in his or her own handwriting, often revealing nuances of the person's self-identity. The second, typeset lettering at the bottom, listed the person's racial makeup. Altogether, the frames presented an immensely diverse group of ages, professions, social stations. The presence of each model's writing made each very personal, amplifying the subjects' humanity far more than similar anthropological photography ever did.[16]

Every model in Fulbeck's project adopted the same pose, naked and facing forward. The similarity to *Time*'s forty-nine computer-generated faces in "Rebirth of a Nation, Computer Style" was remarkable, especially in the cases where the subject was young. On one hand, this accentuated a high degree of intimacy, but on another, it made the subjects available for the spectator to gaze on, reducing them to their physical appearances, rather than, say, putting them in action with family members, acquaintances, or the world at large. More notably, every model's racial makeup appeared below the photograph, in a typeset font disclosing facts about the subject that were often irrelevant to the autobiographical answer. The subjects' own contributions varied from a toddler's scribbling to full paragraphs. Some showed that they subscribed to utopian notions about the future of racial mixture. For example, the young man (Japanese, French, Chinese, Irish, Swedish, Sioux) in figure 7.1 predicted that everyone would be like him in the year 2500 A.D. Fulbeck explained that he made this choice to "demystify the entire phenotype question by eliminating the mystery itself" and to "purposely celebrate the fact that we do love finding out what each other's heritage is."[17] However, do we all love to find out at first glance? Do we all love telling each other at first glance?

In Fulbeck's introduction to *Part Asian, 100% Hapa*, the project's accompanying book, he levied praise for ambiguity, writing, "What's interesting is ambiguity. What's interesting is the haziness, the blurrings, the undefinables, the space and tension between people, the area between the margins that pushes us to stop, to question."[18] In turn, this was praise of the hapas he photographed, in opposition to the compartmentalized thinking of many Americans. However similar in language to the statements of media executives, these compliments were for others like him. Fulbeck was an insider praising others with similar experiences. However, while the components of "The Hapa Project" provided an affirmation for like-minded individuals, for the outside world they were likely to do something different, providing racial makeups and dissolving the ambiguity that Fulbeck celebrated.

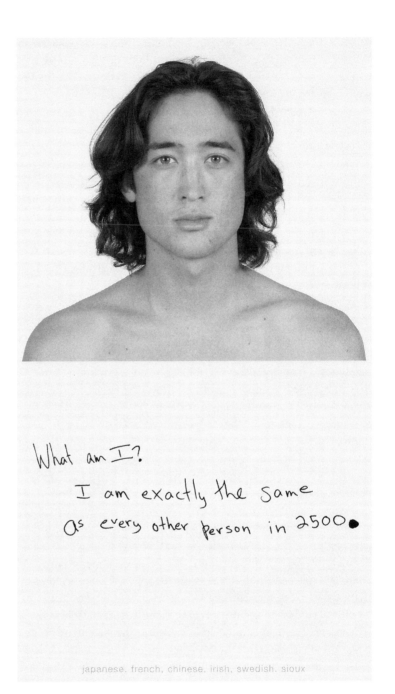

Fig. 7.1. "Japanese, French, Chinese, Irish, Swedish, Sioux"; Kip Fulbeck, "The Hapa Project," 2006

"The Hapa Project" appeared as an exhibition at the Japanese American National Museum from June 8 through October 29, 2006. Here, the curators presented an interesting variation on Fulbeck's method, allowing patrons to post their own Polaroid photo and handwritten caption. Many did share their racial makeup, but some did not. Unlike the typeset revelations, they were able to phrase their statement however they liked, sometimes in very creative ways. A few were not even racially mixed in the conventional sense, but they used the space to reflect on some kind of mixture in their lives. Some snapshots contained more than one person, demonstrating that subjects considered their companions part of their identities. All the samples in this growing collection showed people in their daily wear, rather than naked, and all the samples featured expressions of the models' own choosing, rather than blank faces (see figure 7.2).[19]

By the early twenty-first century, D.N.A. had became a sort of celebrity. It played a prominent role in the O. J. Simpson case, even if an unreliable one. It entered the public imagination again upon the announcement that Scottish scientists had cloned an adult sheep. Every week on detective shows, a forensic scientist would explain that D.N.A. was the blueprint for the human body. And in early 2001, two teams announced that they had mapped and sequenced 90% of the three billion nucleotides in the human genome and had identified all the genes present in it. A boon for biotechnology, the findings of both the international, publicly funded effort and the private, corporate team aimed to gain deeper understanding of predispositions to illness, the specific genes associated with diseases, and possible therapeutic procedures. Additionally, the completion of the Human Genome Project offered greater understanding of humanity, cleaving once and for all the connection between science and a functional understanding of race. Upon the findings of the National Human Genome Research Institute, Francis Collins, director of the international effort, reiterated that the concept of race had no scientific basis. As he said in one interview,

> We are 99.9 percent the same at the D.N.A. level. Regardless of what ethnic or racial group we self-identify with, that statement is true. That's because we are a young species. We are descended from a common ancestral pool about 100,000 years ago when we were all black Africans. Our differences that we place such intense focus on in terms of skin color or hair texture or facial features are a tiny fraction of the differences that exist. What we are learning is there is no scientific basis for drawing boundaries around particular ethnic groups and saying, "They're different."[20]

I am a 26 year old woman who is also a 4th generation Japanese American (yousei!) with an equal amount of Afro. American/creole heritage AND roots in east LA!

♡ full hapa ♡

Fig. 7.2. "Japanese American, Afro. American/Creole" (Photo courtesy of DiscoverNikkei.org, a project of the Japanese American National Museum)

Yet everyday talk about genes and race attributed much more to this 0.1%. At the same time that there was praise of ambiguity, tests claimed to determine clients' racial makeup with exact percentages, reentrenching essentialist ideas about race.

The leader in this field, DNAPrint, had been an enterprise that would use D.N.A. to help doctors best prescribe medical treatments, such as chemotherapy, but then the company began to publicly sell its stock and patented two tests specifically for military and law enforcement use in 2002. One promised to reveal the eye color of crime suspects solely on a D.N.A. sample, and the other, hair color. Even at this point, Tony Frudakis, the company's C.E.O., admitted that skin color would be much harder to determine, an admission that, while they could divine some signs of physical appearance from D.N.A., more complex markers of racial/ethnic identity were harder to ascertain. After all, many factors beyond gene sequences determine one's skin color. In reality, while ancestry influences one's genes, our physical appearances may differ from what our genes indicate. Even though many contemporary geneticists have attempted to deemphasize the relationship between human diversity and physical appearances, much of the public considers genes to be the ingredients of the differences they perceive. Many people know that genes gather to make physical characteristics, and they also believe that groups that share these characteristics belong to the same race. Even with all the coverage of scientific advances, it is easy for people to believe that genes are what race is made of. But their understanding remains at a murky level, allowing genes to replace what blood did for eighteenth- and nineteenth-century thinkers on heredity, resulting in correlations that are direct, causal, and inevitable.[21]

The disconnect between genes, ancestry, and physical appearance grows when we consider racially mixed people. With DNAPrint's test results, it is questionable whether a person has parents from different racial groups or simply has racial mixture in his or her family history. Many people who look mixed are not, and many who are mixed may not look it. Or, depending on the observer, one can squarely look like something one is not. These complications become even more complex when we consider American racial groups that have a great deal of racial mixture in their histories. For example, the history of Latinos has made them a mixture of indigenous, European, African, and in some cases, Asian descent. But is Hispanic/Latino D.N.A. just Indo-European D.N.A. plus Native American D.N.A., as DNAPrint's leading spokespeople were willing to propose to their law enforcement clients? The same is true of African Americans, 80% of whom have some racial mixing in their background. Likewise, people with Native American descent make up one of the largest groups that checked two or more races in the 2000 census. In terms of genetic material, how does this kind of mixture differ from someone whose immediate family has members from any of these groups? With unreliable correlation between physical features and genes, how reliable can any test results be? Judging from census data on racial mixing alone, these are relevant questions for all these racial groups, as well as for others who checked two or more races.[22]

All the while, as Tony Frudakis said, the tests "belie the myths on which racism is based" by proving that "in all of us, especially in the U.S., there is a continuum of ancestries."[23] His business partner, Mark Shriver, added, "By showing the continuum of genetic variation among people, our test dispels race as a scientific way of categorizing people."[24] In April 2005, an article about Samuel M. Richards, a sociology professor who offered students this test to reveal how racially diverse they are, gives an example of how it can complicate students' racial thinking. One student who identified as black found out she had more European D.N.A. than African D.N.A. She wondered how much the country has progressed in regard to race, saying, "I think the test is really interesting; I had to know. But it makes me question, why are we doing this? Why do people, especially in this country, want to know? Why are we, as a people, so caught up in race?"[25] However, DNAPrint was ill equipped to answer these questions. A visit to the website for their most profitable product, AncestryByDNA, led to a statement acknowledging how hard it was to separate culture and biology from the concept of race "in general use." In the "Frequently Asked Questions" section, the company took a position antagonistic to the idea of race as a social construction: "Over the past few decades there has been a movement in several fields of science to oversimplify the issue declaring that race is 'merely a social construct.' While, indeed this may often be true, depending on what aspect of variation between people one is considering, it is also true that there are biological differences between the populations of the world."[26] In so many words, the company took a position against the major interventions of the past fifty-odd years. The statement cited skin color as a "clear example of biological difference." This was ironic, given that skin color was one of the hardest things to determine by genes alone, and the one area DNAPrint was having troubles developing a test to determine. The statement on race closes by attempting to divorce race from ancestry:

> Race is a complex and multivariate construct that we tend to over simplify but in our analysis, we are measuring a person's genetic ancestry and not their race. Your D.N.A. has no recorded history of your political, social,

personal or religious beliefs. It is a simple four letter code that records all of the changes in the D.N.A. from one generation to the next. We report those changes, they are like finger prints and snowflakes, unique and wildly complex.[27]

Just as it was the advertiser's, marketer's, and casting agent's job to reach audiences rather than to promote racial interaction, it was the consumer geneticist's job to sell D.N.A. tests, not to explain the difference between race, culture, genotype, and phenotype. The company preferred to leave customers to their own beliefs, regardless of their implications. Genes became the indivisible starting point for each person's creation, coming together like water molecules in a snowflake. In the end, the company's professions against race seemed disingenuous. They offered certainty about race, even if they defined it as ancestry. By confirming the perceived links between physical appearance, geography, and inheritance, they made ancestry very close to race.

For many people, the tests gave quantifiable answers from the natural sciences and mathematics, forsaking history, whether the discipline itself or knowledge about the experiences of peoples. These positivist fields give authority to the results, rather than an understanding of migration, immigration, or intergroup relations in the United States, which can be far more ambiguous. A blue-eyed man in Appalachian Tennessee would never question how he ended up with D.N.A. that was "45 percent Northern European, 25 percent Middle Eastern, 25 percent Mediterranean (Greek/Turkish), and 5 percent South Asian."[28] Even if the results were accurate, D.N.A. tests neglected to explore the history behind the results. Customers could delve further, or they could be content to let DNAPrint's count lie. It was also possible that people wanted concrete affirmation that they were "unique and wildly complex" via the fractions produced by their popular test, AncestryByDNA. With five major geographic groups, there were countless combinations that the test could report, especially since the proportions did not follow the binary standards (halves, quarters, eighths, etc.) common when talking about people's parentage. Perhaps users got some kind of satisfaction from results that showed they were as unique as *Time*'s New Face of America or more complex than Tiger Woods.

While some people sought DNAPrint's services to learn more about their family histories, others admitted that they were seeking material gain. For example, one white father with white adopted twins of "slightly tan-tinted skin" got results that said they were 9% Native American and 11% northern African. He planned to use this information for obtaining college financial aid. The father said, "Naturally when you're applying to college you're looking at how your genetic status might help you. . . . I have three kids going now, and you can bet that any advantage we can take we will."[29] This was a clear case where customers used the tests to gain access to resources, a sort of possessive investment in D.N.A. As one woman who traced part of her ancestry back to a Scottish oil magnate said, "There's a kind of checkmate-ness to the D.N.A." In other words, she wanted to use the D.N.A. results to trump any claims that she did not deserve any of the industrialist's estate. Overall, what the public wanted from DNAPrint's tests was definite racial makeup, not ambiguity or the jettisoning of racial thinking. To date, there are a handful of companies that have joined DNAPrint in the field of consumer genomics, including D.N.A. Heritage and GeneTree. People looking for exact answers find the companies' answers satisfactory.[30]

The activity around Census 2000 prepared Americans for a shift in language around racial enumeration. Racially ambiguous figures trained Americans in looking at racially mixed people. The rising popularity of consumer genomics tests overlaid the Human Genome Project's technological breakthrough onto old racial thought. The emergence of Barack Obama, who became president of the United States, followed close behind. At Harvard Law School, Obama became the first black editor of the *Harvard Law Review*, which gave him his first taste of national recognition and a book deal with Random House.

His memoir, *Dreams from My Father: A Story of Race and Inheritance* (1995), followed the conventions of a *bildungsroman*, focusing on a missing father as much as constructing a racial identity. As Obama described himself as a boy: "I would not have known at the time, for I was too young to realize that I was supposed to have a live-in father, just as I was too young to know that I needed a race."[31] His upbringing in a white family in Hawaii and then an interracial family in Indonesia accentuated his mixed experience. As an adolescent, he began to notice that Bill Cosby never got the girl on *I Spy* and that no one looked like him in the Sears Roebuck catalog. Barack decided that he was black, different from most African Americans but black nonetheless.

From that point, Obama had to assimilate into blackness, and assimilation involves subscription to the dominant group's ways but not a full surrender of one's own. The three main ways he did this were in his dating choices, his choice of religion, and his choice of community. Of the third, he wrote about receiving an invitation from his father during his college years,

And if I had come to understand myself as a black American, and was understood as such, that understanding remained unanchored to place.

What I needed was a community, I realized, a community that cut deeper than the common despair that black friends and I shared when reading the latest crime statistics, or the high fives I might exchange on a basketball court. A place where I could put down stakes and test my commitments.[32]

He chose to reject his father's offer, along with the alternative: returning to Hawaii. He had chosen a race, rather tenuously, as the "if" indicates. However, he was most affirmative about Chicago. Public service would be his proving grounds. Along with marrying Michelle Robinson and joining the Trinity United Church of Christ, this activism shaped his assimilation into conventional African Americanness.

However, after the 2004 introduction to *Dreams from My Father*, in which Obama referred to himself during his Senate campaign as "a black man with a funny name," he did not explicitly call himself black again.[33] His follow-up book, *The Audacity of Hope*, made no such statement. None of the major speeches of his political career have featured him calling himself black, whether the Democratic National Convention in 2004, the launch of his 2008 presidential campaign, the "More Perfect Union" speech during the Jeremiah Wright controversy, the acceptance of the Democratic nomination, the remarks on Election Day, or his inaugural address. He repeated the story of his black father from Kenya and his white mother from Kansas but never called himself "the black son." He consistently used this sort of multiple-checking way of addressing his makeup, which allowed for a number of extrapolations but avoided any clear assertions. In January 2008, upon arriving in Rock Hill, South Carolina, to campaign for that state's Democratic primary, he addressed concerns that an African American candidate could not be effective in Washington. Here, he used another device, answering, "If I came to you and I had polka dots, but you were convinced that I was going to put more money in your pockets and help you pay for college and keep America safe, you'd say, 'Okay, I wish he didn't have polka dots, but I'm still voting for him.'"[34] He did not insert his own identity into statements like this, but the American public did. His assimilation, a sort of racial passing with full disclosure, was successful.[35]

National praise for how the politician worked across racial groups began when journalist and novelist Scott Turow described his modus operandi as a product of his makeup, as if it is an inborn talent. Writing from the perspective of Obama's early political career, Turow ended his piece by suggesting that Obama may "become the embodiment of one of America's most enduring dreams."[36] The apotheosis continued with a cover article in *Time* describing the freshman senator as "the political equivalent of a rainbow—a sudden preternatural event inspiring awe and ecstasy," praising his ability to find common ground with political opponents but also suggesting that he brought together all colors.[37] Articles such as these suggested that his political method was a product of his racial makeup rather than a well-learned strategy. "He transcends the racial divide so effortlessly," Joe Klein wrote, "that it seems reasonable to expect that he can bridge all the other divisions—and answer all the impossible questions—plaguing American public life."[38] The challenges Obama faced matched and surpassed the special talents his racial makeup has conferred on him. Just as mixed-race children were supposed to fix the strife in their families, a mixed-race politician was supposed to fix the whole nation's divisions.

Obama's manifesto, *The Audacity of Hope*, came to bookstores in October 2006. In January 2007, he formed an exploratory committee to consider running for president, a customary move indicating strong intentions. Even before he announced his candidacy the next month, some people declared that he was not really black. Peter Beinart, former editor of the *New Republic*, called him a "good black" with less support from most African Americans than authentic "bad blacks" received. Stanley Crouch conceded that Obama was black but clarified that he was not black like he was, a descendant of western Africans in the Atlantic slave trade. He refused to consider Obama "one of us." Journalist and author Debra Dickerson went further with the criteria for blackness, emphasizing the genealogical difference. She suggested that categorizing Obama as African American demeaned the racial experience that many true African Americans had and allowed his supporters to disregard the legacy of slavery. He was an outsider, free of the weight of that legacy. Just three years before, she had written *The End of Blackness*, a book that argued, "'Blackness' must be updated so that blacks can free themselves from the past and lead America into the future."[39] Now she was drawing a line between African Americans and immigrants of African descent, calling the experiences of the latter invalid because their pasts were different. By association, her view of racially mixed African Americans may have been the same.[40]

After Dickerson made this proclamation, she appeared on Stephen Colbert's news satire show *The Colbert Report* to defend it. His interview revealed the weaknesses of her position initially by suggesting that if Obama did not have the adequate descent to be black, then he should run as a white guy. Colbert knew that Obama's physical appearance made that untenable, and the impossibility of claiming white descent only made Dickerson's protection of black descent absurd. She had to acknowledge that he was black, but a different kind of black, maybe an "African African American." Then Colbert pointed out that had he never heard her distinction, he might have gotten a sense of fulfillment from supporting a black candidate, without being a racist:

DICKERSON: This is a critique of white self-congratulation, of saying we're embracing a black person when we're not really.

COLBERT: Listen, if you hadn't told me he wasn't black I would have thought that I was supporting a black person. And then I would have been supporting all black people. But now I won't because he's not.

DICKERSON: Well, then that would make you a racist.

COLBERT: If I were white. But I don't see race, because I've moved beyond that. I've developed beyond that. I'm so not a racist that I don't see race. People tell me I'm white and I believe them because I think Barack Obama is black.[41]

Here, Colbert further showed his familiarity with Dickerson's assumptions about race and posed the notion that he did not fit within her understanding of whiteness. Lampooning color-blind rhetoric, which dismisses race as irrelevant, he pointed out that her distinctions about blackness could be irrelevant to him or to any other voter. Finally, if the criteria for blackness in the U.S. arena depended on the lived experience of slavery, Colbert proposed, "What if, for just a brief period of time, he were enslaved," perhaps to a real black person, to gain "all the street cred he needs?"[42] This ruse served the coup de grace to Dickerson's narrow conception of blackness, which though it was easy to construct, excluded anyone outside of its narrow parameters. Obama would have to be a slave to satisfy it. Even if the coverage of the sentiment that Obama was not black enough waned, it returned later. It seemed that the public rejected it, rather than incorporating it into their understanding of him. His physical appearance, his dating choices, his beliefs, and his politics outweighed the arguments of naysayers.

In the weeks following Obama's initial announcement of his presidential run, a few outlets published writers on race articulating how he was mixed as well as black. Some emphasized that even with a monoracial self-descriptor, Obama faced expectations from both blacks and whites. This created a double jeopardy in which it was possible that he could disappoint more sets of constituents. Shelby Steele, the mixed black opponent of affirmative action, also argued that Obama would have to make a choice between being a bargainer and a challenger. The former (for example, Oprah Winfrey) let the public forget about racial differences. The latter (for example, Al Sharpton) always emphasized them. Steele suggested, "He has to drop all masks, all obsessions with identity, all his fears of being called a sell-out, and very carefully come to reveal what he truly believes as an individual."[43] This was a statement on political strategy but also advice on how to manage one's position as a racial minority. James Hannaham, one of the few columnists refusing to reduce Obama's mixed identity to one traditional label or two warring bloods, reminded us that Obama's racial reality was complex, even if he and others tried to simplify it. Appreciating this complexity required leaving questions unanswered, an exercise contrary to centuries of racial categorization in the United States.[44]

During the spring of 2008, some news pieces emphasized Obama's mixed background and appreciated his black identity by focusing on his family. A *New York Times* interview with Maya Soetoro-Ng, Obama's half sister, focused on the values their mother upheld in their upbringing, namely, open-mindedness and inclusion. The educator made sure to describe the role of religion in their childhood, to quell any fear that he was a secret Muslim. She characterized her mother's spirituality as agnostic, appreciating all the world religions, rather than atheist, another taboo influence for any political candidate. Soetoro-Ng also explained that she thought of her brother as black, "because that is how he has named himself. Each of us has a right to name ourselves as we will."[45] Her willingness to appear in a major U.S. newspaper, speaking about their upbringing, reminded readers that his was a mixed family with stations all around the world.

Major profiles of Obama's mother, Ann Dunham, followed. They characterized her as a free spirit who found something special wherever she went. Born in 1942 at Fort Leavenworth, Kansas, her father gave her his first name, Stanley, but she began going by her middle name after the family settled in Hawaii and she started at University of Hawaii at Manoa. She met the university's first African student, Barack Obama, Sr., in Russian class as a freshman. After some objection from both families, they were married on February 2, 1961. The younger Barack was born on August 4, 1961, the elder enrolled for graduate study at Harvard University in 1962, and Ann filed for divorce in January 1964. Dunham married again, this time to Lolo Soetoro, an Indonesian student. Maya, her second child, was born in 1970. The family moved to Indonesia, and Ann pushed young Barack to develop his English skills, then sent him back to Hawaii to attend the prestigious Punahou School. Her desire to gain a graduate degree led to her separation from her second husband but ultimately a Ph.D. in anthropology. She followed a career in economic development, focusing on Indonesian village industries. She died of ovarian and uterine cancer at age fifty-two. Along with his sister's interview, these pieces helped familiarized the public with Obama's background.[46] As opposed to The New Face, which came from Morph 2.0 tinkering, he came from a family with idiosyncrasies, geographic connections, and histories. Obama was a member of a cohort of "racialized, transnational children of globalization" who had the potential to reshape social change on an international level.[47] However, any portion of his unconventional upbringing could be a target for critics. Those who wanted to simplify his background had to omit large facets of his makeup to fit their molds.

During the months between the Jeremiah Wright controversy and Election Day, fewer pieces describing Obama as mixed appeared. Still, his candidacy drew more attention to common mixed-race people, their marginalization, and the social networks available to them. Gary Kamiya reminded readers of Salon that Obama was the first black candidate and the first mixed-race candidate. While Obama was operating on a level of public scrutiny greater than that of most racially mixed people, his negotiations still resembled the balancing act that many engaged with. I emphasize that he let the public apply this label to him, rarely using it to identify himself. Both the experiences from Obama's past and the need to satisfy a broad base of voters had led him to this acquiescence. As an adult who assimilated into blackness, his private feelings may have been more complex. Using his candidacy as a case for the end of the one-drop rule was premature. In fact, the choice to let others categorize him as black showed that hypodescent still held sway over public figures' (and regular mixed folks') lives.[48]

An even smaller minority of commentators held Obama's mixture paramount. Richard Rodriguez, an intellectual descendant of José Vasconcelos, was the most articulate of these. In his National Book Award–nominated title Brown: The Last Discovery of America, he described the phenomenon "brown" as a cultural visual murkiness similar to Latin American comfort with mestizaje. As with Vasconcelos's cosmic race, Rodriguez's conception also indicated a higher level of development. Following this argument, he expressed his disappointment with the persistence of the black-and-white paradigm in our public discourse. He acknowledged that historically the one-drop rule had narrowed choices for African Americans, but he also wondered,

> Is it possible, I wonder, after centuries of slavery and injury, after illicit eroticism between black and white, after lynchings, and children who had to choose between one parent or another, . . . is it possible to say brown? Barack Obama is brown. Mixed. There are millions of us in America who similarly belong to more than one race. There are millions of us who belong to contending races or religions or tribes.[49]

As he had argued before, *brown* was an apt term to describe the mixture that had become so visible in the United States. However, brown had been relevant for generations. Rodriguez believed that Obama, like Gloria Anzaldúa's new *mestiza*, possessed an ability to cross borders, to appreciate disparate facets of identity, and to bring transformative consciousness to a society steeped in binary thinking. Rodriguez urged Obama to "help us imagine lives larger than racial designations. A politician might win the day, if he or she were able to speak of the ways our lives are mixed."[50] Rodriguez dared us to leave the matter unsettled, but this was a task few in the United States undertook.

On election night, upon the projections that Obama would win, news programs focused mostly on the reactions of African Americans, whether in Grant Park in Chicago, Spelman College in Atlanta, or Harlem. Camera work showcased blacks celebrating: Oprah Winfrey in tears, clinging to the white man who happened to be standing next to her; Jesse Jackson also in tears, whether joyous, jealous, or regretful of saying he wanted to cut Obama's "nuts out" four months prior; and college students at Spelman, a historically black women's school, rather than Rutgers, which topped *U.S. News & World Report*'s ranking of ethnically diverse universities. These images obscured the fact Americans of all origins had worked on the campaign, that many racial minorities felt gratification over his victory, and that millions of whites had voted for him. The choices that network directors made added "president of the blacks" to the label "the black president."[51]

On November 7, 2008, at Barack Obama's first press conference as president-elect, he spoke about the economy, the federal stimulus package, and his transition team's objectives. The tone of the event changed during the question-and-answer period, when Obama gave a glimpse into his family's adjustment. Of particular interest was their choice of pet for the White House. He answered, deadpan yet jovial,

> With respect to the dog, this is a major issue. I think it's generated more interest on our website than just about anything. We have—we have two criteria that have to be reconciled. One is that Malia is allergic, so it has to be hypo-allergenic. There are a number of breeds that are hypo-allergenic. On the other hand, our preference would be to get a shelter dog. But obviously, a lot of shelter dogs are mutts, like me. So the—so, whether we're going to be able to balance those two things, I think, is a pressing issue on the Obama household.[52]

This was the first time he had addressed his racial makeup beyond his usual formulation, and many people found his spontaneity refreshing. His humor indicated comfort with his racial identity, and it bolstered hopes that a mixed president with an international background would rectify issues that past administrations had mismanaged. The first family ultimately chose a hypoallergenic breed, rather than a mixed dog from a shelter, but for a while it seemed that the new president and the new dog would reflect Crèvecoeur's formulation of the American.[53]

During these weeks following Obama's victory, especially after his "mutts like me" statement, media spaces hosted further discussion of mixed-race identity in general. National Public Radio's Farai Chideya hosted two interviews on the topic. Lise Funderburg, author of *Black, White, Other*, a 1994 collection of interviews with mixed black-and-white Americans, discussed the history of the one-drop rule, the Multiracial Movement, and Obama's candidacy. Funderburg argued that voices for mixed identity and interracial families expanded with the post–World War II baby boom. Some soldiers' international marriages, the repeal of some state anti-intermarriage laws, and the civil rights movement brought more attention to their concerns even before the *Loving v. Virginia* case. Later, Ralina Joseph, a professor at the University of Washington, and Jungmiwha Bullock, president of the Association for MultiEthnic Americans, made two interventions during their interview on N.P.R.: First, just because A.M.E.A. was founded in 1985 did not mean that people in mixed families had not constructed mixed identities in previous periods. Bullock introduced listeners to the Manasseh Society as evidence. (Bullock also discouraged the use of the term *mutt*, as it suggested that mixed offspring were mistakes, less worthy, or mere animals.) Second, Joseph used Barack Obama's racial identity to illustrate how one could be primarily black but also mixed. Such fluidity had advantages over exclusive monoraciality, which diminished one's mixed experience. It also rectified some shortcomings of exclusive multiraciality, which tended to diminish the inequality that parent racial groups experienced.[54]

Some interracial families concurred with these messages, thankful for the attention Obama's racial background was bringing to their issues. Because of the similar experiences they had, they took pride in his success. They also called him multiracial and black, reflecting Joseph's additive labels. Marie Arana, former editor of the *Washington Post*'s Book World, argued that calling Obama black submitted to the one-drop rule. To her, "Progress has outpaced vocabulary."[55] She claimed, "To me, as to increasing numbers of mixed-race people, Barack Obama is not our first black president. He is our first biracial, bicultural president. He is more than the personification of African American achievement. He is a bridge between races, a living symbol of tolerance, a signal that strict racial categories must go."[56] Arana emphasized that Obama's success was one for all Americans. His racial mixture provided lessons in how mixed the United States really is. Following Vasconcelos, Anzaldúa, and Richard Rodriguez, she provided mixed Hispanic/Latino identity as an illustration of this. She also called Obama brown, keeping the ambiguities in focus. In the *American Prospect*, Adam Serwer responded directly to Arana's piece, asserting, "He's black, get over it,"[57] mainly citing Obama's self-identification as black as the basis for this conclusion. Serwer expressed the commonsense understanding of Obama's racial identity, which received widespread validation through the label "black president." But this position also rejected the prospect of ambiguity, even as it acknowledged the distinguishing features of Obama's experience. Serwer's absolutist statement also barred Arana from being able to find a personal connection with Obama.

As a testimony that racial thinking rarely disappears, the idea that Barack Obama was not black returned, this time at the hands of black comedian David Alan Grier, star and creative force behind *Chocolate News*, another news satire show on Comedy Central. On October 2, Grier did a segment questioning whether Obama would be the first black president. Grier emphasized, "Wake up, white America! Barack Obama is not black. He barely even passes the brown paper bag test." In part, this was an exhortation to white voters who may have been resistant to voting for an African American candidate. However, *Chocolate News* was a show mainly targeting a black audience, and Grier spoke on their behalf. The stuff of legends, the "brown paper bag test" marked a line between light-skinned and dark-skinned blacks. But it has been a means for exclusion of both sets, going either way. By invoking that knowledge and dwelling on it, Grier turned the segment into an in-group joke about racial authenticity. As light skin often indicates more racial mixture in one's background, Grier called attention to Obama's mixture as a disqualifying feature. Although comedic in delivery, the segment revealed that the ideas Stanley Crouch and Debra Dickerson defended in February 2007 still had currency. Black comedians take pot shots at mixed black people because they know mixed black people will not retaliate. If they did, they would be racist, as anyone taking shots at black people would be. If mixed blacks object more gently, then black comedians (from H.B.O. to the kitchen table) can accuse them of being unable to take black humor in stride. But this is a double standard exploiting the close relationship between mixed blacks and blacks. It is like having a parent who will accuse you of disobedience if you cry after he or she hits you.[58]

Even with the visibility of mixed-race celebrities, the irrelevance of racial purity on the genetic level, and the election of a black and mixed president, ambiguity remains an elusive concept. In fact, the idea of surpassing race has been easier to grasp. During Obama's 2008 presidential campaign, this idea gained popularity in use of the term *postracial*. This began as a way to describe how his political approach did not cater to any particular racial group. Whereas politicians such as Jesse Jackson and Al Sharpton made their work for their racial constituents primary, Obama focused on universal issues. However, this was an illusion; his advisers considered the race of voters everywhere the campaign led them, even if he rarely addressed it. Just as their approach to the primaries dedicated attention to each state instead of just to the larger ones, they approached interest from every racial group as well as they could, instead of just blacks and whites.[59]

Labeling the Obama campaign postracial was inaccurate, but the descriptor gained momentum as his appeal grew. The media expanded the meaning of postracial to describe the state the country would achieve with an Obama victory. The term's most naive conceptions held that racial distinctions did not matter at all, suggesting that mere visibility of mixed-race people was a sign of the end of race. This resembled philosopher Naomi Zack's belief that mixed was a stopover before racelessness. For example, columnist Mohammad Ali Salih described an encounter with his mixed black-and-white son, in which he wanted to hear the young man identify with two races. The father realized, "His message is now clear: not only that race doesn't matter, but mixed race also doesn't matter. And the new 'post-race' thinking could be equivalent to 'no race.' A country without racial divisions. What a concept."[60] Salih mistook one youth's identity formation with a whole nation's racial organization.

John McWhorter deployed the idea in a more nuanced way. Rather than "mere magazine-cover rhetoric," the linguist and critic argued that an Obama victory would bring us even closer to the goal of the end of race. He cited the influence that eight (presumptive) years of an Obama presidency would have on today's youth, suggesting that his presence would change their perception of success, racial authenticity, and racism. Inequality would still exist, but the next generation's understanding of its solutions would move away from the identity politics that the present and past generations had employed to address it.[61]

David Hollinger, the historian who, in the 1990s, suggested that the mere presence of interracial marriage, double-minority mixed-race people, and the Multiracial Movement corroded monoracial thinking, used Obama's victory as a chance to revive his formulation *postethnic*, which he preferred over *postracial*, even though the meanings were similar. As with the promise of a postracial United States, a postethnic society would "encourage individuals to devote as much—or as little—of their energies as they wished to their community of descent, and would discourage public and private agencies from implicitly telling citizens that the most important thing about them was their descent community."[62] He believed that Obama's ease in either asserting or understating his racial identity was a model for postethnic affiliation. As before, Hollinger overlooked that this kind of flexibility was easier to practice if one had options. If one moves between different social sets and has the luxury of productive alone time, one can pick and choose communities. This kind of mobility comes with privilege; it is much easier to practice with more resources within reach. In the years since the first publication of *Postethnic America*, Hollinger had better formulated his analysis of inequality. In 1995, he dwelled more on freedom of choice than fighting inequality, saying that mixed-race Americans naturally practiced that freedom of affiliation. In his 2008 essay, Hollinger pointed out that inequality persisted, but he decried fixed ideas of community as the primary way to describe it. His praise of mixed race remained, and he concluded, "Obama's destabilization of color lines will be hard to forget."[63] Once again, reliance on Du Bois's catch phrase emphasized physical appearance even though race has little to do with color. Hollinger was not the first, and he would not be the last, to call Obama a racial hero. But of those heralding a postracial America, he had the most grounded arguments, offering a new perspective rather than ignoring problems.

During the 2008 campaign, Obama did name experiences from his own background that gave him a broader perspective. He preferred to call Americans to action collectively, rather than call himself a bridge between races. But he was running for president of the United States, a position that unifies disparate groups, leads us toward progress, and embodies the nation's higher ideals—positive roles that some people have cast racially mixed people into since the early republic. But that was the job any president would have, mixed or not.

Conclusion

Even with a cursory knowledge of U.S. history, many people are familiar with prohibitions to interracial marriage and the characterization of racially mixed people as a threat to society. This project has focused on the lesser-known position, which casts these as benefits to the nation as a whole. Although those voices have been in the minority, they have deployed their message in every period of the nation's history. Evoking our founding documents, they argued that racial mixing was the way to fulfill our destiny as a multicultural democracy. They often addressed the issues of their time but had the goal of universal equality in mind. Rather than considering racially mixed people a population of degenerates, these spokespeople considered them as a sign of progress. An increase in interracial marriage and mixed offspring would indicate that we had reached our secular, utopian goals. Their wish for progress was hopeful, even if it was simplistic.

While some of these spokespeople celebrated the promise of mixed race, I have avoided arguing for progress, especially since one of my main goals has been to interrogate the notion that racial mixing indicates progress. Instead, following conventions in the liberal arts, I have presented cases from different periods to avoid triumphalism. Without obvious connections between them, it may seem that they are random. However, this scattering of examples reflects the resilience of the optimist tradition. While the prosecution of intermarriage, the protection of monoracial categories, and the demonization of mixed-race people have overpowered the defenders of interracialism, that less popular opinion has consistently reappeared. Sometimes, as with Wendell Phillips, the defenders utilized nationally recognized media, and sometimes, as with Caroline Bond Day, they remained unknown until a scholar compiled someone's unpublished papers. However, progress does happen. Over time, through activism, legislation, and other social forces, conditions can improve, not just change. (I am thinking of the span between 1896 and now, not 1967 and now.) Merely recording the mutations of racism is a safe way to practice evenhanded analysis, but it is shortsighted—and masochistic. I eschew equating progress with mixture, but I also want to convey that optimism is reasonable.

So how do we distinguish wishful thinking from real gains, tokenism from collective advances, or (in the case of politicians who use mixed-race success as proof that reparative policies are unnecessary) praise from dismissal. In *Ideology and Utopia*, Karl Mannheim defined *utopia* as "that type of orientation which transcends reality and which at the same time breaks the bonds of the existing order."[1] Whenever optimists gave their vision of a utopian, improved America, it was usually in the future—the newest of the new, or the new-to-come. To distinguish the utopian from the ideological, Karl Mannheim suggested that we can tell by looking into the past:

> Ideas which later turned out to have been only distorted representations of a past or potential social order were ideological, while those which were adequately realized in the succeeding social order were relative utopias. . . . The extent to which ideas are realized constitutes a supplementary and retroactive standard for making distinctions between facts which as long as they are contemporary are buried under the partisan conflict of opinion.[2]

In other words, "A state of mind is utopian when it is incongruous with the state of reality within which it occurs."[3] This seems to defend success of any new regime but actually calls for vigilance toward that which goes on around us in the present. If a position maintains an existent status quo, it is probably more ideological than utopian. But all kinds of ideologies wrestle on the ground, crusading to gain the privilege of securing their own versions of utopia. The imagined future with far more mixed people may as easily be ideological as it may be utopian.

Later I provide a scale to aid in detecting ideologies in the guise of a comely face. But first let us remember that the terms in this conversation have shifted and changed across time and place. At different moments, the definition of what a "race" is has relied on kinship, biology, and culture. The set of "races" prevalent in the United States has fluctuated between three and five or more, depending on who has done the classification. Similarly, the meaning of "mixture" has applied to marriages between European nationalities; types of humans considered different species; and the fusion of culinary, musical, and linguistic idioms. Even with these complexities, mixed race is a useful site of analysis because of the intersections there. What happens if we put intimate exchanges between racial groups at the center of the examination of race and citizenship in the United States? That is, how would discussions of those themes expand by utilizing the ambiguities arising from interracial intimacy? Is it possible to pursue this conversation without casting it as the one hope for the United States, and racially mixed people as the heroes of American race relations? I argue that this approach brings together more themes than food-groupism does, by definition. Interracial intimacy (the sexual relations between people considered members of disparate origins) is a site where multiple historical themes intersect. Thus, thoughtful conversations about mixed race can produce narratives that keep more themes in view.

However, rather than consider this methodology a separate new field that corrects the ills of existing focuses in African American, Latino/Chicano, Asian American, and American Studies, I emphasize that the study of mixed race is integral to each of them. Rather than the successor to implicitly obsolete approaches, it can be a thread that runs through any or all of them, just as the analytic lenses of gender, class, and the like are. This is especially true when antiracist ends motivate the scholarship on race in the United States. Following the examples of the more effective historical defenders of racial mixture, I argue that mixed-race studies is most effective as one aspect of an array of reform, rather than a good in and of itself.

On one hand, this approach emphasizes that talk about racial mixture is old, not new. It has been an issue whites have tried to discipline and minorities have tried to hush. It is a spark neither for celebration nor for repugnance. On the other hand, it sharpens other analytic lenses, magnifying the textures of the United States' seemingly dyadic racial fabric. Most importantly, it brings into focus past and present formations around citizenship and equality.

The contexts for the positive position on mixed race have changed in each period of U.S. history. But they had three characteristics in common. Most apparently, many who espoused this view were men of privilege. Women, the poor, the laboring, and minorities could also construct similar opinions, but the evidence of this unpopular position was more likely to survive coming from men with access to outlets that would disseminate their views. This gender position influenced the features of the discourse they produced. From T.T.'s reverie in the *Liberator* to Scott Turow's praise of Barack Obama, they often cast racially mixed men as agents of change. From William Short's 1798 letter to Thomas Jefferson to the use of racially mixed women in advertising, they often cast mixed women as objects of beauty, and mixed children as symbols of reconciliation.

Marriage, rather than mere interracial intimacy, was the goal. From William Short onward, these spokespeople knew that illegitimate racial mixing was happening. But they all focused on marriage, our society's sanctioned form of relationship. During the Civil War era, the abolitionists decried sexual exploitation as a crime of the slave system. In principle, at least, they preferred matrimony over that type of relationship. More fundamentally, though, they understood special aspects of marriage that were true before then and remain true to this day: marriage involves a romance between two consenting adults that results in a committed relationship. Interracial marriages can inspire the nation to be interracial, consensual, and committed. This thinking, which can place all the responsibility on the mixed, was apparent in Maria Root's "quiet revolution."[4] By promoting diversity and equality, interracial marriages would increase. This was the crux of Wendell Phillips's "United States of the United Races." Rather than mixed race causing the nation's racial problems to disappear, the nation's living up to what he interpreted as the founding fathers' commitment to "the right of all men to life, liberty, and the pursuit of happiness" would inevitably lead to Fum Hoam marrying your cousin and running for Congress.[5] At this point, Phillips stipulated that this Chinese newcomer learn English and adopt Christianity. Six years later, he removed those criteria, but many of the people discussed in this book have praised interracial marriage and racially mixed people—as long as they conformed to respectable American standards.

More often than not, vanguards had no formal connection to allies before or after them. They had to rearticulate their positions from scratch, receive backlash from the majority, and perhaps fade away. Short's proposal remained in private correspondence. Crèvecoeur's novel marked the peak of his popularity with European readers, but his binding of mixture and novelty to American character remained, even after Ralph Waldo Emerson carried on the smelting metaphor in an 1845 journal entry, first published later, in 1912. Phillips and Douglass influenced Tourgée. Haitian refugees to New Orleans influenced the Comité des Citoyens' conception of public rights. If Zangwill had read Crèvecoeur and Frederick Jackson Turner's "The Significance of the Frontier in American History," then he possibly echoed those works.[6] Zangwill's trope quickly gained attention from thinkers on American diversity. Robert Park and his followers absorbed the playwright's inchoate notions toward racial minorities yet praised mixture as the engine of progress. On the other hand, both Jean Toomer and José Vasconcelos offered alternatives to the melting pot that critiqued race in the United States. Scholars rediscovered Toomer in the 1970s, mainly through his novel *Cane*, which was a classic of the Harlem Renaissance. Beyond that, both his writing after, which turned toward mysticism, and his unpublished journals remained obscure until the 1990s. On the other hand, the Chicano movement credited Vasconcelos for their appreciation of *mestizaje*. In turn, Gloria Anzaldúa echoed his ideas in her *Borderlands/La Frontera*, and Richard Rodriguez did the same in his concept of brownness. *Time* magazine's Miscegenation

Matrix resembles colonial Mexico's *casta* paintings, even though two centuries and different traditions separate them. However, fascination with mixed race in the New World may adopt similar forms regardless of the disparate contexts.

Using Mannheim's tenet as a starting point, I offer a checklist for evaluating fascination with racial mixing in the United States: At the most basic level, does the speaker praise racially mixed people for their physical appearance? Doing so is common in our current, post-civil-rights era, tying racially ambiguous physical appearance to exoticism. Similarly, it is easy to flatter people in interracial relationships by predicting that their children will be beautiful merely because of mixture. However, these kinds of statements have existed for centuries, often independent of meaningful approval of interracial intimacy. Some examples of those who inhabited this level alone: William Short praised the "the perfect mixture of the rose & the lilly" in defusing the danger of acknowledging racial mixture in Virginia, but he also proposed emancipation and equality. The Tragic Mulatto figure was either handsome or winsome, gaining sympathy from white viewers and readers. This was true for works indifferent to slavery (which killed off mixed characters) or even antislavery works such as *Uncle Tom's Cabin* (which recolonized them in Africa). The abolitionists who deployed fair-skinned mixed girls on postcards relied heavily on their physical appearance to build sympathy for their cause. One of the most notable uses of physical appearance alone came with The New Face of America on the fall 1993 special issue of *Time* magazine. As a computer-generated image, the woman existed wholly as physical appearance. As the post-civil-rights period progressed, the visibility of racially mixed models corroborated the idea that acceptance of racial mixture has increased. However, with little more than a presentation of the physical appearance of the models, images of them do not take acceptance to the next level.

Does the speaker praise racially mixed people as superior to one of their parent racial groups? This is a sort of backhanded compliment. Today, this comes out in such statements as "You're not like those other people," whether the others be black, Hispanic/Latino, or whatever, hinting at improvement. But it has been prevalent in writing about particular racial groups. For example, those who wished to assimilate Native Americans considered mixed offspring worth educating, while their nonmixed kin would fade into extinction. Most prominently, pupils of Robert E. Park believed that mulattoes were superior to unmixed blacks. His pupil Edward B. Reuter cited specific African Americans with visible mixture (e.g., Du Bois), claiming that their mixture made them the leadership class for blacks as a whole. Everett

Stonequist also suggested that minority progress depended on the life cycle of the marginal mixed man. On one hand, these scholars recognized that white parentage could bring advantages. But on the other, they ignored less mixed leaders and unremarkable mixed folks. The myth of mixed superiority persists to this day when news outlets focus on educated, privileged interracial families, ignoring poor, working mixed folks. This flatters one segment while denigrating another.

Does the speaker suggest that an increase in racially mixed people is a direct correlation to societal change? In other words, is their mere presence, without anything else, proof of progress? This can go hand in hand with the notion that the existence of mixed people can uplift a particular minority group. Croly's hoax pamphlet *Miscegenation* went this far, posing that "the Miscegens of the Future" would populate the whole earth.[7] However, with sensationalism as his goal, he stopped at this level. Israel Zangwill's *The Melting-Pot* suggested that the mere act of love and intermarriage would heal the differences between David and Vera. Park and the social scientists following him continued this line of reasoning by considering rates of intermarriage a prime indicator of progress for minorities. If they could intermarry, then they could progress. From that point, all you have to do is cite statistics to argue how different groups are progressing. Even by the 1960s, Moynihan and Glaser noticed that assimilation was working differently than Zangwill and Park imagined it, leading to one melded white race that refrained from marrying out. Still, intermarriage rates remain the premier indicator of assimilation. Writers praise Asians and Hispanics/Latinos for intermarrying and puzzle over why blacks do not do so at the same rate.

Does the speaker propose that racial mixture will bring about the end of race altogether? This criterion requires a critical eye to detect. Wendell Phillips predicted the end of race as a tool for making distinctions, yet he never predicted the end of races. Neither did he predict that one ambiguous race would populate America. Similarly, the *Plessy* team used a racially mixed plaintiff to challenge Louisiana's use of racial classification, yet they recognized racial identity as something people possessed. Creoles of color were very aware of how the privileges of their identity changed with the United States' acquisition of Louisiana. Still they held on to it rather than announce themselves raceless. Albion Tourgée argued for "colorblind justice," which would make citizenship primarily a national matter, protect all equally, and avoid onerous outcomes for any class. Yet he constantly called attention to race and mixture in his arguments before the Supreme Court. John Marshall Harlan adopted his term *color-blind* to describe the Constitution, but he did believe in a racial hierarchy.

Our postmodern times seem to have amplified the idea of the complete disappearance of race via mixture. Some people believe that figures like *Time* magazine's New Face of America dissolve race, but I argue that like real-world racially mixed people, she is full of race. Through an emphasis on racial makeup, *Time* placed her abundance of racial and ethnic identity alongside middle-class values to "return America to an unhyphenated whole."[8] In the academic realm, Naomi Zack predicted that mixed race was the last step before racelessness. Along with Kwame Kenneth Appiah and others, she argued that racial categories were invalid anyway. Arthur Schlesinger posed Tiger Woods's ascendancy as proof of the curative powers or interracial intimacy. David Hollinger praised the destabilizing potential of racially mixed people, nearly suggesting that it was an inherent trait. With Barack Obama's election successes, writers were giddy to recycle the notion that race no longer mattered, that the United States had reached a postracial level. However, his race influenced every step of his campaign. Immediately after his inauguration, opponents questioned his authority in racial terms, even doubting whether he was a U.S. citizen. To this day, inequality persists, reflecting historical oppression. Wishing away others' ethnic identities via mixture is paternalistic. The well-meaning white wish to blend away all white people by mixture is narcissistic. But declaring that the nation is postracial because of a few successful racially mixed people is fantastical.

At the summit of my scale, does the speaker offer a more developed vision of utopia with peace, racial equality, and interracial families/racially mixed people participating as full citizens? This is the ultimate criterion because it measures the thoughtfulness of the speaker's fascination with mixed race against his or her appreciation for inequality. Often, this correlates with having a sophisticated vision of reform. In this project, William Short intimated at a society without slavery, with recognition of mixed offspring, and with citizenship for blacks. Wendell Phillips spoke and wrote about the ideal American republic on different occasions. Albion Tourgée lived a lifestyle that flouted social norms in Greensboro, North Carolina, and he populated his Supreme Court brief with interracial families practicing a wide array of public rights.

Some people would contend that the events of the time compelled these figures to construct comprehensive visions of a multicultural democracy. I disagree. After all, how do you measure the difference in tumult between the early republic, the Civil War, and Reconstruction? Anyone concerned with his or her times considers those times with the utmost seriousness. Short, Phillips, and Tourgée were lawyers, and I credit the idioms they used to that common denominator. We recognize the clarity of their ideas because of their training to communicate in clear ways. But speakers from other fields shaped ideas as sophisticated as theirs. For example, as a creative writer, Jean Toomer opposed Israel Zangwill's inchoate praise of racial mixture, using symbols such as the stomach to describe how minorities could participate in a diverse nation. His philosophical development led him to focus on enlightenment, creativity, and aesthetics rather than laws, policies, and amendments. As an educator involved with national politics in Mexico, José Vasconcelos applied philosophical thought to mixture, producing a schema that addressed the philosophical themes Toomer addressed as well. These two men wrote in more lyric forms, which took their arguments in different directions.

Instead of the times or the training being the most important factor, I suggest that examples in this final set had an attention to politics in the United States. For example, in addition to Short, Phillips, and Tourgée, the more sophisticated thinkers in the Multiracial Movement saw their actions as an extension of longstanding civil rights struggles. They considered racial identification on the census as a small, private act that could transform racial thinking in the short term. In the long term, mixed-race identity could "provide the basis for new and varied forms of bonding and integration" between the different aspects of one's background without denying the less advantageous ones.[9] In opposition to the traditional modes of identification, G. Reginald Daniel characterized "multiracial consciousness" as "the next logical step in the progression of civil rights, the expansion of our notion of affirmative action to include strategies not only for achieving socioeconomic equity, but also for affirming a nonhierarchical identity that embraces a 'holocentric' racial self."[10] This required the creation of "new identities, new collective subjectivities, and new meanings"[11] A new consciousness would "ensure that wealth, power, privilege, and prestige were more equitably distributed than has ever been the case before in this country. Such a transformation in thought and behavior would move the United States closer to the ideal of a land of equal opportunity for all."[12] It also suggested that multiracial identity could fulfill the nation's promise of equality. In other words, vocal mixed-race Americans can bring about fulfilling the secular values invoked by other vanguards discussed in this book. Interracial intimacy does affect society, but alone its potential is minimal. People who praise mixture without a comprehensive program place mixed people and interracial relationships on pedestals without taking any further responsibility.

Sometimes, a statement that appears to operate on a superficial level actually works on many levels. In the 1998 motion picture *Bulworth*, Warren Beatty plays a U.S. senator sure that assassins will kill him during a campaign weekend. In an interview on network news, he goes on a truth-speaking spree about race, class, wealth, and politics. His rap ends with the following prescription:

> Rich people have always stayed on top by dividing white people from colored people
> But white people got more in common with colored people then they do with rich people
> We just gotta eliminate them. White people, black people, brown people, yellow people, get rid of 'em all
> All we need is a voluntary, free spirited, open-ended program of pro-creative racial deconstruction
> Everybody just gotta keep fuckin' everybody til they're all the same color.[13]

At first consideration, this is an example par excellence of the hope that widespread racial mixing would eliminate racial identity, with whites as the first on the list. In this, whiteness is nothingness, a pathological nonentity with no culture that could disappear with a huff and a puff. I resist reification of the idea *whiteness*, and I recognize that who is white shifts by time and place. But whiteness is a useful tool for understanding the practice of white supremacy. Bulworth believed that white supremacy would disappear just because the white people have become tawny.

Bulworth continues rapping at a fundraiser, elucidating the ills of the country: the rich control economics, politics, and the media. Their greed targets Americans broadly but especially the more vulnerable in society: the poor and minorities. More than one critic likened the senator's transformation to the jeremiad, a distinctively American form of rhetoric that chastises an audience for straying from a covenant and absolves them if they rededicate themselves to traditional values. In this case, the movie preaches "from the left to the center of the Democratic Party, calling the flock home, hoping to rekindle vanished idealism and compassion, hoping to reignite the fire of activism and, by massive applications of shock, to stir up the juice of energy."[14] In particular, the movie harks back to a previous political era, namely, 1968, between the deaths of Martin Luther King Jr. and Robert F. Kennedy.[15]

Bulworth's ideological roots were apparent, its catalog of transgressions thorough, and its solution to racial problems provocative. Within the jeremiad was a list of transgressions, along with nearly as many commandments:

Thou shalt not steal from the taxpayer. Thou shalt not bribe politicians. Thou shalt not be afraid of socialized medicine. However, dramatic conventions required the movie to stop endorsing the senator's suggestions as viable. As Tom DeLuca and John Buell wrote, this political thriller was a "morality play of (failed) social redemption."[16] It succeeded because the viewers recognized its fulfillment of genre expectations. In this, Jay Bulworth is "the redeemable (indeed redeemed by love), caring, if adorably quirky, white guy who redis-covers his true self." However, the "wholly unsympathetic forces of evil" con-tributing to the story's dramatic tension far outweigh the protagonist.[17] Even at the beginning of the film, it is too late for Jay Bulworth. He would have to die, just as King and Kennedy did in 1968.

Along with others who have noted that widespread racial mixing has left white supremacy intact, Whitehead Senior Fellow at the New America Foun-dation Michael Lind posited in his 1995 book *The Next American Nation* that Asian and Latino acceptance of intermarriage will lead to "a white-Asian-Hispanic melting-pot majority—a hard-to-differentiate group of beige Americans—offset by a minority consisting of blacks who have been left out of the melting pot once again."[18] He subscribed to the quantifiable scale that praises those who intermarry as more assimilable, while selectively denigrat-ing some who do not. His dystopia hinged on an explosive rate of mixture over the coming decades, much like *Time*'s New Face. He further predicted "a troubling new division, one between beige and black,"[19] with the more privileged and presumably lighter-complexioned feeling entitled and insen-sitive to the continued marginalization of darker-complexioned Americans.

Lind's example is particularly useful because he does consider inequal-ity a problem to get rid of. However, to emphasize that racial inequality will remain even if racial mixture increases, Lind took the more pessimistic route. Greed would undermine any transformation that mixture could bring to the United States. This is a worthwhile admonition, considering the urge to believe intermarriage is a catalyst for equality in and of itself. Most impor-tantly, though, Lind insisted that race had ceased to be instrumental. Rather than perfect the system of racial categorization that the federal government used to enforce civil rights legislation, "American law should be brought into line with the reality of the transracial cultural majority, by altogether elimi-nating race as a category from law and politics. . . . Americans should think of themselves as belonging to only one race—the human—and to only one nationality—the American."[20] But race remains an important analytic tool, along with gender, class, and so on. As opposed to nurturing racelessness, color-blindness, or postraciality, interracial intimacy is a robust analytic tool for understanding race, citizenship, and equality in the United States.

Like Schlesinger, Lind wrote in critique of the multiculturalism movement of the 1980s and 1990s, emphasizing American universality over particular identities. However, ethnic identity, as in a perceived connection to collective experiences, remains with us. No one can dictate others' ethnic identities, affiliations, and practices. The assimilation of ethnic whites showed that the practice of symbolic ethnicity and ethnic options happens after social mobility. In addition to white privilege, social mobility came about by opportunity and political participation. Those are the starting points toward equality, not the praise of mixed race and the abandonment of race.

Instead, as with my analysis of The New Face of America, I suggest that mixed-race figures symbolize an abundance of race. I argue that, as opposed to nurturing racelessness, color-blindness, or postraciality, forming a racial identity can be a preliminary step toward antiracist activity. Note that I have pointed out the potential of that path, not the certainty, just as Lani Guinier praised the possibility that "being forced to identify with a group of people can be an unexpected blessing."[21] By no means do I wish to enforce a particular, permanent identity on anyone, especially not one based on unreliable criterion such as physical appearance, the identity of one's associates, or a checklist of authentic experiences. However, the concept Guinier and Gerald Torres introduced in their book The Miner's Canary: Enlisting Race, Resisting Power, Transforming Democracy is instructive: that race relations are much like the birds that used to accompany miners as they dug deeper into the earth. If the canary's sensitive lungs succumbed to dangerous gases, then the human workers would know that the environment was dangerous. Keeping the canary healthy also kept the miners healthy. Similarly, the well-being of disadvantaged groups indicates the toxicity of inequality, which poisons the privileged as well. Hopeful for social change through our democratic avenues, Guinier and Torres argued for "political race," a concept that was diagnostic, aspirational, and activist. As Torres reflected, as a teenager, he had hoped that dating interracially would eliminate racial differences, and producing mixed offspring would eliminate color differences, as a number of the inchoate notions discussed in this book had maintained. He admitted that he was hoping for a type of erasure. As a legal scholar recognizing the potential of racial identification, he realized there was a third way: "through political action that builds from the liberatory energy of culture and community. This alternative approach does not attempt to hide the heavy social lifting that clear black and white categories do. Those categories are political, not just physical. And they call for a political response, not a physical erasure."[22] As Guinier and Torres reiterated, anyone could practice political race, and solutions would come from coalitions, flexibility, and imaginative thinking.[23]

Building on their model, I suggest political mixed race as a tool toward racial equality. Rather that acquiescing to "being forced to identify with a group of people," one can identify with multiple groups. But this must take place within the realm of political action, not merely cultural mixture (via music, food, or language proficiency) or social affiliation (via token friends). For example, those who are committed to grassroots activism can exercise political mixed race in that realm, aligning with causes that look different than they do. Those who are unable to do more than vote can cast their ballots to the benefit of more than one community. Come up with ways to sympathize with people different than yourself. See the relations between yourself and others. On an interpersonal scale, political mixed race can challenge acquaintances' preconceptions about race. This can happen by letting someone assume you identify a certain way—or calling out someone who has assumed you do not identify a certain way. On a national scale, political mixed race can trouble racial hierarchies through unforeseen, innovative, adaptive means. In the end, attention to mixed race across U.S. history shows that instability has always existed in racial meanings, but it should not be a fetish. We can find figurative power in racial mixing, but as an end in itself, it is insufficient. Mixed race can disrupt the status quo, but not on its own. We have to do work.

Notes

NOTES TO THE INTRODUCTION

1. Maria P. P. Root, "A Bill of Rights for Racially Mixed People," in *The Multiracial Experience: Racial Borders as the New Frontier*, ed. Maria P. P. Root (Thousand Oaks, Calif.: Sage, 1996).

2. Werner Sollors, *Beyond Ethnicity: Consent and Descent in American Culture* (New York: Oxford University Press, 1986), 41; see also Ursula Brumm, *American Thought and Religious Typology* (New Brunswick: Rutgers University Press, 1970), 27.

3. Michael Omi and Howard Winant, *Racial Formation in the United States: From the 1960s to the 1990s*, 2nd ed. (New York: Routledge, 1994), 55.

4. Ibid., 54.

5. Ibid., 60.

6. Eduardo Bonilla-Silva, *White Supremacy and Racism in the Post–Civil Rights Era* (Boulder, Colo.: Rienner, 2001), 48.

7. A. Leon Higginbotham, Jr., "The Ten Precepts of American Slavery Jurisprudence: Chief Justice Roger Taney's Defense and Justice Thurgood Marshall's Condemnation of the Precept of Black Inferiority," *Cardozo Law Review* 17 (1996): 1695.

8. Thomas Jefferson, *Notes on the State of Virginia* (Boston: Lilly and Wait, 1832), 151.

9. J. Hector St. John de Crèvecoeur, *Letters from an American Farmer; and, Sketches of Eighteenth-Century America*, ed. Albert E. Stone (Harmondsworth, UK: Penguin Books, 1981), 69–70.

10. Brief of Plaintiff in Error, *Plessy v. Ferguson*, 163 U.S. 537 (1896), in Albion Winegar Tourgée, *Undaunted Radical: The Selected Writings and Speeches of Albion W. Tourgée*, ed. Mark Emory Elliott and John David Smith (Baton Rouge: LSU Press, 2010), 303.

11. Jean Toomer, "Just Americans," *Time*, March 28, 1932.

12. Robert Ezra Park and Ernest Watson Burgess, *Introduction to the Science of Sociology* (Chicago: University of Chicago Press, 1921), 736.

13. Donna Jeanne Haraway, *Modest_Witness@Second_Millennium.FemaleMan©_Meets_ OncoMouse™: Feminism and Technoscience* (New York: Routledge, 1997); Mike Hill, *After Whiteness: Unmaking an American Majority* (New York: NYU Press, 2004); David R. Roediger, *Colored White: Transcending the Racial Past*, American Crossroads 10 (Berkeley: University of California Press, 2002).

NOTES TO CHAPTER 1

1. Georges Louis Leclerc, Count de Buffon, *Natural History, General and Particular, by the Count Buffon*, trans. William Smellie (London: T. Cadell and W. Davies, 1812).

2. Thomas F. Gossett, *Race: The History of an Idea in America*, new ed., Race and American Culture (New York: Oxford University Press, 1997); George W. Stocking,

Race, Culture, and Evolution: Essays in the History of Anthropology (Chicago: University of Chicago Press, 1982).

3. A. Leon Higginbotham, Jr., and Barbara K. Kopytoff, "Racial Purity and Interracial Sex in the Law of Colonial and Antebellum Virginia," *Georgetown Law Journal* 77, no. 6 (1989); Randall Kennedy, *Interracial Intimacies: Sex, Marriage, Identity, and Adoption* (New York: Pantheon, 2003); Gordon S. Wood, *Empire of Liberty: A History of the Early Republic, 1789–1815* (Oxford: Oxford University Press, 2009).

4. Andrew Burstein, *Jefferson's Secrets: Death and Desire at Monticello* (New York: Basic Books, 2005); Joseph J. Ellis, *American Sphinx: The Character of Thomas Jefferson* (New York: Knopf, 1997); Betsy Erkkila, "Radical Jefferson," *American Quarterly* 59, no. 2 (2007); Annette Gordon-Reed, *The Hemingses of Monticello: An American Family* (New York: Norton, 2008); Annette Gordon-Reed, *Thomas Jefferson and Sally Hemings: An American Controversy* (Charlottesville: University of Virginia Press, 1997); Thomas Jefferson, Adrienne Koch, and William Harwood Peden, *The Life and Selected Writings of Thomas Jefferson* (New York: Modern Library, 1998); Barry Shank, "Jefferson, the Impossible," *American Quarterly* 59, no. 2 (2007); Daniel Whitman, "Slavery and the Rights of Frenchmen: Views of Montesquieu, Rousseau, and Raynal," *French Colonial Studies* 1, no. 1 (1977).

5. Andrew Burstein, "Jefferson's Rationalizations," *William and Mary Quarterly* 57, no. 1 (2000); Christa Dierksheide, "'The Great Improvement and Civilization of That Race': Jefferson and the 'Amelioration' of Slavery, ca. 1770–1826," *Early American Studies: An Interdisciplinary Journal* 6, no. 1 (2008); Ari Helo and Peter Onuf, "Jefferson, Morality, and the Problem of Slavery," *William and Mary Quarterly* 60, no. 3 (2003).

6. St. John de Crèvecoeur, *Letters from an American Farmer*, 69.

7. Gay Wilson Allen and Roger Asselineau, *St. John de Crèvecoeur: The Life of an American Farmer* (New York: Viking, 1987); Fawn McKay Brodie, *Thomas Jefferson, an Intimate History* (New York: Norton, 1974); Bruce Chadwick, *"I Am Murdered": George Wythe, Thomas Jefferson, and the Killing That Shocked a New Nation* (Hoboken, N.J.: Wiley, 2009); Joseph J. Ellis, *His Excellency: George Washington* (New York: Vintage Books, 2005); Julia Post Mitchell Kunkle, *St. Jean de Crèvecoeur* (New York: AMS Press, 1966); Andrew Levy, *The First Emancipator: The Forgotten Story of Robert Carter, the Founding Father Who Freed His Slaves* (New York: Random House, 2005); Thomas Philbrick, *St. John de Crèvecoeur* (New York: Twayne, 1970); J. Hector St. John de Crèvecoeur, *Journey into Northern Pennsylvania and the State of New York* (Ann Arbor: University of Michigan Press, 1964); J. Hector St. John de Crèvecoeur, *Eighteenth-Century Travels in Pennsylvania & New York*, trans. and ed. Percy G. Adams (Lexington: University of Kentucky Press, 1961); J. Hector St. John de Crèvecoeur, *More Letters from the American Farmer: An Edition of the Essays in English Left Unpublished by Crèvecoeur*, ed. Dennis D. Moore (Athens: University of Georgia Press, 1995); St. John de Crèvecoeur, *Letters from an American Farmer*.

8. R. Bowman, "Monticello Report: Thomas Jefferson and William Short," Thomas Jefferson Foundation, http://www.monticello.org/reports/people/short.html; James R. Bullington, "The Diplomat and the Duchess," *Foreign Service Journal* 86, no. 10 (2009); Gordon-Reed, *The Hemingses of Monticello*; Marie Goebel Kimball, "William Short, Jefferson's Only 'Son,'" *North American Review* 223, no. 832 (1926); George

Green Shackelford, "William Short: Diplomat in Revolutionary France, 1785–1793," *Proceedings of the American Philosophical Society* 102, no. 6 (1958); George Green Shackelford, *Jefferson's Adoptive Son: The Life of William Short, 1759–1848* (Lexington: University Press of Kentucky, 1993).

9. Ira Berlin and Leslie M. Harris, eds., *Slavery in New York* (New York: New Press, 2005); David Nathaniel Gellman, *Emancipating New York: The Politics of Slavery and Freedom, 1777–1827*, Antislavery, Abolition, and the Atlantic World (Baton Rouge: LSU Press, 2006); Leslie M. Harris, *In the Shadow of Slavery: African Americans in New York City, 1626–1863*, Historical Studies of Urban America (Chicago: University of Chicago Press, 2003); Shane White, *Somewhat More Independent: The End of Slavery in New York City, 1770–1810* (Athens: University of Georgia Press, 1991).

10. Bryce Traister, "Criminal Correspondence: Loyalism, Espionage and Crèvecoeur," *Early American Literature* 37, no. 3 (2002).

11. David Carlson, "Farmer versus Lawyer: Crèvecoeur's 'Letters' and the Liberal Subject," *Early American Literature* 38, no. 2 (2002): 270.

12. Doreen Alvarez Saar, "Crèvecoeur's 'Thoughts on Slavery': Letters from an American Farmer and the Rhetoric of Whig Thought," *Early American Literature* 22, no. 2 (1987): 195.

13. St. John de Crèvecoeur, *Letters from an American Farmer*, 166, 179.

14. Jeff Osborne, "American Antipathy and the Cruelties of Citizenship in Crèvecoeur's *Letters from an American Farmer*," *Early American Literature* 42, no. 3 (2007): 541.

15. Carlson, "Farmer versus Lawyer"; Osborne, "American Antipathy"; Norman A. Plotkin, "Saint-John de Crèvecoeur Rediscovered: Critic or Panegyrist?," *French Historical Studies* 3, no. 3 (1964); Elayne Antler Rapping, "Theory and Experience in Crèvecoeur's America," *American Quarterly* 19, no. 4 (1967); Saar, "Crèvecoeur's 'Thoughts on Slavery.'"

16. Brumm, *American Thought and Religious Typology*, 27; Herbert David Croly, *The Promise of American Life* (New York: Macmillan, 1909); Eric Foner, *The Story of American Freedom* (New York: Norton, 1998); Gary Gerstle, *American Crucible: Race and Nation in the Twentieth Century* (Princeton: Princeton University Press, 2001); Philip Gleason, "The Melting Pot: Symbol of Fusion or Confusion?," *American Quarterly* 16, no. 1 (1964); Milton Myron Gordon, *Assimilation in American Life: The Role of Race, Religion, and National Origins* (New York: Oxford University Press, 1964); Daniel Hoffman, *Form and Fable in American Fiction* (New York: Norton, 1973); D. H. Lawrence, *Studies in Classic American Literature* (New York: T. Seltzer, 1923); Dana D. Nelson, *National Manhood: Capitalist Citizenship and the Imagined Fraternity of White Men*, New Americanists (Durham: Duke University Press, 1998); Arthur M. Schlesinger, *The Disuniting of America: Reflections on a Multicultural Society*, rev. and enlarged ed. (New York: Norton, 1998); Sollors, *Beyond Ethnicity*, 40–65; Frederick Jackson Turner, *The Frontier in American History* (New York: Dover, 1996).

17. St. John de Crèvecoeur, *Letters from an American Farmer*, 69.

18. Lucia C. Stanton, "Monticello Jefferson-Hemings Report: Appendix H," Thomas Jefferson Foundation, http://www.monticello.org/plantation/hemingscontro/appendixh.html.

19. Thomas Jefferson, *Notes on the State of Virginia*, ed. Frank Shuffelton (New York: Penguin Books, 1999), 150.

20. Ibid., 151.

21. Charles A. Cerami, *Benjamin Banneker: Surveyor, Astronomer, Publisher, Patriot* (New York: Wiley, 2002).

22. Jefferson, *Notes on the State of Virginia*, 168.

23. Ibid.; Mitch Kachun, "Antebellum African Americans, Public Commemoration, and the Haitian Revolution," *Journal of the Early Republic* 26, no. 2 (2006): 270n. 27; Frank Shuffelton, "Thomas Jefferson: Race, Culture, and the Failure of Anthropological Method," in *A Mixed Race: Ethnicity in Early America*, ed. Frank Shuffelton (New York: Oxford University Press, 1993).

24. Stanton, "Monticello Jefferson-Hemings Report."

25. Bruce David Baum and Duchess Harris, "Jefferson's Legacies: Racial Intimacies and American Identity," in *Racially Writing the Republic: Racists, Race Rebels, and Transformations of American Identity*, ed. Bruce David Baum and Duchess Harris (Durham: Duke University Press, 2009); Annette Gordon-Reed, "Engaging Jefferson: Blacks and the Founding Father," *William and Mary Quarterly*, 3rd series, 57, no. 1 (2000); Martha Elizabeth Hodes, *Sex, Love, Race: Crossing Boundaries in North American History* (New York: NYU Press, 1999); Gary B. Nash, "The Hidden History of Mestizo America," *Journal of American History* 82, no. 3 (1995); Clarence Earl Walker, *Mongrel Nation: The America Begotten by Thomas Jefferson and Sally Hemings* (Charlottesville: University of Virginia Press, 2009).

26. Richard B. Bernstein, *Thomas Jefferson: The Revolution of Ideas*, Oxford Portraits (Oxford: Oxford University Press, 2004); Burstein, *Jefferson's Secrets*; Ellis, *American Sphinx*; Gordon-Reed, *Thomas Jefferson and Sally Hemings*; Gordon-Reed, *Hemingses of Monticello*.

27. William Short to Thomas Jefferson, December 25, 1789, in *The Papers of Thomas Jefferson Digital Edition*, ed. Barbara B. Oberg and J. Jefferson Looney (Charlottesville: University of Virginia Press, Rotunda, 2008).

28. William Doyle, *The Oxford History of the French Revolution*, 2nd ed. (Oxford: Oxford University Press, 2002); Christopher Hibbert, *The Days of the French Revolution* (New York: Morrow Quill, 1981).

29. Gordon S. Brown, *Toussaint's Clause: The Founding Fathers and the Haitian Revolution* (Jackson: University Press of Mississippi, 2005); Laurent Dubois, *Avengers of the New World: The Story of the Haitian Revolution* (Cambridge: Belknap Press of Harvard University Press, 2004); C. L. R. James, *The Black Jacobins; Toussaint L'Ouverture and the San Domingo Revolution*, 2d ed. (New York: Vintage Books, 1963); Tim Matthewson, *A Proslavery Foreign Policy: Haitian-American Relations during the Early Republic* (Westport, Conn.: Praeger, 2003); Short to Jefferson, December 25, 1789.

30. Dubois, *Avengers of the New World*; John D. Garrigus, *Before Haiti: Race and Citizenship in French Saint-Domingue*, The Americas in the Early Modern Atlantic World (New York: Palgrave Macmillan, 2006); Stewart R. King, *Blue Coat or Powdered Wig: Free People of Color in Pre-Revolutionary Saint Domingue* (Athens: University of Georgia Press, 2001); William Short to John Jay, March 3, 1790, in *Papers of Thomas Jefferson*; William Short to Thomas Jefferson, September 26, 1790, in *Thomas Jefferson and William Short Correspondence*, transcribed and ed. Gerard W. Gawalt, Manuscript Division, Library of Congress, Washington, D.C.; William Short to Thomas Jefferson, October 21, 1790, in *Papers of Thomas Jefferson*.

31. William Short to Thomas Jefferson, May 3, 1791, in *Papers of Thomas Jefferson*; William Short to Thomas Jefferson, November 21, 1791, in ibid.

32. Short to Jefferson, May 3, 1791; Short to Jefferson, November 21, 1791.

33. Magali Marie Carrera, *Imagining Identity in New Spain: Race, Lineage, and the Colonial Body in Portraiture and Casta Paintings*, Joe R. and Teresa Lozano Long Series in Latin American and Latino Art and Culture (Austin: University of Texas Press, 2003); María Concepción García Saiz, *Las Castas Mexicanas: Un Género Pictórico Americano* (Milan: Olivetti, 1989); Ilona Katzew, *Casta Painting: Images of Race in Eighteenth-Century Mexico* (New Haven: Yale University Press, 2004).

34. William Short to Thomas Jefferson, February 27 [1798], in *Papers of Thomas Jefferson*.

35. William Short to Thomas Jefferson, August 24, 1798, in *Papers of Thomas Jefferson*; William Short to Thomas Jefferson, July 2, 1799, in ibid.; William Short to Thomas Jefferson, August 6, 1800, in ibid.; William Short to Thomas Jefferson, September 18, 1800, in ibid.

36. William Short to Thomas Jefferson, February 27 [1798], in *Papers of Thomas Jefferson*.

37. Ibid.

38. Ibid.

39. Ibid.

40. Ibid.

41. Tom Costa and Rector and Visitors of the University of Virginia, "The Geography of Slavery," http://www2.vcdh.virginia.edu/gos/laws1751-1800.html; Peter Kolchin, *American Slavery, 1619–1877*, 1st rev. ed. (New York: Hill and Wang, 2003); James Sidbury, *Ploughshares into Swords: Race, Rebellion, and Identity in Gabriel's Virginia, 1730–1810* (New York: Cambridge University Press, 1997); Rector and Visitors of the University of Virginia, "Historical Census Browser," http://mapserver.lib.virginia.edu/.

42. Costa and University of Virginia, "Geography of Slavery"; Kachun, "Antebellum African Americans"; University of Virginia, "Historical Census Browser."

43. Elise Virginia Lemire, *"Miscegenation": Making Race in America*, New Cultural Studies (Philadelphia: University of Pennsylvania Press, 2002).

44. Kachun, "Antebellum African Americans"; Matthewson, *Proslavery Foreign Policy*.

45. Brodie, *Thomas Jefferson*; Chadwick, *"I Am Murdered."*

46. Thomas Jefferson to Henri Grégoire, February 25, 1809, in *The Works of Thomas Jefferson in Twelve Volumes: Federal Edition*, collected and ed. Paul Leicester Ford (Washington, D.C.: Library of Congress, 1809).

47. Quoted in "Early History of the American Colonization Society," *African Repository* 12 (1836): 51.

NOTES TO CHAPTER 2

1. Thomas Jefferson to John Holmes, April 22, 1820, in the Thomas Jefferson Papers, Series 1, General Correspondence, 1651–1827, Library of Congress, Washington, D.C.

2. Ibid.; Thomas Jefferson to William Short, April 13, 1820, in *Thomas Jefferson and William Short Correspondence*.

3. Jefferson to Holmes, April 22, 1820.

4. Gordon-Reed, *Thomas Jefferson and Sally Hemings*; Gordon-Reed, *Hemingses of Monticello*; Lucia C. Stanton, "Brief Biography of Sally Hemings," Thomas Jefferson Foundation, http://www.monticello.org/plantation/lives/sallyhemings.html; Stanton, "Monticello Jefferson-Hemings Report."
5. Quoted in Scot French, *The Rebellious Slave: Nat Turner in American Memory* (Boston: Houghton Mifflin, 2004), 29.
6. William Lloyd Garrison, "The Marriage Law," *Liberator*, May 7, 1831.
7. Ibid.; see also Sollors, *Beyond Ethnicity*, 60–65.
8. Robert H. Abzug, *Cosmos Crumbling: American Reform and the Religious Imagination* (New York: Oxford University Press, 1994), 6–7; Perry Miller, *Errand into the Wilderness: An Address* (Williamsburg, VA: William and Mary Quarterly for the Associates of the John Carter Brown Library, 1952); Gilbert Osofsky, "Wendell Phillips and the Quest for a New American Identity," *Canadian Review of Studies in Nationalism* 1 (1973).
9. William Lloyd Garrison, "The Marriage Law," *Liberator*, February 15, 1839.
10. Wendell Phillips, *Speeches, Lectures, and Letters: Second Series*, Anti-Slavery Crusade in America (New York: Arno, 1969), 11.
11. T.T., "A Dream, *Liberator*, April 2, 1831.
12. John Stauffer, "In the Shadow of a Dream: White Abolitionists and Race," in *Proceedings of the Fifth Annual Gilder Lehrman Center International Conference* (New Haven: Yale University Press, 2003); James B. Stewart, "The Emergence of Racial Modernity and the Rise of the White North, 1790–1840," *Journal of the Early Republic* 18, no. 2 (1998); T.T., "A Dream."
13. T.T., "Another Dream," *Liberator*, April 2, 1831.
14. Quoted in Louis Ruchames, "Race, Marriage, and Abolition in Massachusetts," *Journal of Negro History* 40, no. 3 (1955): 33.
15. Quoted in William Lloyd Garrison, "Marriage Law," *Liberator*, April 30, 1831.
16. Leon F. Litwack, "The Abolitionist Dilemma: The Antislavery Movement and the Northern Negro," *New England Quarterly* 34, no. 1 (1961); William H. Pease and Jane H. Pease, "Antislavery Ambivalence: Immediatism, Expediency, Race," *American Quarterly* 17, no. 4 (1965); Ruchames, "Race, Marriage, and Abolition."
17. William Lloyd Garrison, "The Insurrection," *Liberator*, September 3, 1831.
18. Pennsylvania Hall Association (Philadelphia) and Samuel Webb, *History of Pennsylvania Hall* (Philadelphia: Merrihew and Gunn, 1838); Josiah Clark Nott, "The Mulatto a Hybrid—Probable Extinction of the Two Races If the Whites and Blacks Are Allowed to Intermarry," *American Journal of the Medical Sciences* 6, no. 11 (1843); Samuel Morton, "Hybridity in Animals, Considered in Reference to the Question of the Unity of the Human Species," *American Journal of Science* 3 (1847); Louis Agassiz, *The Diversity of Origin of the Human Races* ([Boston?], 1850); John Bachman, *The Doctrine of the Unity of the Human Race Examined on the Principles of Science* (Charleston, S.C.: C. Canning, 1850); Josiah Clark Nott and George R. Gliddon, *Types of Mankind; or, Ethnological Researches Based upon the Ancient Monuments, Paintings, Sculptures, and Crania of Races, and upon Their Natural, Geographical, Philological and Biblical History: Illustrated by Selections from the Inedited Papers of Samuel George Morton and by Additional Contributions from L. Agassiz, W. Usher, and H. S. Patterson*, 6th ed. (Philadelphia: Lippincott, Grambo, 1854).

19. Harris, *In the Shadow of Slavery*, 197–98; Eric Lott, *Love and Theft: Blackface Minstrelsy and the American Working Class*, Race and American Culture (New York: Oxford University Press, 1993), 131–35.

20. Harriet Martineau, *Society in America*, 2 vols. (New York: Saunders and Otley, 1837), 2:328–29; Harriet Martineau, *Retrospect of Western Travel*, 3 vols. (London: Saunders and Otley, 1838), 1:228–30.

21. Ira V. Brown, "Racism and Sexism: The Case of Pennsylvania Hall," *Phylon* 37, no. 2 (1976); Pennsylvania Hall Association and Webb, *History of Pennsylvania Hall*; James Brewer Stewart, "Modernizing 'Difference': The Political Meanings of Color in the Free States, 1776–1840," *Journal of the Early Republic* 19, no. 4 (1999).

22. "Constitution of the New England Anti-Slavery Society," *Abolitionist*, January 1833; Ruchames, "Race, Marriage, and Abolition," 254–55.

23. "Speech of Wendell Phillips," *Liberator*, June 11, 1858.

24. Garrison, "The Marriage Law," *Liberator*, February 15, 1839.

25. Ibid.

26. Ibid.; Ruchames, "Race, Marriage, and Abolition," 257–63.

27. Ann Warren Weston, quoted in James Brewer Stewart, *Wendell Phillips, Liberty's Hero* (Baton Rouge: LSU Press, 1986), 72–73.

28. "Marriage Law"; Thayer quoted in Stewart, *Wendell Phillips*, 72–73.

29. William Lloyd Garrison, "Interracial Marriage," *Liberator*, February 8, 1839.

30. Garrison, "The Marriage Law," *Liberator*, February 15, 1839.

31. Quoted in ibid.

32. Wendell Phillips, "Speech of Wendell Phillips, Esq. at the Anniversary of the American Anti-Slavery Society in the Cooper Institute, New York," *Liberator*, May 29, 1863.

33. Ibid.

34. Betty Fladeland, *James Gillespie Birney: Slaveholder to Abolitionist* (New York: Greenwood, 1969).

35. Quoted in William Lloyd Garrison, "Fear of Interracial Marriage (Anti Abolitionists)," *Liberator*, January 1, 1841.

36. Phillips, "Speech of Wendell Phillips, Esq. at the Anniversary of the American Anti-Slavery Society."

37. Maria Diedrich, *Love across Color Lines: Ottilie Assing and Frederick Douglass* (New York: Hill and Wang, 1999); Frederick Douglass, "The Future of the Negro Race," *North American Review* 142 (May 1886); Frederick Douglass, *Autobiographies* (New York: Library of America, 1994); Waldo E. Martin, *The Mind of Frederick Douglass* (Chapel Hill: University of North Carolina Press, 1984); William S. McFeely, *Frederick Douglass* (New York: Simon and Schuster, 1992).

38. Ottilie Assing and Frederick Douglass, *Radical Passion: Ottilie Assing's Reports from America and Letters to Frederick Douglass*, ed. and trans. Christoph K. Lohmann, New Directions in German American Studies (New York: Lang, 1999); Diedrich, *Love across Color Lines*.

39. Lydia Maria Francis Child, *Fact and Fiction: A Collection of Stories* (New York: C. S. Francis, 1847); Werner Sollors, *Neither Black nor White yet Both: Thematic Explorations of Interracial Literature* (New York: Oxford University Press, 1997).

40. William Ragan Stanton, *The Leopard's Spots: Scientific Attitudes toward Race in America, 1815–59* (Chicago: University of Chicago Press, 1960); Harriet Beecher Stowe, *Uncle Tom's Cabin; or, Life among the Lowly* (Boston: John P. Jewett, 1852).

41. Irving H. Bartlett, *Wendell Phillips, Brahmin Radical* (Westport, Conn.: Greenwood, 1973); Stewart, *Wendell Phillips.*

42. Wendell Phillips, "The United States of the United Races," *National Era*, September 15, 1853.

43. Ibid.

44. Ibid.

45. Wendell Phillips, "Speech of Wendell Phillips," *Liberator*, July 16, 1858; W. Caleb McDaniel, "The Fourth and the First: Abolitionist Holidays, Respectability, and Radical Interracial Reform," *American Quarterly* 57, no. 1 (2005); Wendell Phillips, "Speech of Wendell Phillips at the Celebration of the 1st of August at Abington," *Liberator*, August 14, 1857.

46. Wendell Phillips, "Address by Wendell Phillips," *Liberator*, October 7, 1859.

47. Ibid.

48. Wendell Phillips, "Speech of Wendell Phillips," *Liberator*, February 10, 1860.

49. Phillips referred to John Sella Martin, a black abolitionist who shared the stage with him that day. Ibid.

50. "Democracy and Black Republicanism," *Vermont Patriot*, April 21, 1860.

51. "Alabama. Our Montgomery Correspondence," *New York Herald*, January 25, 1861.

52. Phillips, "Speech of Wendell Phillips, Esq. at the Anniversary of the American Anti-Slavery Society."

53. Ibid.

54. Wendell Phillips, "Speech of Wendell Phillips Delivered before the Sixteenth Ward Republican Association at the Cooper Institute, New York," *Liberator*, June 5, 1863.

55. Mary Niall Mitchell, "'Rosebloom and Pure White,' or So It Seemed," *American Quarterly* 54, no. 3 (2002): 373.

56. "The Union Convention in Concord, N.H.," *Daily Advertiser*, June 18, 1863.

57. Quoted in Montgomery Blair, "Speech of Montgomery Blair, U.S. Postmaster General," *Liberator*, June 26, 1863.

58. Quoted in ibid.

59. Wendell Phillips, "Speech of Wendell Phillips, Esq. at Framingham, July 4, 1863," *Liberator*, July 10, 1863.

60. "Wendell Phillips on the Fourth," *New York Herald*, July 7, 1863.

61. "The Radicals and Their Committees—the Antics of the Drunken Committee," *New York Herald*, July 8, 1863; see also "The Great Question of the Restoration of the Southern States," *New York Herald*, August 25, 1863; "The Maryland Election and the Next Congress—the Contest for the Speakership," *New York Herald*, August 27, 1863; "Amalgamation," *Newark Advocate*, August 28, 1863; William Lloyd Garrison, "The War of the Cabinet—Conservative Manifesto Issued through the Postmaster General," *Liberator*, October 16, 1863.

62. Quoted in "The Negro Question," *Daily Advertiser*, August 12, 1863. The *Herald* agreed, calling political and social equality "the most absurd, visionary, and impracticable idea that ever entered the mind of man." "Negro Question"; see also "Great Question of the Restoration of the Southern States."

63. David G. Croly, *Miscegenation: The Theory of the Blending of the Races, Applied to the American White Man and Negro* (New York: Dexter, Hamilton, 1864), 5.

64. Sidney Kaplan, "The Miscegenation Issue in the Election of 1864," *Journal of Negro History* 34, no. 3 (1949): 284.

65. Ibid.
66. Croly, *Miscegenation*, 8–9.
67. Ibid., 11.
68. Ibid., 64.
69. Ibid., 34.
70. Ibid., 27.
71. "General Intelligence," *Newark Advocate*, April 15, 1864.
72. "The New Doctrine of Miscegenation," *San Francisco Evening Bulletin*, May 7, 1864.
73. Kaplan, "Miscegenation Issue," 291.
74. Quoted in ibid., 290.
75.   75.Samuel Sullivan Cox, *Eight Years in Congress, from 1857 to 1865* (New York: Appleton, 1865), 354.
76. John Van Evrie, *New York Weekly Day-Book*, March 12, 1864.
77. *National Antislavery Standard*, March 5, 1864.
78. Kaplan, "Miscegenation Issue," 305; R. Edward Lee, "Miscegenation: The Theory of the Blending of the Races Applied to the American White Man, and the Negro," *Blacfax*, 1999.

NOTES TO CHAPTER 3

1. Caryn Cossé Bell, *Revolution, Romanticism, and the Afro-Creole Protest Tradition in Louisiana, 1718–1868* (Baton Rouge: LSU Press, 1997); George Washington Cable and Joseph Pennell, *The Creoles of Louisiana* (New York: Scribner, 1884); Rodolphe Lucien Desdunes, *Our People and Our History: Fifty Creole Portraits* (Baton Rouge: LSU Press, 2001); Kimberly S. Hanger, *Bounded Lives, Bounded Places: Free Black Society in Colonial New Orleans, 1769–1803* (Durham: Duke University Press, 1997); Saidiya V. Hartman, *Scenes of Subjection: Terror, Slavery, and Self-Making in Nineteenth-Century America*, Race and American Culture (New York: Oxford University Press, 1997); Shirley Elizabeth Thompson, *Exiles at Home: The Struggle to Become American in Creole New Orleans* (Cambridge: Harvard University Press, 2009).
2. Thompson, *Exiles at Home*.
3. Thomas J. Davis, "More than Segregation, Racial Identity: The Neglected Question in *Plessy v. Ferguson*," *Washington and Lee Race and Ethnicity Ancestry Law Journal* 10 (2004); Mark Elliott, "Race, Color Blindness, and the Democratic Public: Albion W. Tourgée's Radical Principles in *Plessy v. Ferguson*," *Journal of Southern History* 67, no. 2 (2001); Mark Emory Elliott, *Color-Blind Justice: Albion Tourgée and the Quest for Racial Equality from the Civil War to "Plessy v. Ferguson"* (Oxford: Oxford University Press, 2006); Mark Golub, "Plessy as 'Passing': Judicial Responses to Ambiguously Raced Bodies in *Plessy v. Ferguson*," *Law & Society Review* 39, no. 3 (2005); Blair Murphy Kelley, *Right to Ride: Streetcar Boycotts and African American Citizenship in the Era of "Plessy v. Ferguson"* (Chapel Hill: University of North Carolina Press, 2010); Jules Lobel, *Success without Victory: Lost Legal Battles and the Long Road to Justice in America*, Critical America (New York: NYU Press, 2003); Charles A. Lofgren, *The "Plessy" Case: A Legal-Historical Interpretation* (New York: Oxford University Press, 1987); Rebecca J. Scott, "The Atlantic World and the Road to *Plessy v. Ferguson*," *Journal of American History* 94, no. 3 (2007); Rebecca J. Scott, "Public Rights, Social Equality, and the Conceptual Roots of the Plessy Challenge," *Michigan*

Law Review 106 (March 2008); Tourgée, *Undaunted Radical*; C. Vann Woodward, "The Case of the Louisiana Traveler," in *Quarrels That Have Shaped the Constitution*, ed. John A. Garraty (New York: Harper and Row, 1964).

4. Martha Menchaca, *Recovering History, Constructing Race: The Indian, Black, and White Roots of Mexican Americans*, Joe R. and Teresa Lozano Long Series in Latin American and Latino Art and Culture (Austin: University of Texas Press, 2001); David J. Weber, *The Mexican Frontier, 1821–1846: The American Southwest under Mexico*, Histories of the American Frontier (Albuquerque: University of New Mexico Press, 1982); David J. Weber, *Foreigners in Their Native Land: Historical Roots of the Mexican Americans*, 30th anniversary pbk. ed. (Albuquerque: University of New Mexico Press, 2003).

5. Neil Foley, *The White Scourge: Mexicans, Blacks, and Poor Whites in Texas Cotton Culture*, American Crossroads (Berkeley: University of California Press, 1997); Reginald Horsman, *Race and Manifest Destiny: The Origins of American Racial Anglo-Saxonism* (Cambridge: Harvard University Press, 1981), 246; Weber, *Foreigners in Their Native Land*.

6. "The Treaty of Guadalupe Hidalgo (Hispanic Reading Room, Hispanic Division)," Library of Congress, http://www.loc.gov/rr/hispanic/ghtreaty/.

7. Ibid.

8. Tomás Almaguer, *Racial Fault Lines: The Historical Origins of White Supremacy in California* (Berkeley: University of California Press, 1994); Menchaca, *Recovering History*; Weber, *Foreigners in Their Native Land*.

9. Leslie Bow, *Partly Colored: Asian Americans and Racial Anomaly in the Segregated South* (New York: NYU Press, 2010); Lucy M. Cohen, *Chinese in the Post–Civil War South: A People without a History* (Baton Rouge: LSU Press, 1984); Robert G. Lee, *Orientals: Asian Americans in Popular Culture*, Asian American History and Culture (Philadelphia: Temple University Press, 1999), 75–78, 83; James W. Loewen, *The Mississippi Chinese: Between Black and White*, Harvard East Asian Series 63 (Cambridge: Harvard University Press, 1971).

10. Lauren L. Basson, *White Enough to Be American? Race Mixing, Indigenous People, and the Boundaries of State and Nation* (Chapel Hill: University of North Carolina Press, 2008); Frederick E. Hoxie, *A Final Promise: The Campaign to Assimilate the Indians, 1880–1920* (Lincoln: University of Nebraska Press, 1984).

11. Basson, *White Enough to Be American?*; Paul Spruhan, "A Legal History of Blood Quantum in Federal Indian Law to 1935," *South Dakota Law Review* 51, no. 1 (2006); Paul Spruhan, "Indian as Race/Indian as Political Status: Implementation of the Half-Blood Requirement under the Indian Reorganization Act, 1934–1945," *Rutgers Race and Law Review* 8, no. 1 (2006); Kimberly Tallbear, "D.N.A., Blood, and Racializing the Tribe," *Wicazo Sa Review* 18, no. 1 (2003); Terry P. Wilson, "Blood Quantum: Native American Mixed Bloods," in *Racially Mixed People in America*, ed. Maria P. P. Root (Newbury Park, Calif.: Sage, 1992).

12. Marcia Beth Bordman, "Dear Old Golden Day Rules: A Study in the Rhetoric of Separate-but-Equal in *Roberts v. City of Boston* (1849), *Plessy v. Ferguson* (1896), and *Brown v. Board of Education* (1954)" (Ph.D. diss., University of Maryland, 1993); Elliott, "Race, Color Blindness, and the Democratic Public"; Elliott, *Color-Blind Justice*.

13. Elliott, *Color-Blind Justice*, 65.

14. W. E. B. Du Bois, *Black Reconstruction in America: An Essay toward a History of the Part Which Black Folk Played in the Attempt to Reconstruct Democracy in America, 1860–1880* (New York: Oxford University Press, 2007); Eric Foner, *Reconstruction: America's Unfinished Revolution, 1863–1877*, New American Nation Series (New York: Harper and Row, 1988); William Gillette, *Retreat from Reconstruction, 1869–1879* (Baton Rouge: LSU Press, 1979).

15. Elliott, "Race, Color Blindness, and the Democratic Public," 294; Elliott, *Color-Blind Justice*, 32–33.

16. Jane Elizabeth Dailey, *Before Jim Crow: The Politics of Race in Postemancipation Virginia*, Gender & American Culture (Chapel Hill: University of North Carolina Press, 2000); Jane Elizabeth Dailey, Glenda Elizabeth Gilmore, and Bryant Simon, *Jumpin' Jim Crow: Southern Politics from Civil War to Civil Rights* (Princeton: Princeton University Press, 2000); Howard N. Rabinowitz, "More than the Woodward Thesis: Assessing the Strange Career of Jim Crow," *Journal of American History* 75, no. 3 (1988); Howard N. Rabinowitz, *Race Relations in the Urban South, 1865–1890* (Athens: University of Georgia Press, 1996); C. Vann Woodward, "Strange Career Critics: Long May They Persevere," *Journal of American History* 75, no. 3 (1988); C. Vann Woodward, *The Strange Career of Jim Crow*, commemorative ed. (Oxford; New York: Oxford University Press, 2002).

17. Louisiana Constitution, Title I, Article XVIII (1868).

18. Scott, "Public Rights," 782.

19. Foner, *Reconstruction*.

20. Albion Winegar Tourgée, *Bricks without Straw: A Novel* (1880), ed. Carolyn L. Karcher (Durham: Duke University Press, 2009); Albion Winegar Tourgée, *A Fool's Errand* (New York: Fords, Howard, and Hulbert, 1879).

21. George Washington Cable, *Old Creole Days* (New York: Scribner, 1879); George Washington Cable, *The Grandissimes: A Story of Creole Life* (New York: Scribner, 1880); George Washington Cable, *The Negro Question: A Selection of Writings on Civil Rights in the South* (Garden City, N.Y.: Doubleday, 1958); Cable and Pennell, *Creoles of Louisiana*; George Washington Cable, *Madame Delphine* (New York: Scribner, 1881).

22. Cable, *Negro Question*, 99.

23. Ibid., 112.

24. Ibid.

25. Ibid., 113.

26. Elliott, *Color-Blind Justice*; Foner, *Reconstruction*.

27. *Civil Rights Cases*, 109 U.S. 3 (1883).

28. Elliott, *Color-Blind Justice*; Foner, *Reconstruction*; Robert Green Ingersoll, "Civil Rights," in *The Works of Robert G. Ingersoll* (New York: Dresden, C. P. Farrell, 1902).

29. Diedrich, *Love across Color Lines*; Douglass, *Autobiographies*; Martin, *Mind of Frederick Douglass*; McFeely, *Frederick Douglass*.

30. Quoted in Martin, *Mind of Frederick Douglass*, 100.

31. Douglass, "Future of the Negro Race."

32. Martin, *Mind of Frederick Douglass*, 221.

33. Basson, *White Enough to Be American?*

34. Phillips, "United States of the United Races."

35. Elliott, "Race, Color Blindness, and the Democratic Public"; Elliott, *Color-Blind Justice*; Golub, "Plessy as 'Passing'"; Lobel, *Success without Victory*; Lofgren, *"Plessy" Case*; Keith Weldon Medley, *We as Freemen: "Plessy v. Ferguson"* (Gretna, La.: Pelican, 2003); Thomas, *Plessy v. Ferguson*.

36. Affidavit of C. C. Cain, *Ex parte* Plessy, 11 So. 948 (La. 1892) (No. 11,134).

37. *Ex parte* Plessy, 11 So. 948 (La. 1892) (No. 11,134).

38. Ibid.

39. Medley, *We as Freemen*, 132; Otto H. Olsen, *Carpetbagger's Crusade: The Life of Albion Winegar Tourgée* (Baltimore: Johns Hopkins University Press, 1965), 312–23.

40. Elliott, "Race, Color Blindness, and the Democratic Public," 311; Mark Elliott, "The Question of Color-Blind Citizenship: Albion Tourgée, W. E. B. Du Bois and the Principles of the Niagara Movement," *Afro-Americans in New York Life and History* 32, no. 2 (2008).

41. Eric J. Sundquist, "Mark Twain and Homer Plessy," *Representations*, no. 24 (1988); Mark Twain, *The Tragedy of Pudd'nhead Wilson; and, the Comedy, Those Extraordinary Twins* (1894; repr., New York: Oxford University Press, 1996).

42. Sundquist, "Mark Twain and Homer Plessy," 103.

43. Lofgren, *Plessy Case*, 152–55.

44. Brief of Plaintiff in Error, *Plessy v. Ferguson*, 163 U.S. 537 (1896), in Tourgée, *Undaunted Radical*, 301.

45. Lofgren, *Plessy Case*, 156–62.

46. Brief of Plaintiff in Error, 303.

47. Ibid., 310.

48. *Plessy v. Ferguson*, 163 U.S. 537 (1896).

49. Ibid.

50. Gabriel J. Chin, "The Plessy Myth: Justice Harlan and the Chinese Cases," *Iowa Law Review* 82, no. 151 (1996); Gabriel J. Chin, "The First Justice Harlan by the Numbers: Just How Great Was the Great Dissenter?," *Akron Law Review* 33, no. 629 (1999); *Fong Yue Ting v. United States*, 149 U.S. 698, 717; *United States v. Wong Kim Ark*, 169 U.S. 649 (1898).

51. Thomas Stewart Denison, *Patsy O'Wang, an Irish Farce with a Chinese Mix-Up*, in *The Chinese Other, 1850–1925: An Anthology of Plays*, ed. Dave Williams (Lanham, Md.: University Press of America, 1997), 126.

52. Ibid., 148.

1. W. E. Castle, "Mendel's Law of Heredity," *Science* 18, no. 456 (1903); W. E. Castle, "The Explanation of Hybrid Vigor," *Proceedings of the National Academy of Sciences of the United States of America* 12, no. 1 (1926); W. E. Castle, "Biological and Social Consequences of Race-Crossing," *American Journal of Physical Anthropology* 9 (1926); C. B. Davenport, "Race Crossing in Jamaica," *Scientific Monthly* 27, no. 3 (1928); C. B. Davenport, "Some Criticisms of 'Race Crossing in Jamaica,'" *Science* 72, no. 1872 (1930); F. Scott Fitzgerald, *The Great Gatsby*, ed. Matthew J. Bruccoli (New York: Scribner, 1996), 12; William B. Provine, "Geneticists and the Biology of Race Crossing," *Science* 182, no. 4114 (1973); Lothrop Stoddard, *The Rising Tide of Color against White World-Supremacy* (New York: Scribner, 1920).

2. Charles Benedict Davenport and Florence Harris Danielson, *Heredity of Skin Color in Negro-White Crosses* (Washington, D.C.: Carnegie Institution of Washington, 1913); Sollors, *Beyond Ethnicity*, 105.

3. F. James Davis, *Who Is Black? One Nation's Definition*, 10th anniversary ed. (University Park: Pennsylvania State University Press, 2001).

4. W. E. B. Du Bois, *Dusk of Dawn: An Essay toward an Autobiography of a Race Concept* (New York: Harcourt, Brace, 1940); W. E. B. Du Bois, *The Autobiography of W. E. B. Du Bois: A Soliloquy on Viewing My Life from the Last Decade of Its First Century* (New York: International, 1968); W. E. B. Du Bois, *W. E. B. Du Bois: A Reader*, ed. David L. Lewis (New York: Holt, 1995); W. E. B. Du Bois, *The Oxford W. E. B. Du Bois Reader*, ed. Eric J. Sundquist (New York: Oxford University Press, 1996); David L. Lewis, *W. E. B. Du Bois*, 2 vols. (New York: Holt, 1993).

5. W. E. B. Du Bois, "The Conservation of Races," in *W. E. B. Du Bois: A Reader*, 10.

6. Anthony Appiah, *In My Father's House: Africa in the Philosophy of Culture* (New York: Oxford University Press, 1992); Kwame Anthony Appiah, "The Uncompleted Argument: Du Bois and the Illusion of Race," in *"Race," Writing, and Difference*, ed. Henry Louis Gates, Jr. (Chicago: University of Chicago Press, 1986); Bernard W. Bell, Emily Grosholz, and James B. Stewart, *W. E. B. Du Bois on Race and Culture: Philosophy, Politics, and Poetics* (New York: Routledge, 1996).

7. Du Bois, "Conservation of Races," 10.

8. Ibid., 14.

9. Ibid., 26.

10. Adolph L. Reed, *W. E. B. Du Bois and American Political Thought: Fabianism and the Color Line* (New York: Oxford University Press, 1997).

11. Robert Reid-Pharr, *Once You Go Black: Choice, Desire, and the Black American Intellectual*, Sexual Cultures (New York: NYU Press, 2007), 17.

12. Du Bois, *Dusk of Dawn*, 100.

13. W. E. B. Du Bois, *The Souls of Black Folk: Essays and Sketches* (Chicago: A. C. McClurg, 1903); Du Bois, "Conservation of Races"; Du Bois, "The Talented Tenth: Memorial Address," in *W. E. B. Du Bois: A Reader*, 347–53.

14. Du Bois, *Dusk of Dawn*, 101.

15. Ibid., 101–2.

16. W. E. B. Du Bois, "The Twelfth Census and the Negro Problems," *Southern Workman*, 1900, 305–9.

17. Israel Zangwill, *The East African Question: Zionism and England's Offer*, Zionist Essays and Addresses (New York: Maccabaean, 1904), 52.

18. "Zangwill, Israel, 1864–1926," ProQuest Information and Learning Company, http://gateway.proquest.com.content.lib.utexas.edu:2048/openurl?ctx_ver=Z39.88-2003&xri:pqil:res_ver=0.2&res_id=xr i:lion-us&rft_id=xri:lion:rec:ref:5876; Joseph Leftwich, *Israel Zangwill* (New York: T. Yoseloff, 1957); Meri-Jane Rochelson, *A Jew in the Public Arena: The Career of Israel Zangwill* (Detroit: Wayne State University Press, 2008); Maurice Wohlgelernter, *Israel Zangwill: A Study* (New York: Columbia University Press, 1964); Zangwill, *East African Question*; Israel Zangwill, *Without Prejudice* (New York: Century, 1896), 83–85.

19. Israel Zangwill, *The Melting-Pot: Drama in Four Acts*, new and rev. ed. (New York: Macmillan, 1914), 33.

20. Ibid., 34.

21. Ibid., 184.
22. Leftwich, *Israel Zangwill*, 252.
23. Elsie Bonita Adams, *Israel Zangwill* (New York: Twayne, 1971); Internet Broadway Database, "The Melting Pot Production Credits," http://www.ibdb.com/production. asp?ID=6834; Joe Kraus, "How the Melting Pot Stirred America: The Reception of Zangwill's Play and Theater's Role in the American Assimilation Experience," in "Varieties of Ethnic Criticism," *Melus* 24, no. 3 (1999); Guy Szuberla, "Zangwill's *The Melting Pot* Plays Chicago," in "History and Memory," *Melus* 20, no. 3 (1995).
24. Zangwill, *Melting-Pot*, 207.
25. Ibid.
26. "Zangwill, Israel, 1864–1926"; Nathan Glazer and Daniel P. Moynihan, *Beyond the Melting Pot: The Negroes, Puerto Ricans, Jews, Italians, and Irish of New York City* (Cambridge: MIT Press, 1963), 290; Wohlgelernter, *Israel Zangwill*.
27. Horace Meyer Kallen, "Democracy versus the Melting-Pot," *Nation*, February 25, 1915, 220.
28. Randolph Silliman Bourne, *History of a Literary Radical, and Other Essays*, ed. Van Wyck Brooks (New York: Huebsch, 1920); Gleason, "Melting Pot"; John Higham, *Strangers in the Land: Patterns of American Nativism, 1860–1925* (New Brunswick: Rutgers University Press, 2002), 248.
29. Gleason, "Melting Pot," 27.
30. Philip Gleason, *Speaking of Diversity: Language and Ethnicity in Twentieth-Century America* (Baltimore: Johns Hopkins University Press, 1992); Gleason, "Melting Pot," 45.
31. Robert Ezra Park, "Racial Assimilation in Secondary Groups with Particular Reference to the Negro," *American Journal of Sociology* 19, no. 5 (1914); Stow Persons, *Ethnic Studies at Chicago, 1905–45* (Urbana: University of Illinois Press, 1987); Dorothy Ross, *The Origins of American Social Science*, Ideas in Context (Cambridge: Cambridge University Press, 1991).
32. Edward Franklin Frazier, *The Negro in the United States* (New York: Macmillan, 1949); Persons, *Ethnic Studies at Chicago*, 105–6.
33. Robert Ezra Park and Ernest Watson Burgess, *Introduction to the Science of Sociology* (Chicago: University of Chicago Press, 1921), 736.
34. Ibid., 737–38.
35. Edward Byron Reuter, *The Mulatto in the United States: Including a Study of the Rôle of Mixed-Blood Races throughout the World* (Boston: Badger, 1918); Edward Byron Reuter, *The American Race Problem: A Study of the Negro* (New York: Thomas Y. Crowell, 1927); Edward Byron Reuter, *Race Mixture: Studies in Intermarriage and Miscegenation* (New York: Whittlesey House, McGraw-Hill, 1931).
36. Robert E. Park, "Human Migration and the Marginal Man," *American Journal of Sociology* 33, no. 6 (1928): 1.
37. Everett V. Stonequist, "The Problem of the Marginal Man," *American Journal of Sociology* 41, no. 1 (1935): 6.
38. Ibid.; Everett V. Stonequist, *The Marginal Man: A Study in Personality and Culture Conflict* (New York: Scribner, 1937).
39. Trudier Harris-Lopez and Thadious M. Davis, *Afro-American Writers from the Harlem Renaissance to 1940*, Dictionary of Literary Biography 51 (Detroit: Gale Research, 1987), 274–88; Nellie McKay, "Jean Toomer in Wisconsin," in *Jean Toomer: A Critical*

Evaluation, ed. Therman B. O'Daniel (Washington, D.C.: Howard University Press, 1988), 47–55; Peter Quartermain, *American Poets, 1880–1945, First Series*, Dictionary of Literary Biography 45 (Detroit: Gale Research, 1986), 405–9; Jean Toomer, "The Maturing Years," in *The Wayward and the Seeking: A Collection of Writings by Jean Toomer*, ed. Darwin T. Turner (Washington, D.C.: Howard University Press, 1980), 84–98; Jean Toomer, "A New Race in America," in *A Jean Toomer Reader: Selected Unpublished Writings*, ed. Frederik L. Rusch (New York: Oxford University Press, 1993), 105.

40. Jean Toomer, "Americans and Mary Austin," *New York Call*, October 10, 1920.

41. Ibid.

42. Jean Toomer, "The Crock of Problems," in *Jean Toomer: Selected Essays and Literary Criticism*, ed. Robert B. Jones (Knoxville: University of Tennessee Press, 1996), 58.

43. Toomer, "Americans and Mary Austin."

44. Toomer, "Crock of Problems," 58–59; Jean Toomer, "Race Problems and Modern Society," in *Jean Toomer: Selected Essays and Literary Criticism*, 69.

45. Conversations with Margo J. Anderson, University of Wisconsin–Milwaukee Department of History; Jennifer L. Hochschild and Brenna Marea Powell, "Racial Reorganization and the United States Census, 1850–1930: Mulattoes, Half-Breeds, Mixed Parentage, Hindoos, and the Mexican Race," *Studies in American Political Development* 22 (2008); H. L. Mencken, "Designations for Colored Folk," *American Speech* 19, no. 3 (1944); Kelly Miller, "Review of the Mulatto in the United States," *American Journal of Sociology* 25, no. 2 (1919); Bureau of the Census, U.S. Department of Commerce, *Population, 1920, Volume III, Fourteenth Census of the United States, Taken in the Year 1920* (Washington, D.C.: U.S. Government Printing Office, 1922), 10.

46. Marcus Garvey, *Philosophy and Opinions of Marcus Garvey*, ed. Amy Jacques Garvey (New York City: Atheneum, 1969), 17.

47. Malcolm X and Alex Haley, *The Autobiography of Malcolm X* (New York: Grove, 1965), 1.

48. Garvey, *Philosophy and Opinions of Marcus Garvey*, 26.

49. Ibid., 286.

50. Ibid.

51. W. E. B. Du Bois, "The Social Equality of Whites and Blacks," *Crisis*, November 1920.

52. Ibid.

53. Ibid.

54. Warren G. Harding, "Address of the President of the United States at the Celebration of the Semicentennial of the Founding of the City of Birmingham, Alabama" (Washington, D.C.: U.S. Government Printing Office, 1921).

55. Ibid.

56. Ibid.

57. W. E. B. Du Bois, "President Harding and Social Equality," *Crisis*, December 1921.

58. Ibid.

59. William Wells Brown, *Narrative of William W. Brown, a Fugitive Slave* (Boston: Anti-Slavery Office, 1847); Lydia Maria Francis Child, *Incidents in the Life of a Slave Girl* (Boston: author, 1861); Lewis Garrard Clark and Milton Clark, *Narratives of the Sufferings of Lewis and Milton Clarke, Sons of a Soldier of the Revolution, during a Captivity of More than Twenty Years among the Slaveholders of Kentucky, One of the So Called Christian States of North America. Dictated by Themselves* (Boston: B. Marsh, 1846).

60. Jean Toomer to Waldo Frank, October 9, 1922, in *The Letters of Jean Toomer, 1919-1924* (Knoxville: University of Tennessee Press, 2006), 86.

61. Jean Toomer to Horace Liveright, September 5, 1923, in *Jean Toomer Reader*, 94.

62. Harry L. Jones, "Jean Toomer's Vision: 'Blue Meridian,'" in O'Daniel, *Jean Toomer: A Critical Evaluation*, 337.

63. Jean Toomer to James Weldon Johnson, July 11, 1930, in *Jean Toomer Reader*, 105-6.

64. Gabriella De Beer, *José Vasconcelos and His World* (New York: Las Americas, 1966); John H. Haddox, *Vasconcelos of Mexico, Philosopher and Prophet* (Austin: University of Texas Press, 1967); José Vasconcelos, *The Cosmic Race: A Bilingual Edition*, trans. Didier Tisdel Jaén (Baltimore: Johns Hopkins University Press, 1997).

65. Quoted in Haddox, *Vasconcelos of Mexico*, 61-62.

66. De Beer, *José Vasconcelos and His World*; Haddox, *Vasconcelos of Mexico*; Vasconcelos, *Cosmic Race*.

67. Jean Toomer, "A New Race in America," in *Jean Toomer Reader*, 105.

68. Jean Toomer, "Outline of an Autobiography," in *The Wayward and the Seeking*, 120-21.

69. "Just Americans," *Time*, March 28, 1932.

70. Ibid.

71. Ibid.

72. Jean Toomer, "The Americans," in *Jean Toomer Reader*, 107.

73. Ibid.

74. Ibid.

75. Ibid., 107-10.

76. Jean Toomer, "Not Typically American," in *Jean Toomer Reader*, 96.

77. Ibid., 100.

78. Ibid., 95-101.

79. Jean Toomer, "The Blue Meridian," ll. 816-23, in *The Collected Poems of Jean Toomer*, ed. Robert B. Jones and Margery Toomer Latimer (Chapel Hill: University of North Carolina Press, 1988), 74.

80. Ibid., 72, l. 739; Frederik L. Rusch, "Editor's Note," in *Jean Toomer Reader*, 79-80.

81. Bernard W. Bell, "Jean Toomer's 'Blue Meridian': The Poet as Prophet of a New Order of Man," in O'Daniel, *Jean Toomer: A Critical Evaluation*, 347; Harris-Lopez and Davis, *Afro-American Writers from the Harlem Renaissance to 1940*, 274-88; Jones, "Jean Toomer's Vision," 337-38; Toomer, "The Cane Years," in *The Wayward and the Seeking*, 120-21.

82. Vasconcelos, *Cosmic Race*, 4.

83. Glazer and Moynihan, *Beyond the Melting Pot*, 289.

NOTES TO CHAPTER 5

1. Matthew Frye Jacobson, *Whiteness of a Different Color: European Immigrants and the Alchemy of Race* (Cambridge: Harvard University Press, 1998); George Lipsitz, *The Possessive Investment in Whiteness: How White People Profit from Identity Politics*, rev. and exp. ed. (Philadelphia: Temple University Press, 2006); David R. Roediger, *Working toward Whiteness: How America's Immigrants Became White: The Strange Journey from Ellis Island to the Suburbs* (New York: Basic Books, 2005); Nell Irvin Painter, *The History of White People* (New York: Norton, 2010).

2. Langston Hughes, *The Ways of White Folks* (New York: Vintage Books, 1990); Ronald T. Takaki, *Double Victory: A Multicultural History of America in World War II* (Boston: Little, Brown, 2000).

3. Laura Pulido, *Black, Brown, Yellow, and Left: Radical Activism in Los Angeles*, American Crossroads (Berkeley: University of California Press, 2006).

4. G. Reginald Daniel, *More than Black? Multiracial Identity and the New Racial Order* (Philadelphia: Temple University Press, 2002), 93–124; St. Clair Drake, *Black Metropolis: A Study of Negro Life in a Northern City* (New York: Harcourt, 1945), 129–73; Clotye Murdock Larsson, *Marriage across the Color Line* (Chicago: Johnson, 1965), 58–61.

5. Heidi Ardizzone, "'Such Fine Families': Photography and Race in the Work of Caroline Bond Day," *Visual Studies* 21, no. 2 (2006): 110; Caroline Bond Day, "C.B. Day Mss.," untitled draft, n.d., in Caroline Bond Day Papers, Peabody Museum of Archeology and Ethnology, Harvard University, Cambridge, Massachusetts.

6. Ardizzone, "Such Fine Families"; Caroline Bond Day, "Selections from a Study of Some Negro-White Families in the United States," in *Blacks at Harvard: A Documentary History of African-American Experience at Harvard and Radcliffe*, ed. Werner Sollors, Caldwell Titcomb, and Thomas A. Underwood (New York: NYU Press, 1993); Sollors, *Neither Black nor White yet Both*.

7. Reid-Pharr, *Once You Go Black*, 123.

8. David Gutiérrez, *Walls and Mirrors: Mexican Americans, Mexican Immigrants, and the Politics of Ethnicity* (Berkeley: University of California Press, 1995), 77–78.

9. Alberto Urista, "El Plan Espiritual de Aztlán," in *Aztlan: An Anthology of Mexican American Literature*, ed. Luis Valdez and Stan Steiner (New York: Knopf, 1972), 403.

10. Ibid.

11. Velia García Hancock, "La Chicana, the Chicano Movement, and Women's Liberation," *Chicano Studies Newsletter*, February–March 1971; Edward Murguía, *Chicano Intermarriage: A Theoretical and Empirical Study* (San Antonio, Tex.: Trinity University Press, 1982); Vicki Ruíz, *From out of the Shadows: Mexican Women in Twentieth-Century America*, 10th anniversary ed. (New York: Oxford University Press, 2008), 99–126.

12. Vine Deloria, *Custer Died for Your Sins: An Indian Manifesto* (New York: Macmillan, 1969), 172.

13. Ibid., 48–49.

14. Ibid., 3.

15. Leonard Peltier, *Prison Writings: My Life Is My Sundance*, ed. Harvey Arden (New York: St. Martin's, 1999), 93.

16. Peter Matthiessen, *In the Spirit of Crazy Horse* (New York: Viking, 1983); Russell Means and Marvin J. Wolf, *Where White Men Fear to Tread: The Autobiography of Russell Means* (New York: St. Martin's, 1995); Paul Chaat Smith and Robert Allen Warrior, *Like a Hurricane: The Indian Movement from Alcatraz to Wounded Knee* (New York: New Press, 1996).

17. W. E. B. Du Bois, "The Color Line Belts the World," in *W. E. B. Du Bois: A Reader*, 42.

18. Glenn Omatsu, "The 'Four Prisons' and the Movements of Liberation: Asian American Activism from the 1960s to the 1990s," in *Asian American Studies Now: A*

Critical Reader, ed. Jean Yu-wen Shen Wu and Thomas C. Chen (New Brunswick: Rutgers University Press, 2010), 306.

19. Fred Wei-han Ho and Bill Mullen, *Afro Asia: Revolutionary Political and Cultural Connections between African Americans and Asian Americans* (Durham: Duke University Press, 2008); Michael Liu, Kim Geron, and Tracy A. M. Lai, *The Snake Dance of Asian American Activism: Community, Vision, and Power in the Struggle for Social Justice, 1945–2000* (Lanham, Md.: Lexington Books, 2008); Vijay Prashad, *Everybody Was Kung Fu Fighting: Afro-Asian Connections and the Myth of Cultural Purity* (Boston: Beacon, 2001); Heike Raphael-Hernandez and Shannon Steen, *Afroasian Encounters: Culture, History, Politics* (New York: NYU Press, 2006).

20. Frank H. Wu, *Yellow: Race in America beyond Black and White* (New York: Basic Books, 2002), 261.

21. Darryl Frears and Claudia Deane, "Biracial Couples Report Tolerance: Survey Finds More Are Accepted by Families," *Washington Post*, July 5, 2001, quoted in Wu, *Yellow*, 268.

22. Yen Le Espiritu, "Possibilities of a Multiracial Asian America," in *The Sum of Our Parts: Mixed-Heritage Asian Americans*, ed. Teresa Williams-León and Cynthia L. Nakashima (Philadelphia: Temple University Press, 2001), 25.

23. Thomas Borstelmann, *The Cold War and the Color Line: American Race Relations in the Global Arena* (Cambridge: Harvard University Press, 2001); Mary L. Dudziak, *Cold War Civil Rights: Race and the Image of American Democracy*, Politics and Society in Twentieth-Century America (Princeton: Princeton University Press, 2000).

24. Michael C. Thornton, "The Quiet Immigration: Foreign Spouses of U.S. Citizens, 1945–1985," in *Racially Mixed People in America*, ed. Maria P. P. Root (Newbury Park, Calif.: Sage, 1992).

25. Thomas Cripps, *Making Movies Black: The Hollywood Message Movie from World War II to the Civil Rights Era* (New York: Oxford University Press, 1993).

26. Mary Beltrán and Camilla Fojas, *Mixed Race Hollywood* (New York: NYU Press, 2008); Donald Bogle, *Toms, Coons, Mulattoes, Mammies, and Bucks: An Interpretive History of Blacks in American Films*, 4th ed. (New York: Continuum, 2001); Susan Courtney, *Hollywood Fantasies of Miscegenation: Spectacular Narratives of Gender and Race, 1903–1967* (Princeton: Princeton University Press, 2005).

27. Rudolph P. Byrd, ed., *The World Has Changed: Conversations with Alice Walker* (New York: New Press, 2010); Jane Lazarre, *Beyond the Whiteness of Whiteness: Memoir of a White Mother of Black Sons* (Durham: Duke University Press, 1996); Herbert Randall and Bobs M. Tusa, *Faces of Freedom Summer* (Tuscaloosa: University of Alabama Press, 2001); Diane DeCesare Ross, "Mississippi Freedom Summer Photograph by Herbert Randall," Special Collections, University of Southern Mississippi Libraries, University of Southern Mississippi; Danzy Senna, *Where Did You Sleep Last Night? A Personal History* (New York: Farrar, Straus, and Giroux, 2009); Rebecca Walker, *Black, White, and Jewish: Autobiography of a Shifting Self* (New York: Riverhead Books, 2001); Evelyn C. White, *Alice Walker: A Life* (New York: Norton, 2004).

28. Joseph Carroll, "Most Americans Approve of Interracial Marriages," Gallup, August 16, 2007, http://www.gallup.com/poll/28417/Most-Americans-Approve-Interracial-Marriages.aspx; Kennedy, *Interracial Intimacies*; Rachel F. Moran, *Interracial Intimacy: The Regulation of Race and Romance* (Chicago: University of Chicago Press,

2001); Phyl Newbeck, *Virginia Hasn't Always Been for Lovers: Interracial Marriage Bans and the Case of Richard and Mildred Loving* (Carbondale: Southern Illinois University Press, 2004); Peggy Pascoe, *What Comes Naturally: Miscegenation Law and the Making of Race in America* (Oxford: Oxford University Press, 2009); Renee Christine Romano, *Race Mixing: Black-White Marriage in Postwar America* (Cambridge: Harvard University Press, 2003).

29. Sara Bullard, *Free at Last: A History of the Civil Rights Movement and Those Who Died in the Struggle* (New York: Oxford University Press, 1993); Clayborne Carson, ed., *The Eyes on the Prize: Civil Rights Reader: Documents, Speeches, and Firsthand Accounts from the Black Freedom Struggle, 1954–1990* (New York: Viking, 1991); John Hope Franklin and Alfred A. Moss, *From Slavery to Freedom: A History of African Americans*, 8th ed. (New York: Knopf, 2000); Henry Hampton, Steve Fayer, and Sarah Flynn, *Voices of Freedom: An Oral History of the Civil Rights Movement from the 1950s through the 1980s* (New York: Bantam Books, 1990); Michael J. Klarman, *From Jim Crow to Civil Rights: The Supreme Court and the Struggle for Racial Equality* (Oxford: Oxford University Press, 2004); Steven F. Lawson and Charles M. Payne, *Debating the Civil Rights Movement, 1945–1968*, 2nd ed., Debating Twentieth-Century America (Lanham, Md.: Rowman and Littlefield, 2006); Ellen Levine, *Freedom's Children: Young Civil Rights Activists Tell Their Own Stories* (New York: Putnam, 1993); Aldon D. Morris, *The Origins of the Civil Rights Movement: Black Communities Organizing for Change* (New York: Free Press, 1984); Harvard Sitkoff, *The Struggle for Black Equality*, 25th anniversary ed. (New York: Hill and Wang, 2008); Juan Williams, *Eyes on the Prize: America's Civil Rights Years, 1954–1965* (New York: Viking, 1987).

30. Mary C. Waters, *Ethnic Options: Choosing Identities in America* (Berkeley: University of California Press, 1990), 167; see also Ross Chambers, "The Unexamined," in *Whiteness: A Critical Reader*, ed. Mike Hill (New York: NYU Press, 1997); Richard Dyer, *White* (London: Routledge, 1997).

31. Richard D. Alba, *Ethnic Identity: The Transformation of White America* (New Haven: Yale University Press, 1990), 3.

32. Ibid.; Waters, *Ethnic Options*.

33. Bonilla-Silva, *White Supremacy and Racism*, 157–66; Eduardo Bonilla-Silva, *Racism without Racists: Color-Blind Racism and the Persistence of Racial Inequality in the United States*, 3rd ed. (Lanham, Md.: Rowman and Littlefield, 2010), 53–74; Census-Scope, "CensusScope—Population by Race," http://www.censusscope.org/us/chart_race.html; Bureau of the Census, U.S. Department of Commerce, "Hispanic Origin and Race of Coupled Households (Phc-T-19)," http://www.census.gov/population/www/cen2000/phc-t19.html.

34. Albert Murray, *The Omni-Americans: New Perspectives on Black Experience and American Culture* (New York: Outerbridge and Dienstfrey, 1970), 22.

NOTES TO CHAPTER 6

1. Margo J. Anderson and Stephen E. Fienberg, *Who Counts? The Politics of Census-Taking in Contemporary America* (New York: Russell Sage Foundation, 2001); Clara E. Rodriguez, *Changing Race: Latinos, the Census, and the History of Ethnicity in the United States*, Critical America (New York: NYU Press, 2000); Kim M. Williams,

Mark One or More: Civil Rights in Multiracial America, Politics of Race and Ethnicity (Ann Arbor: University of Michigan Press, 2006).

2. Because of the associations of the term *multiracial* with the Multiracial Movement, I use it only in connection with the movement's endeavor. As such, I capitalize it.

3. Michael Omi and Howard Winant, *Racial Formation in the United States: From the 1960s to the 1990s*, 2nd ed. (New York: Routledge, 1994), 5.

4. Andrew Hacker, *Two Nations: Black and White, Separate, Hostile, Unequal* (New York: Scribner, 2003).

5. Bonilla-Silva, *White Supremacy and Racism*, 48.

6. Ibid.; Eduardo Bonilla-Silva, *Racism without Racists: Color-Blind Racism and the Persistence of Racial Inequality in the United States*, 3rd ed. (Lanham, Md.: Rowman and Littlefield, 2006); Hacker, *Two Nations*; Omi and Winant, *Racial Formation in the United States*.

7. Frances Fox Piven and Richard A. Cloward, *The Breaking of the American Social Compact* (New York: New Press, 1997); Barbara Vobejda, "Clinton Signs Welfare Bill amid Division," *Washington Post*, August 23, 1996.

8. Arthur Meier Schlesinger Jr., *The Disuniting of America: Reflections on a Multicultural Society*, rev. and enlarged ed. (New York: Norton, 1998), 21.

9. Carlos A. Fernandez, "A.M.E.A. Mission Statement" (Tucson, Ariz.: Association of MultiEthnic Americans, 1990), 14.

10. Nancy G. Brown and Ramona E. Douglass, "Evolution of Multiracial Organizations: Where We Have Been and Where We Are Going," in *New Faces in a Changing America: Multiracial Identity in the 21st Century*, ed. Loretta I. Winters and Herman L. DeBose (Thousand Oaks, Calif.: Sage, 2003); G. Reginald Daniel, "Beyond Black and White: The New Multiracial Consciousness," in *Racially Mixed People in America*, ed. Maria P. P. Root (Newbury Park, Calif.: Sage, 1992); Carlos A. Fernandez, "A.M.E.A. Mission Statement" (Tucson, Ariz.: Association of MultiEthnic Americans, 1990).

11. Project R.A.C.E., "About Project RACE: Why We Need a Multiracial Classification—Biracial Mixed Race," http://www.projectrace.com/aboutprojectrace/ (accessed December 8, 2003).

12. Robert Anthony Watts, "Not Black, Not White, but Biracial," *Atlanta Journal-Constitution*, December 1, 1991.

13. Minkah Makalani, "A Biracial Identity or a New Race? The Historical Limitations and Political Implications of a Biracial Identity," *Souls* 3, no. 4 (2001); Paul R. Spickard, "Does Multiraciality Lighten? Me-Too Ethnicity and the Whiteness Trap," in *Crossing Lines: Race and Mixed Race across the Geohistorical Divide*, ed. Marc Coronado, Rudy P. Guevarra, Jr., Jeffrey Moniz, and Laura Furlan Szanto (Santa Barbara, Calif.: Multiethnic Student Outreach, 2003).

14. Nathan Glazer, *We Are All Multiculturalists Now* (Cambridge: Harvard University Press, 1997), 14; see also Todd Gitlin, *The Twilight of Common Dreams: Why America Is Wracked by Culture Wars* (New York: Metropolitan Books, 1995).

15. Rebecca Chiyoko King, "Race, Racialization, and Rights: Lumping and Splitting Multiracial Asian Americans in the 2000 Census," *Journal of Asian American Studies* 3, no. 2 (2000): 194.

16. Ana Mari Cauce, Yumi Hiraga, Craig Mason, Tanya Aguilar, Nydia Ordonez, and Nancy Gonzales, "Between a Rock and a Hard Place: Social Adjustment of Biracial

Youth," in *Racially Mixed People in America*, ed. Maria P. P. Root (Newbury Park, Calif.: Sage, 1992); Jewelle Taylor Gibbs and Alice M. Hines, "Negotiating Ethnic Identity: Issues for Black-White Adolescents," in ibid.; Christine C. Ijima Hall, "Please Choose One: Ethnic Identity Choices for Biracial Individuals," in ibid.; James H. Jacobs, "Identity Development in Biracial Children," in ibid.; Helena Jia Hershel, "Therapeutic Perspectives on Biracial Identity Formation and Internalized Oppression," in *American Mixed Race: The Culture of Microdiversity*, ed. Naomi Zack (Lanham, Md.: Rowman and Littlefield, 1995).

17. Maria P. P. Root, "Within, Between, and Beyond Race," in Root, *Racially Mixed People in America*, 3.
18. Ibid.
19. Ibid.
20. Root, "Bill of Rights for Racially Mixed People," 9.
21. Naomi Zack, "Life after Race," in Zack, *American Mixed Race*, 300.
22. Naomi Zack, introduction to Zack, *American Mixed Race*, x.
23. Ibid.
24. Zack, "Life after Race," 301.
25. Omi and Winant, *Racial Formation in the United States*; Ronald R. Sundstrom, "'Racial' Nominalism," *Journal of Social Philosophy* 33, no. 2 (2002): 195.
26. Appiah, "Uncompleted Argument," 39; David A. Hollinger, *Postethnic America: Beyond Multiculturalism* (New York: Basic Books, 1995), 19–50.
27. Appiah, "Uncompleted Argument," 45.
28. Paul Gilroy, *The Black Atlantic: Modernity and Double Consciousness* (Cambridge: Harvard University Press, 1993), xi.
29. Barbara Vobejda, "Categorizing the Nation's Millions of 'Other Race,'" *Washington Post*, April 29, 1991.
30. Lena Williams, "In a 90's Quest for Black Identity, Intense Doubts and Disagreement," *New York Times*, November 30, 1991.
31. Susan R. Graham, "Grassroots Advocacy," in Zack, *American Mixed Race*, 189.
32. Gabrielle Sandor, "The 'Other' Americans," *American Demographics*, June 1994, 189.
33. Rogers Worthington, "Between Black and White the Old Questions of Origin and Race No Longer Add Up," *Toronto Star*, July 7, 1994.
34. Daniel, *More than Black?*, 137.
35. Reginald Daniel gives an extensive history of the Multiracial Movement and his role as liaison between A.M.E.A. and Project R.A.C.E. Ibid., 125–51.
36. Ibid., 137.
37. *Time* 142, no. 21 (Fall 1993).
38. James R. Gaines, "From the Managing Editor," *Time* 142, no. 21 (Fall 1993): 2.
39. Ibid., 2.
40. Carroll, "Most Americans Approve of Interracial Marriages"; Jeffrey M. Jones, "Americans' Views of Immigration Growing More Positive," Gallup, July 10, 2006, http://www.gallup.com/poll/23623/Americans-Views-Immigration-Growing-More-Positive.aspx.
41. George G. Sanchez, "Face the Nation: Race, Immigration, and the Rise of Nativism in Late Twentieth Century America," *International Migration Review* 31, no. 4 (1997).
42. Pico Iyer, "The Global Village Finally Arrives: The New World Order Is a Version of the New World Writ Large: A Wide-Open Frontier of Polyglot Terms and Post

National Trends," *Time*, November 18, 1993; Thomas McCarroll, "It's a Mass Market No More: The New Ethnic Consumer Is Forcing U.S. Companies to Change the Ways They Sell Their Wares," *Time*, December 2, 1993.

43. Christopher John Farley, "The Art of Diversity: Hyphenated-Americans Can Be Found along the Cutting Edge of All the Arts," *Time*, December 2, 1993.

44. Ibid.

45. John Elson, "Sometimes the Door Slams Shut," *Time*, December 2, 1993; Bruce W. Nelan, "Not Quite So Welcome Anymore: As Reflected in a Time Poll, the Public Mood over Immigration Is Turning Sour Again," *Time*, December 2, 1993; Richard Brookhiser, "Three Cheers for the WASPs: When It Comes to Being American, They Wrote the Book," *Time*, December 2, 1993.

46. Steve Liss, "America's Immigrant Challenge," *Time*, December 2, 1993.

47. Jill Smolowe, "Intermarried . . . with Children," *Time*, Fall 1993.

48. Ibid.

49. Ibid.

50. Ibid.

51. "Rebirth of a Nation, Computer Style," *Time*, Fall 1993.

52. Carrera, *Imagining Identity in New Spain*; Ilona Katzew, "Casta Painting: Identity and Social Stratification in Colonial Mexico," *Laberinto*, Fall 1997, http://www.gc.maricopa.edu/laberinto/fall1997/casta1997.htm (accessed January 31, 2007); Katzew, *Casta Painting*; Nash, "Hidden History of Mestizo America."

53. John Berger, *Ways of Seeing* (New York: Viking, 1973).

54. Laura Mulvey, "Visual Pleasure and Narrative Cinema," *Screen* 16, no. 3 (1977).

55. Lauren Gail Berlant, *The Queen of America Goes to Washington City: Essays on Sex and Citizenship* (Durham: Duke University Press, 1997); Haraway, *Modest_Witness@ Second_Millennium*; Michael Paul Rogin, *Blackface, White Noise: Jewish Immigrants in the Hollywood Melting Pot* (Berkeley: University of California Press, 1996); Caroline A. Streeter, "The Hazards of Visibility: 'Biracial' Women, Media Images, and Narratives of Identity," in *New Faces in a Changing America: Multiracial Identity in the 21st Century*, ed. Loretta I. Winters and Herman L. DeBose (Thousand Oaks, Calif.: Sage, 2003).

56. John O'Sullivan, "Losing Face," *National Review*, February 21, 1994, 8.

57. Ibid.

58. "Who Is the Face of America?," *Mirabella*, September 1994, 2.

59. Ibid.

60. Carla K. Bradshaw, "Beauty and the Beast: On Racial Ambiguity," in Root, *Racially Mixed People in America*, 77.

61. Hollinger, *Postethnic America*, 45.

62. Ibid., 166.

63. Stanley Crouch, "Race Is Over," *New York Times Magazine*, September 29, 1996.

64. Schlesinger, *Disuniting of America*, 49.

65. Ibid., 140.

66. Gary Smith, "The Chosen One," *Sports Illustrated*, December 23, 1996.

67. Ibid.

68. Ibid.

69. Jack E. White, "I'm Just Who I Am," *Time*, May 5, 1997.

70. John Leland and Gregory Beals, "In Living Colors," *Newsweek*, May 5, 1997.

71. Ibid.
72. James K. Glassman, "A Dishonest Campaign," *Washington Post*, September 17, 1996.
73. "Tiger, Tiger, Burning Bright," *Economist*, June 16, 2001.
74. "Golfer Says Comments about Woods 'Misconstrued,'" CNN.com, April 21, 1997, http://www.cnn.com/US/9704/21/fuzzy/.
75. Ibid.
76. "Black America and Tiger's Dilemma," *Ebony*, July 1997.
77. Ibid.
78. Lisa Jones, "Are We Tiger Woods Yet? America Buys Social Change," *Village Voice*, July 22, 1997; Gary Kamiya, "Cablinasian Like Me," *Salon*, April 30, 1997.
79. Liliana Chen and Tomio Geron, "The 25 Most Influential Asian Americans," *A. Magazine*, January 31, 1997.
80. "The aList 1997," *A. Magazine*, January 31, 1998; "The A. 100: 100 Most Influential Asian Americans of the Decade," *A. Magazine*, November 30, 1999; Jennifer Abbassi and Chris Fan, "aList 2001: Their Achievements Span Fields Ranging from Sports to Business to Entertainment to Activism," *A. Magazine*, January 31, 2002; Corey Takahashi, "Checking Off the Future," *A. Magazine*, March 31, 1998; Jan R. Weisman, "The Tiger and His Stripes: Thai and American Reactions to Tiger Woods's (Multi-) 'Racial Self,'" in *The Sum of Our Parts: Mixed-Heritage Asian Americans*, ed. Teresa Williams-León and Cynthia L. Nakashima (Philadelphia: Temple University Press, 2001).
81. Jay Nordlinger, "Tiger Time," *National Review*, April 20, 2001.
82. Root, "Bill of Rights for Racially Mixed People."
83. "Forbes Celebrity 100 2004," Forbes.com, 2004, http://www.forbes.com/celebrities2004/LIRWR6D.html?passListId=53&passYear=2004&passListType=Person&uniqueId=WR6D&datatype=Person; "World's 50 Highest-Paid Athletes 2004," Forbes.com, 2004, http://www.forbes.com/athletes2004/LIRWR6D.html?passListId=2&passYear=2004&passListType=Person&uniqueId=WR6D&datatype=Person; Cynthia L. Nakashima, "Servants of Culture: The Symbolic Role of Mixed-Race Asians in American Discourse," in Williams-León and Nakashima, *Sum of Our Parts*, 42.
84. Itabari Njeri, "The Last Plantation," in *"Mixed Race" Studies: A Reader*, ed. Jayne O. Ifekwunigwe (London: Routledge, 2004), 300.
85. Lisa Jones, *Bulletproof Diva: Tales of Race, Sex, and Hair* (New York: Anchor Books, 1995), 61–62.
86. Jon Michael Spencer, *The New Colored People: The Mixed-Race Movement in America* (New York: NYU Press, 1997), 75.
87. Ibid., 73.
88. Ibid.; Hanna Rosin, "Count Us In: Multiracial Groups Don't Want to Be Boxed Out by Census," *Rocky Mountain News*, January 2, 1994; Daryl Strickland, "Interracial Generation: 'We Are Who We Are' . . . ," *Seattle Times*, May 5, 1995; Linda Mathews, "Beyond 'Other': A Special Report," *New York Times*, July 6, 1996; Haya El Nasser, "Panel: 'Multiracial' Census Label Unneeded; Suggests Allowing Multiple Checks in Race Categories," *USA Today*, July 9, 1997; Laura Flores, "Multiracial Groups Seek Identity: U.S. Census Urged to Add Category," *New Orleans Times-Picayune*, December 10, 1995.
89. Ann Morning, "New Faces, Old Faces: Counting the Multiracial Population Past and Present," in Winters and DeBose, *New Faces in a Changing America*.

90. Scott Shepard, "Moving from 'Other' to 'Multiracial,'" *Atlanta Journal-Constitution*, July 7, 1997.

91. Susan A. Graham, "Multiracial Life after Newt," Project RACE website, November 9, 2001, http://www.projectrace.com/fromthedirector/archive/fromthedirector-110998.php.

92. Newt Gingrich, "Letter to OMB Re: Multiracial Census Category" (July 1, 1997), *Multiracial Activist*, last updated October 19, 2005, http://multiracial.com/site/content/view/975/29/.

93. Steven A. Holmes, "Gingrich Outlines Plan on Race Relations," *New York Times*, June 19, 1997; Williams, *Mark One or More*, 21.

94. Haya El Nasser, "Measuring Race: Varied Heritage Claimed and Extolled by Millions," *USA Today*, May 8, 1997; Suzann Evinger, "How to Record Race: Categories of Race and Ethnicity and the 2000 Census," *American Demographics*, May 1996; Mathews, "Beyond 'Other'"; Kerry Ann Rockquemore, "Deconstructing Tiger Woods: The Promises and the Pitfalls of Multiracial Identity," in *Tripping on the Color Line: Black-White Multiracial Families in a Racially Divided World*, ed. Heather M. Dalmage (New Brunswick: Rutgers University Press, 2000); Shepard, "Moving from 'Other' to 'Multiracial'"; Gary Younge, "Multiracial Citizens Divided on Idea of Separate Census Classification," *Washington Post*, July 19, 1996.

95. Candy Mills, "Interrace Matters: Mixed Blessings," *Interrace*, September 30, 1997.

96. Steven A. Holmes, "People Can Claim One or More Races on Federal Forms," *New York Times*, October 30, 1997.

97. Mills, "Interrace Matters."

98. Ibid.

99. Wiley A. Hall, "Denying Our Diversity Makes No Census," *Baltimore Afro-American*, July 12, 1997.

100. Ramon McLeod, "2000 Census Sets Compromise for Mixed Races . . . ," *San Francisco Chronicle*, October 30, 1997.

101. Aziz Haniffa, "Listing under More than One Race to Be Allowed," *India Abroad*, November 7, 1997; Mills, "Interrace Matters."

102. D'Vera Cohn and Darryl Fears, "Multiracial Growth Seen in Census; Numbers Show Diversity, Complexity of U.S. Count," *Washington Post*, March 13, 2001; Kirk Kicklighter, "Millions Claim Multiple Races: Census Broadens Its Range of Racial Classifications," *Atlanta Journal-Constitution*, March 13, 2001; Eric Schmitt, "For 7 Million People in Census, One Race Category Isn't Enough," *New York Times*, March 13, 2001.

NOTES TO CHAPTER 7

1. Karn Williams, "Hollywood Action Star and Sex Symbol Remains a Modest Guy from New York," *Afro-American*, August 23, 2002.

2. Crouch, "Race Is Over"; Davenport and Danielson, *Heredity of Skin Color*; Caroline Day and Earnest Albert Hooton, *A Study of Some Negro-White Families in the United States* (Westport, Conn.: Negro Universities Press, 1970); Kip Fulbeck, "The Hapa Project Samples," Seaweed Productions, http://www.seaweedproductions.com/the-hapa-project/samples/; Kip Fulbeck, *Part Asian, 100% Hapa* (San Francisco: Chronicle Books, 2006); Katzew, *Casta Painting*.

3. Stephen Jay Gould, *The Mismeasure of Man*, rev. and exp. ed. (New York: Norton, 1996); Ashley Montagu, *Statement on Race*, 3d ed. (New York: Oxford University Press, 1972); Robert A. Nye, "The Rise and Fall of the Eugenics Empire: Recent Perspectives on the Impact of Biomedical Thought in Modern Society," *Historical Journal* 36, no. 3 (1993).

4. Scott Turow, "The New Face of the Democratic Party—and America," *Salon*, March 30, 2004, http://dir.salon.com/story/news/feature/2004/03/30/obama/index.html.

5. Barack Obama, *Dreams from My Father: A Story of Race and Inheritance* (New York: Three Rivers, 2004); Barack Obama, "Keynote Address at the 2004 Democratic National Convention," July 27, 2004, http://www.barackobama.com/2004/07/27/keynote_address_at_the_2004_de.php.

6. Streeter, "Hazards of Visibility," 316.

7. Leland and Beals, "In Living Colors."

8. Ibid.

9. Conversation with Gia Madeiros, K. K. Branding, November 13, 2004.

10. Alison Stein Wellner, "Finding the Future Face of America," *Forecast*, February 2003.

11. Ibid.; David Whelan, "Casting Tiger Woods: Multiracials Step into the Advertising Spotlight," *Forecast*, May 7, 2001.

12. Ruth La Ferla, "Generation E.A.: Ethnically Ambiguous," *New York Times*, December 28, 2003.

13. Ibid.

14. Christine Bittar, "The New Face of Beauty," *Brandweek*, January 19, 2004.

15. LeiLani Nishime, "Hapas and Hawaii: Claiming Multiracial and (Trans) National Identities" (paper presented at American Studies Association National Conference, Oakland, Calif., 2006).

16. Kip Fulbeck, "Hapa Project Samples."

17. Fulbeck, *Part Asian, 100% Hapa*, 16.

18. Ibid., 13.

19. Discover Nikkei, "The Hapa Collection | Nikkei Album," Japanese American National Museum, http://www.discovernikkei.org/nikkeialbum/node/86.

20. John Fauber, "Genetic Research Shows People Are Very Similar," *Milwaukee Journal Sentinel*, March 29, 2001.

21. "D.N.A. Test Could Beat Suspects by a Hair," *Chemistry and Industry*, November 19, 2001; Christopher Cole, "D.N.A. Paints Portrait of Crime Suspects: Testing of Genetic Sample Can Determine Eye Color, Other Details, Firm Says," *Milwaukee Journal Sentinel*, July 14, 2002.

22. Bureau of the Census, U.S. Department of Commerce, "Population by Race and Hispanic or Latino Origin, for the United States, Regions, Divisions, and States, and for Puerto Rico: 2000," http://factfinder.census.gov/home/en/datanotes/expplu.html; Melville J. Herskovits, *The American Negro: A Study in Racial Crossing* (New York: Knopf, 1928); Marcos Mocine-McQueen, "D.N.A. Test Suggests Race of Woman's Killer in '97," *Denver Post*, January 21, 2004; Cindy Rodriguez, "'Latino' D.N.A. Finding Rooted in Imprecision," *Denver Post*, January 26, 2004; Dana Hawkins Simons, "Getting D.N.A. to Bear Witness," *U.S. News & World Report*, June 23, 2003; Nicholas Wade, "For Sale: A D.N.A. Test to Measure Racial Mix," *New York Times*, October 1, 2002; Joel Williamson, *New People: Miscegenation and Mulattoes in the United States* (New York: Free Press, 1980).

23. Simons, "Getting D.N.A. to Bear Witness."

24. Wade, "For Sale."

25. Emma Daly, "D.N.A. Tells Students They Aren't Who They Thought," *New York Times*, April 13, 2005.

26. DNAPrint, "What Is Race?," http://www.ancestrybydna.com/ancestry-by-dna-faq.php.

27. Ibid.

28. Brent Kennedy of Kingsport, Tennessee, received these results. Gregory M. Lamb, "Mixed Roots: Science Looks at Family Trees," *Christian Science Monitor*, April 28, 2005.

29. Amy Harmon, "Seeking Ancestry, and Privilege, in D.N.A. Ties Uncovered by Tests," *New York Times*, April 12, 2006.

30. Steve Connor, "The Missing Link? Oprah Winfrey Says She Has Zulu Blood. She's Not Alone," *Independent*, June 29, 2005; Harmon, "Seeking Ancestry"; Lamb, "Mixed Roots"; Joanna Weiss, "Black History, through Family Trees," *Boston Globe*, February 1, 2006.

31. Obama, *Dreams from My Father*, 27.

32. Ibid., 115.

33. Ibid., viii.

34. Dana Milbank, "Who's Ready for Change?," *Washington Post*, January 24, 2008, http://www.washingtonpost.com/wp-dyn/content/article/2008/01/23/AR2008012303655.html.

35. Obama, "Keynote Address at the 2004 Democratic National Convention"; Barack Obama, "Full Text of Senator Barack Obama's Announcement for President," BarackObama.com, February 10, 2007, http://www.barackobama.com/2007/02/10/remarks_of_senator_barack_obam_11.php; Barack Obama, "Barack Obama, Illinois," Democratic National Convention website, 2008, http://www.demconvention.com/barack-obama/; Barack Obama, "A More Perfect Union," BarackObama.com, March 18, 2008, http://my.barackobama.com/page/content/hisownwords; Barack Obama, "Remarks of President-Elect Barack Obama: Election Night," BarackObama.com, November 4, 2008, http://www.barackobama.com/2008/11/04/remarks_of_presidentelect_bara.php; Barack Obama, "President Barack Obama's Inaugural Address," BarackObama.com, January 20, 2009, http://my.barackobama.com/page/community/post/stateupdates/gGxHZR.

36. Turow, "New Face of the Democratic Party."

37. Joe Klein, "The Fresh Face," *Time*, October 15, 2006, http://www.time.com/time/magazine/article/0,9171,1546302,00.html; Debra J. Dickerson, "Colorblind: Barack Obama Would Be the Great Black Hope in the Next Presidential Race—If He Were Actually Black," *Salon*, January 22, 2007, http://www.salon.com/opinion/feature/2007/01/22/obama/; Rachel L. Swarns, "So Far, Obama Can't Take Black Vote for Granted," *New York Times*, February 2, 2007.

38. Klein, "Fresh Face."

39. Debra J. Dickerson, *The End of Blackness: Returning the Souls of Black Folk to Their Rightful Owners* (New York: Pantheon Books, 2004), 7.

40. Barack Obama, *The Audacity of Hope: Thoughts on Reclaiming the American Dream* (New York: Crown, 2006); Ta-Nehisi Coates, "Is Obama Black Enough?," *Time*, February 1, 2007, http://www.time.com/time/nation/article/0,8599,1584736,00.html; Stanley Crouch, "What Obama Isn't: Black Like Me on Race," *New York Daily News*,

November 2, 2006, http://www.nydailynews.com/archives/opinions/obama-black-race-article-1.585922; Dickerson, "Colorblind."

41. "Debra Dickerson," ColbertNation.com, February 8, 2007, http://www.colbertnation.com/the-colbert-report-videos/81955/february-08-2007/debra-dickerson.

42. Ibid.

43. Shelby Steele, "The Identity Card," *Time*, November 30, 2007, http://www.time.com/time/printout/0,8816,1689619,00.html.

44. James Hannaham, "Multiracial Man," *Salon*, February 2, 2008, http://www.salon.com/opinion/feature/2008/02/02/biracial_obama/print.html; Steele, "Identity Card"; Shelby Steele, *A Bound Man: Why We Are Excited about Obama and Why He Can't Win* (New York: Free Press, 2008).

45. Deborah Solomon, "All in the Family," *New York Times*, January 20, 2008, http://www.nytimes.com/2008/01/20/magazine/20wwln-Q4-t.html?_r=1.

46. Amanda Ripley, "The Story of Barack Obama's Mother," *Time*, April 9, 2008, http://www.time.com/time/nation/article/0,8599,1729524,00.html; Janny Scott, "A Free-Spirited Wanderer Who Set Obama's Path," *New York Times*, March 14, 2008, http://www.nytimes.com/2008/03/14/us/politics/14obama.html?_r=1&pagewanted=all.

47. Robert L. Allen, "Reassessing the Internal (Neo)Colonialism Theory," *Black Scholar* 35, no. 1 (2005): 8.

48. Gary Kamiya, "The Mix Master," *Salon*, June 10, 2008, http://www.salon.com/opinion/kamiya/2008/06/10/obama_race/print.html; Peggy Orenstein, "Mixed Messenger," *New York Times*, March 23, 2008, http://www.nytimes.com/2008/03/23/magazine/23wwln-lede-t.html; Mike Stuckey, "Multiracial Americans Surge in Number, Voice," MSNBC.com, May 28, 2008, http://www.msnbc.msn.com/id/24542138/print/1/displaymode/1098/.

49. Richard Rodriguez, "See the Brown in Us," *Newsweek*, May 24, 2008, http://www.newsweek.com/id/138513.

50. Ibid.

51. Charles Hurt, "Jesse Jackson Says He Wants to Cut Obama's 'Nuts Out,'" *New York Post*, July 9, 2008, http://www.nypost.com/seven/07092008/news/nationalnews/jesse_jackson_sharply_criticizes_obama_119161.htm; Bob Morse, "Rutgers Leads the Way in Ethnic Diversity," *Morse Code: Inside the College Rankings* (blog), *U.S. News & World Report*, September 9, 2008, http://www.usnews.com/blogs/college-rankings-blog/2008/09/09/rutgers-leads-the-way-in-ethnic-diversity.html.

52. Barack Obama, "President-Elect Obama's First News Conference," *New York Times*, November 7, 2008, http://www.nytimes.com/2008/11/07/us/politics/07obama-text.html?_r=1&pagewanted=all.

53. Alan Fram, "'Mutts Like Me' Shows Obama's Racial Comfort," *MSNBC.com*, November 8, 2008, http://www.msnbc.msn.com/id/27606637/.

54. Farai Chideya, "Barack Obama: Face of New Multiracial Movement?," NPR, November 12, 2008, http://www.npr.org/templates/story/story.php?storyId=96916824; Farai Chideya, "A Revealing History of a Multiracial America," November 12, 2008, http://www.npr.org/templates/story/story.php?storyId=96916821.

55. Marie Arana, "He's Not Black," *Washington Post*, November 28, 2008, http://www.washingtonpost.com/wp-dyn/content/article/2008/11/28/AR2008112802219.html.

56. Ibid.

57. Ibid.; Adam Serwer, "He's Black, Get over It," *American Prospect*, December 5, 2008, http://www.prospect.org/cs/articles?article=hes_black_get_over_it.

58. David Alan Grier, "First Black President?," *Chocolate News*, Comedy Central, October 9, 2008; David Alan Grier, "Advice to Obama," *Chocolate News*, Comedy Central, November 5, 2008.

59. Ginger Thompson, "Seeking Unity, Obama Feels Pull of Racial Divide," *New York Times*, February 12, 2008, http://www.nytimes.com/2008/02/12/us/politics/12obama. html?pagewanted=1&_r=2.

60. Mohammad Ali Salih, "A Son's Wisdom on a Post-Racial World," *USA Today*, February 22, 2008, http://blogs.usatoday.com/oped/2008/02/a-sons-wisdom-o.html (accessed July 13, 2009).

61. John McWhorter, "Obamakids," *New York Magazine*, August 10, 2008, http://nymag. com/news/features/49141/.

62. David A. Hollinger, "Obama, the Instability of Color Lines, and the Promise of a Postethnic Future," *Callaloo* 31, no. 4 (2008): 1333.

63. Hollinger, *Postethnic America*; Hollinger, "Obama."

NOTES TO THE CONCLUSION

1. Karl Mannheim, *Ideology and Utopia: An Introduction to the Sociology of Knowledge* (San Diego: Harcourt Brace Jovanovich, 1985), 193.

2. Ibid., 204.

3. Ibid., 192.

4. Root, "Bill of Rights for Racially Mixed People."

5. Phillips, "United States of the United Races."

6. Ralph Waldo Emerson, *The Collected Works of Ralph Waldo Emerson* (Cambridge, Mass.: Belknap, 1971); Turner, *Frontier in American History*.

7. Croly, *Miscegenation*, 58.

8. "Rebirth of a Nation, Computer Style."

9. Daniel, *More than Black?*, 175.

10. Daniel, "Beyond Black and White," 334; Root, "Bill of Rights for Racially Mixed People"; G. Reginald Daniel, "Multiethnic Individual: An Operational Definition" (paper presented at the Kaleidoscope, the Annual Conference of Multiracial Americans of Southern California, Los Angeles, Calif., 1988).

11. G. Reginald Daniel, "Black No More or More than Black? Multiracial Identity Politics and the Multiracial Movement," in *Racial Thinking in the United States: Uncompleted Independence*, ed. Paul R. Spickard and G. Reginald Daniel (Notre Dame, Ind.: University of Notre Dame Press, 2004), 280.

12. Daniel, *More than Black?*, 194.

13. Warren Beatty, *Bulworth* (Twentieth Century Fox, 1998).

14. Stephen Hunter, "Beatty's 'Bulworth': A Call to the Left," *Washington Post*, May 22, 1998.

15. Sacvan Bercovitch, *The American Jeremiad* (Madison: University of Wisconsin Press, 1978); Tom DeLuca and John Buell, *Liars! Cheaters! Evildoers! Demonization and the End of Civil Debate in American Politics* (New York: NYU Press, 2005).

16. DeLuca and Buell, *Liars! Cheaters! Evildoers!*, 42.

17. Ibid., 40–43.
18. Michael Lind, "The Beige and the Black," *New York Times*, August 16, 1998.
19. Ibid.
20. Michael Lind, *The Next American Nation: The New Nationalism and the Fourth American Revolution* (New York: Free Press, 1996), 295–96.
21. Lani Guinier and Gerald Torres, *The Miner's Canary: Enlisting Race, Resisting Power, Transforming Democracy* (Cambridge: Harvard University Press, 2002), 4.
22. Ibid., 9.
23. Ibid., 11–31.

Index

About the Author

Greg Carter is Assistant Professor of History at the University of Wisconsin–Milwaukee. His writing on minstrelsy, racial passing, and mixed-race representation has appeared in *Ethnic Studies Review*, *Journal of American Ethnic History*, and *Mixed Race Hollywood*, edited by Mary Beltrán and Camilla Fojas.